SPIRAL GUIDE W9-CFV-688

Travel With Someone You Trust®

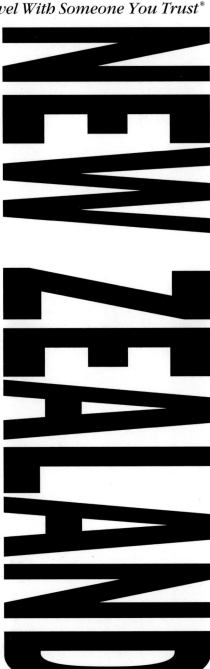

NEW ZEALAND

Contents

Original text by Veronika Meduna and Mavis Airey
Revised and updated by Megan Singleton

Edited, designed and produced by AA Publishing, a trading name
of AA Media Limited, whose registered office is Fanum House,
Basing View, Basingstoke, Hampshire RG21 4EA. Registered
number 06112600.

Published in the United States by AAA Publishing,
1000 AAA Drive, Heathrow, Florida 32746.
Published in the United Kingdom by AA Publishing.

ISBN: 978-1-59508-432-3

Cover design and binding style by permission of AA Publishing
Color separation by AA Digital Department
Printed and bound in China by Leo Paper Products

A04413
Maps in this title produced from map data © New Holland
Publishing (South Africa) (Pty) Ltd, 2009
(except p188)

The Magazine

A great holiday is more than just lying on a beach or shopping till you drop — to really get the most from your trip you need to know what makes the place tick. The Magazine provides an entertaining overview to some of the social, cultural and natural elements that make up the unique character of this engaging country.

SHAKY ISLES

New Zealand is perched on the Pacific Ring of Fire, a collision zone between two gigantic chunks of the Earth's crust. Here, the Pacific and Indo-Australian tectonic plates grind against each other to create unique landscapes and at times their force is released with devastating consequences.

A Dynamic Land

The boundary between the tectonic plates runs right down the country – from the Bay of Plenty through Wellington and along the South Island. The plates move at approximately the same rate as fingernails and hair grow: about 30–60mm (1–2 inches) per year.

In the North Island, this friction has caused volcanic eruptions and earthquakes, but it has also created the extraordinary thermal areas of the Central Plateau (► 82–85) and the spectacular peaks of Tongariro National Park (► 87–89). The South Island also experiences regular tremors and landslides, the most recent being the tragic earthquake that hit Christchurch in early 2011 (see below). The Alpine Fault (which runs along the length of the Southern Alps and continues to push up the mountains) has formed snow-topped peaks, glaciers, lakes and fjords.

The Human Cost

On 22 February 2011, the destructive force of nature was experienced by the inhabitants of Christchruch as an earthquake reaching 6.3 on the Richter scale hit the country's second city with shattering results. While memories of the devastation and human losses caused by the 1931 Napier earthquake (► 93) still linger, and scars in the landscape are testimony to a powerful 1987 tremor at Edgecumbe in the Bay of Plenty, this most recent quake is the worst to have hit the country in over 80

Bubbling and steaming mud pools are just one of the fascinating formations caused by tectonic plate movement. Page 5: Trout fishing in Lake Pukaki

years. Its effects are sure to leave a lasting mark on the city and the tragic loss of life will be felt by the families affected for generations to come.

With growing cities sitting alongside fault lines and volcanoes, the reliance on technology and geologists to monitor the mood of each active volcano is essential. Even the sleeping volcanoes dotting Auckland's cityscape (► 51) are under constant scrutiny. The current cones are considered extinct, but the volcanic field below them is only dormant and could well open up new vents. New Zealand's capital, Wellington, is bracing itself for a spectacle of another kind. The city straddles a fault line

The impressive crater of Mount Tarawera and Lake Rotomahana

that last caused a major earthquake in 1855. The quake, which registered 8.2 on the Richter scale, was felt from Auckland to Dunedin, and added a strip of new land to Wellington's entire southern coastline, uplifting some 5,000sq km (2,000sq miles) of land. The capital is now having to face the growing likelihood of another "big one" sometime soon.

Four Seasons in One Day

As if the threat of earthquakes and volcanoes wasn't enough for its inhabitants to contend with, New Zealand also experiences extremes in weather. The long and narrow islands can suffer freezing hailstorms on one coast at the same time as sunshine burns down on the other. From the subtropical climate of the far north to the freezing southern regions, the difference in temperature can be several degrees. The islands' maritime climate also means that the weather changes with amazing rapidity, and so visitors should come prepared for four seasons in day.

THE LEGEND OF THE VOLCANOES

Maori mythology offers a beautiful and poetic explanation for New Zealand's many volcanoes: Ngatoroirangi, an ancient priest and explorer, was caught in a blinding blizzard while climbing Mount Ngauruhoe. He called on his sisters, in the distant homeland of Hawaiki, to send him fire to keep him warm. The glowing embers sent by his sisters landed first at White Island (► 91), and then where Ngatoroirangi was standing to form the volcanoes of the Central Plateau.

PEOPLE WITH
MANA

"Haere mai, haere mai" are some of the first words you're likely to hear on arriving in New Zealand, welcoming you to Aotearoa, the Land of the Long White Cloud. A renaissance of Maori language and culture is happening.

No official event is complete without a Maori ceremony. Te Reo Maori, the Maori language, is taught in schools and used in parliamentary debates, and many of its words have entered New Zealand English. This renewed interest comes after Maori traditions were discouraged for generations in the ill-conceived belief that Maori would want to assimilate with the European settlers' way of life, and could do so more easily if they forgot their own culture.

A Proud Celebration of Maori Culture

Today, however, the goal is to embrace cultural diversity and to find a way for Maori and Pakeha (people of European descent) – and the many other ethnic groups of New Zealand – to live together in a fairer society. The process is not without tensions: Maori are still disadvantaged in many ways. But they are proud to celebrate the achievements of their cultural heroes – people with mana (spiritual authority).

The traditional *Poi* dance performed at the New Zealand Maori Arts and Crafts Institute

Rebellion

Hone Heke Pokai (*c.*1810–50) became the first tribal chief to add his name to the Treaty of Waitangi in 1840 (➤ 61–62). Before long, though, Maori began to fear that the Europeans would observe the treaty's principles of partnership only until they could seize the land. Hone Heke regretted his role and expressed his growing resentment of British sovereignty by cutting down one of its symbols, a shipping-signal flagstaff on Maiki, overlooking Russell, not once but four times.

In 1887, **Horonuku Te Heuheu Tukino IV** (*c.*1821–88) gave away one of his tribe's most precious possessions – the three sacred peaks that form Tongariro National Park (➤ 87–89). The far-sighted paramount chief of the Ngati Tuwharetoa people realized that giving the land to the government would prevent it being sold off in small slices. The area became New Zealand's first national park.

In 1893, **Sir Apirana Ngata** (1874–1950) became the first Maori to graduate from a New Zealand university. He had grown up in the Ngati Porou communities of the East Coast (➤ 190–193) and saw it as

THE TREATY OF WAITANGI

The Treaty of Waitangi was drawn up in 1840 and eventually signed by more than 500 tribal chiefs. Under its terms, chiefs ceded their sovereignty to the British Queen in exchange for protection and the same rights as British citizens.

However, the meaning of "sovereignty" was muddled in translation and the document remains controversial. The treaty guaranteed Maori the possession of their land and resources, but land was in fact confiscated and relations between the chiefs and the Crown quickly deteriorated.

A lively demonstration of stick dancing

his mission to save his people from social disintegration and eventual extinction. He helped them to develop and farm their land, while also encouraging them to preserve their culture and maintain their own identity.

More Leading Figures

Dame Whina Cooper (1895–1994) founded the Maori Women's Welfare League. She became a national representative of peaceful protest in her 80s, when she led thousands of Maori on a rally. For two months in 1975 she headed the Maori land march from Northland to Parliament in Wellington (▶ 104–106), to dramatize the Maori's determination to retain their land and culture.

Corporal Willie Apiata (*b.*1972) made headlines in 2007 when he was awarded the Victoria Cross for bravery under fire in Afghanistan in 2004. Following a rocket attack on his position, Apiata saved the life of a seriously injured comrade by carrying him 70m (75 yards) to safety under heavy fire. The hero has endeared himself to the nation for his modesty – he says of his act that he was just doing what he is trained for.

MAORI GLOSSARY

Aotearoa New Zealand	*Kai* food, eat	*Marae* meeting place
Aroha love	*Karakia* prayer	*Maunga* mountain
Awa river	*Kia ora* a common	*Moana* lake, sea
Haere mai welcome	greeting	*Pa* fortified village
Haka dance	*Kaumatua* male elder	*Pakeha* person of
Hongi pressing noses	*Kuia* female elder	European descent
in greeting	*Mana* spiritual power,	*Pounamu* greenstone
Iwi people, tribe	authority	*Waka* canoe

A traditional Haka Otaki Te Rahui group in full dress

No More
MEAT AND THREE VEG

From being a gastronomic wilderness up until the 1980s, New Zealand's culinary scene has since undergone a dramatic transformation, to the extent that its chefs are now in hot demand around the world.

New Zealand has always produced superb ingredients – meat, poultry, vegetables, seafood and fruit – but New Zealanders have not always been as open to new culinary ideas as they are today. There was a time when roast lamb with bland vegetables was the most exciting meal. Meat and three veg is still a classic, but as a nation of immigrants, New Zealanders couldn't help but be exposed to outside influences. After simmering in conservative juices, Kiwis have whipped up a fusion of tastes, with the strongest influences from Asia, the Pacific Islands and the Mediterranean.

Cosmopolitan Dining

The number of New Zealand's fully licensed restaurants has more than tripled since the early 1990s, supplemented by hundreds of smaller eateries. From fine dining to sandwich bars, there are plenty of culinary temptations in the cities and a wealth of gastronomic experiences in rural areas. Menus often feature local, seasonal produce, and most eateries usually offer at least a couple of vegetarian options. Dishes that are sure to please include pan-fried fish such as blue cod, tarakihi or snapper; roast venison (sometimes called cervena) or lamb; crayfish (especially in Kaikoura, ► 128–129); and whitebait fritters (best on the West Coast of the South Island, ► 149–151).

WILDFOODS FESTIVAL

Held around March each year in the small West Coast town of Hokitika (► 149–150), the Wildfoods Festival (www.wildfoods.co.nz) is not for those with a timid palate. Here, 100-plus food stalls dish up "bush tucker" delicacies to crowds of around 22,000 adventurous gourmets in what has become a gastronomic highlight of the local social calendar.

Old favourites are possum burgers, crouching grasshoppers, mountain oysters and huhu grubs, 5cm-long (2-inch) insect larvae that taste of peanut butter. To help the digestion, how about a worm slammer – earthworms pickled in vodka?

THE BEST OF NEW ZEALAND WINES

White Wines

- Sauvignon Blanc: New Zealand's most famous wine, especially when it's from Marlborough. Typically, it has a gooseberry character with a dry style.
- Chardonnay: These range from big, buttery and full of oak to lighter styles designed to go with food.
- Riesling: A brilliant food wine, excellent value, and best made in the South Island. Canterbury is a leader in the variety.
- Sparkling: New Zealand sparkling wines range from cheap sweet fizz to traditionally made, bottle-fermented brut in the Champagne style.

Red Wines

- Pinot Noir: New Zealand produces world-class Pinot Noir, which tends to be relatively full-bodied. It's hard to grow and make, so quantities are small and it's expensive. The best comes from Martinborough and Central Otago.
- Cabernet Sauvignon/Merlot: Hawke's Bay is one of the few regions in New Zealand able to ripen Cabernet Sauvignon consistently to produce the distinctive fruity red. Merlot is often blended in to soften it.

Maori Cuisine

Traditionally, Maori gathered food from the land and sea, and also farmed such staples as *kumara* (sweet potato). Favourite dishes include tuna, eel, *kina* (sea urchin) and other *kai moana* (seafood), *titi* (muttonbird) and wild pork, while accompaniments and seasonings include *puha* (a spinach-like vegetable), *horopito* (a peppery-tasting shrub), *kawakawa* (also called bush basil) and *pikopiko* (fern frond, sometimes used in a pesto). These are often barbecued or stewed, or for special occasions are cooked in a *hangi* (earth oven). This is a pit dug in the ground and lined with stones heated in a fire. Leaves are then placed over the stones, and meat, seafood and vegetables layered on top. Finally, the *hangi* is covered over with more leaves and earth, and the food is left to steam. Try a *hangi* at Rotorua (➤ 86).

New Zealand is famous for its lamb, served here with baked onions

Weird and Wonderful
WILDLIFE

The kea is a breed of parrot

New Zealand is a favourite among wildlife tourists, who arrive armed with binoculars, underwater goggles, cameras and high hopes of catching a glimpse of some extraordinary creatures. Few realize that their first wildlife encounter is likely to be with a possum stretched out flat on the road.

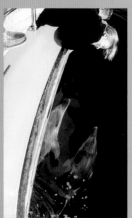

Dolphin cruises are very popular

New Zealand is home to some of the world's rarest and strangest animals: kakapo – plump, bizarrely sweet-smelling parrots that have forgotten how to fly; tuatara – ancient, wrinkly reptiles that once shared the planet with dinosaurs; weta – heavily armoured insects the size of mice; and fluffy, flightless kiwi, the national symbol. The country is like a Noah's Ark, floating in the southern Pacific carrying a precious cargo of unique creatures.

When New Zealand broke off from the super-continent Gondwana millions of years ago, its only animals were birds, reptiles and insects. The only land mammals were bats. Without the threat of predators or competition from opponents, birds didn't need to fly and insects could grow to palm size. But there are now a number of stowaways, like the possum, and to ensure the survival of legitimate passengers many New Zealanders regard it as their civic duty to stand on the accelerator if they see one of these squatters on the road.

The Possum Problem

A yellow-eyed penguin

Possums are the worst. These cute critters were introduced from Australia in 1837 to launch a fur trade, and are now found in more than 90 per cent of the country. The standard joke about New Zealand is that the country has more sheep than people – but possums outnumber both combined.

More than 70 million emerge from their sleeping holes each night to crunch on 19,000 tonnes of vegetation, mostly the shoots of indigenous trees. Australia's eucalyptus trees contain natural toxins but New Zealand's trees have no defence mechanisms. Apart from stripping native forests, possums rob birds of their food supplies. Similarly, stoats, ferrets and rats, which feast on the eggs and chicks of native birds, make any attempt at breeding a difficult undertaking.

While the public roadkill effort may initially come as an unpleasant surprise to visitors, it is but a small part of a huge effort to keep such undesirables in check. At a cost of around NZ$80 million per year, a variety of methods, including poisoning and trapping, are used to keep pests at bay and to help visitors take home memories of truly wild encounters.

An injured kea is cared for at the Willowbank Wildlife Reserve

Feathered Favourites

One of the most memorable wildlife experiences is watching penguins come ashore after their day's fishing. If you are in the right place at the right time, you'll see some of them waddle ashore or perform an elaborate ritual with their mate.

The Otago Peninsula (▶ 174–175) is a good place to see yellow-eyed penguins and at Milford Sound (▶ 166–168) you might encounter Fiordland crested penguins.

There are several other peculiar birds. The cheekiest is the kea (alpine parrot), which you're likely to encounter around Arthur's Pass (▶ 154), where it breeds in rocky crevices.

The flightless and night-active kiwi is almost impossible to see in the wild, unless you venture as far south as Stewart Island; because they nest on the ground, their eggs and chicks are sitting targets for introduced predators such as stoats and ferrets, and all five endemic species are threatened with extinction. But there are several kiwi houses in the country – for example at the Whakarewarewa Thermal Valley in Rotorua (▶ 82–85) and Willowbank in Christchurch (▶ 152–153) – and

A seal basks in the sun at Milford Sound

A bird makes its mark in the Awaroa inlet of Abel Tasman National Park

they've been reintroduced to the Karori Wildlife Sanctuary in Wellington (➤ 110), where you can hear them, and maybe even spot them, during the evening.

New Zealand is surrounded by hundreds of offshore islands. Like lifeboats around a vessel with a valuable load, these islands provide safe havens for endangered species. Kapiti (➤ 111–112) is one of the most accessible island reserves, where you can see rare bird species such as the kokako, stitchbird and saddleback, as well as vivacious kaka (forest parrots) and parakeets.

Marine Mammals

Whales, dolphins and seals live around New Zealand's 15,000km (9,300 miles) of coastline. The best place to see all three is Kaikoura (➤ 128–129) on the east coast of the South Island. Sperm whales are abundant here year-round, chasing giant squid in the deep underwater canyons. Dolphins cruise the bays around Kaikoura in large pods, and they are also reliably found in the Bay of Islands (➤ 60–62).

Hector's dolphins, the smallest species, are unique to New Zealand and regularly visit Kaikoura and Akaroa Harbour (➤ 144) in summer to have their young. If you're looking for seals, follow your nose. The grey torpedoes are so well camouflaged on the rocky coastline that they are hard to spot, but their fishy smell gives them away.

Above: New Zealand's famous kiwi is at risk from non-native predators but several reserves are helping its survival. Below: Bottlenose dolphins swimming just off Stewart Island

Peter Jackson on the set of *The Lord of the Rings: Return of the King*

From
Mansfield to
Middle Earth

Not so long ago, New Zealand writers and painters were convinced that the only way to find fame and fortune was by leaving their island home behind. But things have changed and now movie stars and directors flock to New Zealand, and Kiwi writers and artists are fêted both at home and on the international stage.

Authors in the Limelight

Katherine Mansfield (1888–1923) is regarded as one of New Zealand's finest literary exports and the achievements of her short life continue to be celebrated at her birthplace in Wellington (▶ 107). Also held dear to New Zealanders is Janet Frame (1924–2004), whose autobiographical *An Angel at My Table* (1984) was subsequently turned into an award-winning film by Kiwi director Jane Campion in 1990.

The Chronicles Of Narnia: Prince Caspian was filmed in New Zealand

Keri Hulme is best known as the author of the Booker Prize-winning novel *The Bone People* (1984), but she has also produced many short stories and volumes of poetry. Another Maori writer who is creating waves internationally is Witi Ihimaera. The former diplomat and New Zealand consul to the United States became the country's first Maori writer to publish a novel in English. Since *Tangi* in 1973, he has become a prolific chronicler of social issues affecting Maori through such works as *The Whale Rider* (1987). A more recent Kiwi winner of the Booker Prize is Lloyd Jones, for his *Mister Pip* (2006). This novel tells the harrowing tale of a small community on the Papua New Guinean island of Bougainville caught up in the 1990s civil war.

The Visual Arts
The country's most internationally famous artist is Frances Hodgkins (1869–1947), whose watercolours and oil paintings are part of the permanent exhibitions at galleries in Wellington and Dunedin. Other renowned painters include Colin McCahon (1919–87); Rita Angus (1908–70), famed in particular for her landscapes and self-portraits; Charles Goldie (1870–1947), whose paintings of high-ranking Maori are tinged with sadness; and Ralph Hotere (*b*.1931), one of the country's most respected living artists.

Film Friendly
Filming by Peter Jackson of the hugely successful *Lord of the Rings* trilogy in New Zealand in 1999 and 2000 put the country firmly on the cinematic map, and it continues to be used for its spectacular landscapes, attractive exchange rate and growing movie-production expertise.

Internationally acclaimed and much-loved Kiwi, Dame Kiri Te Kanawa

In 2002, Witi Ihimaera's *Whale Rider* was filmed at Whangara, north of Hawke's Bay (➤ 193), gaining Keisha Castle-Hughes, its 11-year-old star, an Oscar nomination for her role. Since then, the locally produced *In My Father's Den* (2004), based on the novel by Kiwi author Maurice Gee, was released to critical acclaim, and Peter Jackson went on to film his remake of the classic *King Kong* in 2005. New Zealand is also tipped to be the location used for Jackson's *The Hobbit*. The international films *The Chronicles of Narnia: The Lion, the Witch and the Wardrobe* (2005) and *Prince Caspian* (2008), based on CS Lewis's children's books, were filmed in New Zealand, using the country's spectacular scenery to great effect.

In 2010 *Boy,* about growing up in New Zealand in the Michael Jackson-crazed 1980s, became New Zealand's highest-grossing film ever. Written and directed by Taika Waititi, it was shot in the remote town Waihau Bay.

MUSICAL KIWIS

Soprano Dame Kiri Te Kanawa is perhaps New Zealand's best-known singer. Although Dame Kiri has retired from the operatic stage, she still appears at concert halls and open-air venues in New Zealand and abroad. Another Kiwi soprano is Hayley Westenra, who gained international recognition at the age of just 16 in 2003 with the release of her album *Pure*.

Pop music stars include Bic Runga, of Chinese and Maori descent, a singer-songwriter renowned for her haunting ballads; Maori-Niuean hip hop artist Che Fu; and the band Crowded House. Most recently, the Grammy Award-winning comedy music act, *The Flight of the Conchords,* aka Bret McKenzie and Jermaine Clement, have gained success in the UK and US as a result of their television show.

The New Zealand
EXPERIMENT

As a small nation of resourceful people far away from the rest of the world, New Zealand can afford to swim against the stream and try things others might not dare to consider.

Nuclear Free

When New Zealanders decide to tackle an issue, they aren't afraid to stand up and be counted. This can be seen in the country's controversial decision to declare itself nuclear free in 1987, and to spearhead protests against the testing of atomic bombs in the Pacific. Opposition to French nuclear testing at Mururoa and to visits by US nuclear-powered and -armed ships culminated in the sinking of Greenpeace's *Rainbow Warrior* by French secret service agents in 1985. Outrage over the incident is still felt today, and the nation remains staunchly nuclear free.

In a bid to curb climate change New Zealand recently introduced a controversial Emissions Trading Scheme tax to discourage pollutants, and to encourage investment into forests and research.

Necessity is the Mother of Invention

The ingenuity of Kiwis is summed up by the saying that, given a piece of No. 8 fencing wire, they can fix or make just about anything. This stems from the days when spares were hard to come by and farmers had to

make do and mend as best they could.

The film *The World's Fastest Indian* (2005) celebrates this inventiveness, telling the story of Burt Munro (1899–1978) and his 1920 Indian motorcycle. Munro modified the machine over a period of 46 years in his garden shed, eventually taking it to the Bonneville Salt Flats

The sinking of *Rainbow Warrior* still causes outrage today. Right: Anthony Hopkins as Burt Munro

LEADING THE FLOCK

1893 New Zealand is the first country to give women the vote.

1948 Major protests against the exclusion of Maori players from a rugby tour of South Africa.

1981 Protests against a visit by the South African Springbok rugby team divide the country.

1985 New Zealand's anti-nuclear policy leads to the refusal of a visit by the USS *Buchanan* warship.

1994 New Zealand ratifies the Protocol on Environmental Protection to the Antarctic Treaty, banning mining for at least 50 years.

2007 Prime Minister Helen Clark announces plans to make New Zealand the world's first totally carbon-neutral country by 2040.

2010 Prime Minister John Key introduces an Emissions Trading Scheme.

in Utah and setting a world speed record that still stands today. Another well-respected motorbike engineer was John Britten (1950–95), who designed and built record-making machines using revolutionary materials; you can see his V1000 model at Te Papa in Wellington (➤ 108–109). Other famous Kiwi inventors include South Island farmer Richard Pearse (1877–1953), who built his own plane and apparently flew before the Wright brothers did; and the "father of nuclear physics", Sir Ernest Rutherford (1871–1937), who split the atom – rather ironic for nuclear-free New Zealand.

SWEATY JERSEYS and the Auld Mug

Sport is part of everyday life in New Zealand and a major source of national pride. Winning athletes are treated to a hero's welcome when they return, whereas failure to win a coveted trophy sends the nation into collective mourning.

Rugby

Rugby union is the main national sport – some would say obsession – with 150,000 Kiwis playing the game. The professional season starts in February with the Super 15 competition and ends with the National Provincial Championships in late October. The national team, the All Blacks, is among the most successful in the world, and will be vying to take the World Cup when the competition is hosted by New Zealand in 2011. The players' every moves are recorded in the nation's memory, and many New Zealanders can recite the names of All Blacks players going back decades. Like film stars elsewhere, rugby players fill the tabloid pages, especially since the sport turned professional in 1995. The team is famous for performing the haka, a Maori dance, before each match, a tradition dating from the 19th century (see box).

> "Kiwis are natural competitors with a real desire to be the best"

Netball

Almost as popular as rugby is netball, with the ANZ Championship and World Championship both followed closely by avid fans of the sport. The ANZ Championship, inaugurated in 2008, sees 12 regional New Zealand teams competing against five from Australia between April and July. The national team, the Silver Ferns, won the World Netball Championship in Jamaica in 2003, and is looking to regain the title in Singapore in 2011 after losing out to Australia in 2007.

Above right: The All Blacks perform their famous haka prior to a match in Eden Park

Yachting

One of New Zealand's biggest sporting coups took place in 1995 when a group of yachties took home the America's Cup, the world's oldest sporting trophy. In 144 years, the "Auld Mug" had left its case in the USA only one other time, to spend a season with the Australian team in 1983. Five years after its historic 1995 win, Team New Zealand defended the title in the Hauraki Gulf (➤ 58–59), and Auckland's Viaduct Basin (➤ 52) was the place to be for every self-respecting Kiwi. Again, New Zealand won the

---

THE ALL BLACKS' HAKA

The haka performed by the All Blacks was composed by the famous Maori chief Te Rauparaha (c.1760–1849) to commemorate the occasion in 1810 when he escaped his enemies by hiding in a food pit. On emerging from the pit, Te Rauparaha was confronted by another chief, who to his relief turned out to be friendly. Following instruction from the haka leader, All Blacks players join in the actions and words of the chant:

Ka mate, ka mate	I die, I die
Ka ora', ka ora'	I live, I live
Ka mate, ka mate	I die, I die
Ka ora', ka ora'	I live, I live
Tenei te tangata puhuruhuru	This is the hairy man
Nana i tiki mai whakawhiti te ra	Who caused the sun to shine again for me
Upane, upane	Up the ladder, up the ladder
Upane, kaupane	To the top
Whiti te ra!	The sun shines!

race, this time against the Italian Prada team in what was the first final in the cup's history without American competitors.

Outdoor Life

Easy access to wilderness areas and the ocean is one of the reasons for most Kiwis' sporting passion. It would be difficult to grow up in New Zealand without spending significant amounts of time hiking, fishing or

NEW ZEALAND'S SPORTING HEROES

- Jean Batten smashes Amy Johnson's solo flight time between England and Australia by six days in 1934. In 1935, the "Garbo of the Skies" becomes the first woman to make the return flight. In 1936 she makes the first direct flight between England and New Zealand and then the fastest trans-Tasman flight.
- Jack Lovelock wins Olympic gold in the 1,500m at Berlin in 1936.
- Sir Edmund Hillary climbs Mount Everest in 1953.
- Murray Halberg wins Olympic gold in the 5,000m in 1960.
- Yachtsman Sir Peter Blake wins the Whitbread Round the World Race in 1969, and leads Team New Zealand to victory in the America's Cup in 1995 and 2000.
- Mark Todd wins Olympic gold in three-day eventing in 1984 and 1988, and bronze in 2000.
- Hamish Carter wins an Olympic gold in the men's triathlon in 2004; Bevan Docherty takes silver in the same race and then bronze in 2008.
- Golfer Michael Campbell wins the US Open in 2005.
- Twins Caroline and Georgina Evers-Swindell win Olympic gold in 2004 in the women's double sculls, then repeat their feat in Beijing in 2008.
- Valerie Vili takes the women's shot put record at the 2006 Commonwealth Games, wins the World Championship in 2007, and adds gold at the 2008 Olympics.

Left: Valerie Vili receives her gold medal at the 2008 Olympics. Above: Mountain biking is one of the country's most popular and accessible outdoor sports

riding the surf. Another reason is that Kiwis are natural competitors with a real desire to be the best. It's perhaps not surprising that some of the most challenging outdoor endurance competitions and adventure sports began in New Zealand. Whether it's bungy jumping, sailing or extreme endurance races, chances are that a Kiwi holds the record.

NATIONAL BICYCLE NETWORK

There are plans underway to build a national cycleway that will stretch from one end of the country to the other, linking small towns, rural communities, cities, beaches and mountains. The government invested NZ$50 million in 2009 as an initiative to boost tourism. The first portion, Ruapehu-Whanganui Trails Ngā Ara Tūhono, opened in July 2010.

CAN YOU HACKETT?

Bungy jumping veteran AJ Hackett is one of the driving forces behind New Zealand's reputation as an adventure sports destination. However, bungy jumping is no New Zealand invention. On Pentecost, one of the islands in Vanuatu (in the South Pacific), men have been jumping off high wooden towers for centuries – with their feet attached to elastic vines. In the 1970s, this ancient ritual inspired the Oxford University Dangerous Sports Club to try it for themselves. AJ Hackett saw a video and was hooked. He spent some time testing latex rubber cords before making a series of jumps, first from a ski-field gondola 91m (298 feet) above the snow, and then, in June 1987, from the Eiffel Tower, launching an entire industry.

BEST OF...

A country as rich and diverse in natural beauty and cultural charms as New Zealand can make it almost impossible to choose what to see and do first. To help you get the most from your visit here are some of the best experiences.

Best Beaches

With 15,000km (9,300 miles) of coastline, New Zealand is like one big beach. At Tunnel Beach, southwest of Dunedin, you'll find giant sandstone bluffs and a hand-hewn tunnel dating from the 1870s. Ninety Mile Beach in Northland (➤ 67) is a great sunset location, and for a wild surf try Piha Beach west of Auckland (➤ 66), Wharariki Beach on the west coast of Golden Bay (➤ 131) or Gillespies Beach (➤ 189) on the West Coast.

Best Wildlife Views

Swimming with dolphins at Kaikoura (➤ 128–129) or in the Bay of Islands (➤ 60–62) could move you to tears of joy. Watching dolphins ride the bow wave of a boat in Milford Sound (➤ 166–168) comes close, and seeing a sperm whale relaxing in the water off Kaikoura is awe inspiring. Seeing huge royal albatrosses and ungainly yellow-eyed penguins up close on the Otago Peninsula just outside Dunedin (➤ 174) is a highlight for any birdwatcher.

A cruise of Milford Sound offers breathtaking views

Best Exercise

- Hire some inline skates to dart along Wellington's scenic waterfront or squeeze into a pedal-boat for a paddle on the harbour.
- In Auckland, you can be the skipper of a super-yacht for a few hours (➤ 52–54), and see how exhausting it can be.

Kawakawa's public toilets are in a class of their own

- Walk the long-distance Abel Tasman Coastal Track (➤ 126–127), exploring the forested headlands and golden bays, or follow the route offshore in a kayak.

Best City Views

- Mount Victoria and the cable car terminal in Wellington's Botanic Garden (➤ 186) give stunning views over the capital.
- In Auckland, zoom up the Sky Tower (➤ 50–51) or drive up to One Tree Hill (➤ 65).
- In Queenstown, the top station of the gondola is a good place to be in the evening (➤ 164–165).

Best National Parks

- Tongariro National Park, in central North Island (➤ 87–89).
- Abel Tasman National Park, at the top of South Island (➤ 126–127).
- Nelson Lakes National Park (➤ 131).
- Aoraki/Mount Cook National Park, in the Southern Alps (➤ 147–148).
- Fiordland National Park, in the southwest of South Island (➤ 166–168).

Best Public Facility

The grass-roofed public toilets in the small town of Kawakawa, south of the Bay of Islands, were the last piece of artful architecture designed by Friedensreich Hundertwasser (1928–2000). The celebrated eccentric Austrian architect and painter chose the sleepy town as his retirement home and also transformed some of the shopfronts on the main street in his trademark colourful style.

Best Boat Trip

A cruise of Milford Sound (➤ 166–168) is hard to beat as far as the drama of the dripping landscape is concerned, but Doubtful Sound offers a more remote kind of wilderness experience (➤ 168).

TRANZALPINE
Train Adventure

The coast-to-coast traverse of the Southern Alps is one of the great rail journeys of the world. From the Pacific to the Tasman Sea, the TranzAlpine route runs through 224km (139 miles) of the South Island's rugged scenery.

Frontier Travel

The TranzAlpine adventure began life as a few ramshackle railcars travelling along the narrow-gauge track between Christchurch (➤ 142–143) and Greymouth (➤ 149). It provided the sole means of transport for people needing to cross the Main Divide in bad weather. Rain, wind and snow frequently shut down the western leg of State Highway 73, which cuts an almost parallel route through the mountainous immensity of the South Island's alpine spine.

The Modern Journey

Today, the TranzAlpine is still popular with regular travellers between the lush and wild West Coast (➤ 149–151) and the orderly Canterbury Plains, but the comfort level of the modern carriages reflects the growing number

Tranz Scenic trains run on the TranzAlpine route through spectacular scenery

Tranz Scenic

of travellers and rail buffs on the train. About 200,000 people have travelled on the TranzAlpine every year since it was launched as a tourist attraction in 1987.

For the first 20 minutes of the half-day journey to Greymouth, the train speeds – relatively speaking – through suburbia and the city's rural outskirts to Rolleston, where it leaves the main south line to veer west towards the mountains. The train then rumbles through the flat alluvial Canterbury Plains, passing rolling pastures and small rural townships until reaching Springfield, a former railway service centre about an hour from Christchurch, which marks the start of the long alpine haul to Arthur's Pass (► 154). Here, the bush-clad foothills start stretching beyond the tree line, exposing the first raw rock faces and bare summits.

As the TranzAlpine enters a labyrinth of gorges and hills, it crosses the first viaduct, which spans more than 200m (650 feet) across the dry shingle bed of the Kowai River.

Valleys Deep and Mountains High

For the next hour, the journey becomes a scenic and spectacular slide show. No fewer than 16 short tunnels act as the light switch between

---

TRANZALPINE TIPS

■ Christchurch's railway station is to the southwest of Hagley Park and is not very well connected by public transport. The easiest and most inexpensive way to get there is to take one of the 10-seat shuttle buses that provide a door-to-door service throughout the city.

■ There is a licensed buffet on board the train.

■ There is an outdoor viewing platform on the TranzAlpine, a spartan affair but a perfect place to get good views and take photographs.

■ Arrive early for the train, as seats are allocated on check-in not on booking.

stupendous vistas of magnificent deep-cut river canyons and soaring mountains. About 85km (53 miles) from Christchurch, the rust-coloured "T" of the Staircase Viaduct connects two tunnels and, at 73m (239 feet) (3m/10 feet higher than Christchurch Cathedral), marks the highest of a sequence of tall steel bridges the TranzAlpine has to cross, until it emerges into the broad valleys of the Waimakariri and Bealey rivers. In summer, the braided Waimakariri (Maori for "cold water") runs through its wide gravel bed in trickles and streams, but after a storm it swells to a thunderous river that carves the landscape.

Arthur's Pass, 737m (2,417 feet) above sea level, is the end point of the climb and provides a brief stopping point on the journey. As the train starts its steep downhill ride to the West Coast, it disappears into the 8.5km (5-mile) Otira Tunnel for more than 10 minutes.

The Other Side

At the other end the landscape is very different. Dense rainforest hangs over the track and huge flax bushes push against the embankment. Gems on the western leg include the Otira Hotel, the Taramakau River, rich in fish and greenstone, vast patches of rainforest and Lake Brunner.

Upon arrival at Greymouth most passengers opt to stay on for a few days to explore the West Coast. For those eager to experience the stunning views again, the train departs just one hour later for the return journey.

Stunning views of Arthur's Pass can be enjoyed from the train. Opposite: Bungy jumping was made popular in New Zealand

PLANNING YOUR JOURNEY

■ At the time of writing services were cancelled as a result of the Christchurch earthquake. Please check journey times online.

■ Bookings can be made by calling 0800 872 467 (toll free) or 00 64 4 495 0775 from overseas. You can also visit www.tranzscenic.co.nz or buy tickets in person at the reservations centre open daily 7am to 7pm. Advance reservations are recommended during summer.

Finding Your Feet

First Two Hours

New Zealand's three main international airports are at Auckland, Wellington and Christchurch. Some flights from Australia also land at Queenstown, Dunedin, Hamilton and Rotorua.

> ### Ground Transport Fares
> $ under NZ$10 $$ NZ$11–$20 $$$ NZ$21–$30 $$$$ over NZ$30

Travelling by Air

■ All passengers arriving on international flights have to clear customs and immigration and undergo **biosecurity checks**. On your plane, you'll fill in an arrival card and a declaration form for any biosecurity risk goods (meat, dairy products, fruit, plant and animal material) you may be carrying. Sniffer dogs work at the baggage claim area, monitoring luggage for **animal and vegetable products**. Officers from the Ministry of Agriculture and Forestry will check your declaration form and luggage if necessary. Packaged foods are usually acceptable, but if you're unsure it is best to declare what you are bringing in and **check with the MAF officers**. Failure to declare risk goods carries an instant fine of NZ$400, while knowingly or accidentally bringing in such goods can cost you up to NZ$100,000.

■ International travellers departing from Auckland by air are no longer required to pay Departure Tax. However if departing from another city on an international flight a fee of NZ$25 is applicable. Children under 12 are free.

Arriving in Auckland

■ About 80 per cent of flights into New Zealand arrive at **Auckland International Airport** (www.aucklandairport.co.nz), 23km (14 miles) from the city.

■ **Once you exit customs** on the ground floor, there are information and foreign exchange desks, luggage storage facilities, a domestic transfer check-in counter and car hire desks.

■ The best way to get to downtown is on the **Airbus** (tel: 0800 10 30 80 toll free; www.airbus.co.nz, $$), which leaves from the forecourt of the arrivals area. It departs daily every 15 minutes 6am–6pm, every 20 minutes 6pm–8pm, then every 30 minutes until 10pm. The journey takes about 45 minutes to get to the city, stopping at all major hotels and landmarks along the way. It may make extra stops on request if they are en route. Buy your ticket on the bus.

■ Some hotels have **free shuttle services**, so check with your accommodation.

■ Small **door-to-door shuttle buses** (**Supershuttle:** tel: 0800 748 885 toll free; www.supershuttle.co.nz, $$$), which wait for passengers outside the terminal, are only slightly more expensive than the Airbus but can be faster.

■ Taxis ($$$$) are the most expensive means of transport. Both taxis and shuttle buses depart from in front of the terminal.

■ If you are **transferring to a domestic flight**, the domestic terminal is about 800m (880 yards) away. Follow the blue lines painted on the pavement outside the international terminal, or catch the free inter-terminal bus, which departs daily 6am–10:30pm from the arrivals end of the forecourt.

■ Any of the transport options from the airport will drop you off where you need to go, but **orientation is straightforward**. The airport is to the south of the city. The main artery downtown is Queen Street, which stretches from Quay Street at the waterfront to the junction of the city's main motorways.

Auckland Visitor Information Centres

■ The centre at the international terminal is **open daily** while flights are arriving or leaving. The domestic terminal office is open daily 6am–10pm.

■ There are two inner-city information centres; the atrium of Sky City at the corner of Victoria and Federal streets focuses on the capital and is open daily 8–8; the Viaduct Basin branch, 137 Quay Street, Princes Wharf, covers the whole country and is open Nov–Apr daily 8–7; May–Oct 9–5:30 (tel: 0800 AUCKLAND or 0800 2825 5263; www.aucklandnz.com).

■ The centres offer **free maps, brochures and up-to-date timetables**.

Arriving in Wellington

■ **Wellington International Airport** (www.wellingtonairport.co.nz) is about 10km (6 miles) from the inner city. The **international and domestic terminals** are housed in the same building.

■ International passengers arrive on the **ground floor of the terminal building**. Car hire desks and luggage storage facilities are near the baggage claim carousels, and an information desk, shops and cafes are on the first floor.

■ The best way to get to the city is on the Airport Flyer (tel: 0800 801 700 toll free; www.metlink.co.nz; $) which connects the airport with central Wellington and the Hutt Valley. It departs from the southern end of the airport terminal every 15 minutes on weekdays (6:20am–9:30pm).

■ **Taxis** ($$$) and **shuttles** ($$) depart from bays opposite the main exit.

■ **Wellington's inner city** stretches along the waterfront, between Mount Victoria (overlooking Oriental Parade) and the Parliament complex. The main downtown hubs are Lambton Quay and Courtenay Place.

■ Wellington can be **confusing for drivers** because the streets don't follow a regular grid and the inner city is circumnavigated by a one-way system. The motorway runs through Wellington. Beyond the city centre it forks into SH1, going north to the Kapiti Coast, and SH2, to the Hutt Valley.

Wellington Visitor Information Centre

■ The **main centre** is at the corner of Victoria and Wakefield streets, Civic Square (tel: 0800 933 5363 toll free or 04802 4860; www.wellingtonnz.com). The centre has free maps and information about attractions, accommodation and regional transport. Open Mon–Wed, Fri 8:30–5, Thu 9:30–5, Sat–Sun 9:30–4:30, public holidays 11–4:30, with extended hours in peak season (Dec–Apr).

Arriving in Christchurch

■ International flights arrive at **Christchurch International Airport** (www.christchurchairport.co.nz), about 12km (7 miles) northwest of the city centre. The **international and domestic terminals** are close together. Both have information and car hire desks. A new combined international and domestic terminal is due to be completed in 2011.

■ The **Metro Airport Bus** (www.metroinfo.org.nz; $) departs from outside the international terminal, on weekdays every 30 minutes 6:35am–6:35pm and hourly 7:20pm–1am. On weekends buses run every 30 minutes noon–5pm and hourly Sat 8:10am–noon, 5pm–12:55am and Sun 8:40am–noon, 5pm–12:55am. Routes and timings may be subject to change while repairs are made to the city as a result of 2011 earthquake, see details online.

■ **Taxis** ($$$$) and **shuttles** ($$) depart from a lane beginning outside the domestic and international terminals.

■ Christchurch is laid out in a **grid pattern**, with Colombo Street as the main north–south thoroughfare. Hagley Park is a dominant feature, separating the inner city from the western suburbs.

Getting Around

New Zealand's major cities all offer a good network of public transport but there are also domestic flights, long-distance bus services and train services connecting the cities and larger towns. For longer journeys, plan and book ahead for the best prices.

City Transport Fares
$ under NZ$5 $$ NZ$6–$10 $$$ NZ$11–$20 $$$$ over NZ$20

In Auckland

- Auckland has an integrated public transport system that comprises buses, trains and ferries. Contact **MAXX** (tel: (09) 366 6400 or 0800 103080 toll free; www.maxx.co.nz) for all routes and timetables.
- At visitor information centres you can get the **Auckland Busabout Guide**, which lists all destinations, their bus route number and departure point.
- The **Link bus** ($), travelling clockwise and anticlockwise on a loop that includes most of the inner-city attractions, runs every 10 minutes at peak times (Mon–Fri 6am–7pm, Sat 7am–6pm) and every 15 minutes off peak (Mon–Sat 6pm–11:30pm, Sun and public holidays 7am–11:30pm).
- The Link and other buses often connect with **ferries** to Auckland's northern suburbs ($$) and to the Hauraki Gulf islands ($$$$). Ferries depart from the berth between Princes and Queens wharfs. The most frequent connections are the 12-minute ferry to Devonport (every 30 minutes or hourly Mon–Thu 6:10am–11:30pm, Fri–Sat 6:15am–1am, Sun and holidays 7:30am–10:30pm), Birkenhead (every 30 minutes or hourly Mon–Fri 7:15am–11:10pm, Sat–Sun and holidays 7:40am–5:40pm) and Bayswater (every 30 minutes or hourly Mon–Fri 7:15am– 10:40pm, Sat–Sun and holidays 7:40am–5:40pm) in the north, and to Waiheke Island (every 30 minutes or hourly Mon–Fri 5:20am–11:45pm, Sat 6:30am–11:45pm, Sun and holidays 7am–9:30pm). Contact **Fullers** (tel: (09) 367 9111; www.fullers.co.nz) for timetables.
- The metropolitan **commuter train service** (MAXX, tel: (09) 366 6400; www.maxx.co.nz, $–$$) runs west to Waitakere and south to Papakura.

In Wellington

- Wellington has an **excellent public transport network**, with buses running frequently and late into the night. The visitor information centre has maps of the capital's bus network; or contact Metlink (tel: 0800 801 700 toll free; www.metlink.org.nz) for route and timetable details.
- **Buses** connect the inner city with all the suburbs, including Hutt Valley.
- The **Stadium Shuttle** ($) is a special service linking the central city with the Westpac Stadium. For most major events, services commence approximately two hours prior to the start and continue to leave from the stadium about every 10–15 minutes until the crowd has dispersed.
- The **cable car** ($) runs from Lambton Quay up to the Botanic Gardens, every 10 minutes Mon–Fri 7am–10pm, Sat 8:30am–10pm, Sun and public holidays 9am–9pm.
- **Tranz Metro** operates a metropolitan commuter train service ($–$$) in Wellington, connecting the inner city with Upper Hutt in the Hutt Valley and Paraparaumu on the Kapiti Coast north of the capital (tel: 0800 801 700 toll free; www.tranzmetro.co.nz).

In Christchurch

- Most **buses** ($) depart from the Bus Exchange in Lichfield Street, where the Metroinfo counter (tel: (03) 366 8855; www.metroinfo.org.nz) has all route plans and timetables. Staff members are helpful and will book door-to-door **shuttle buses** ($) to destinations not covered by the bus network.
- The **Shuttle** (free) is a bus service that runs along a loop between the town hall and convention centre, through the central city to a shopping mall south of the city. The bus runs every 10–15 minutes (Mon–Fri 7:30am–10:30pm, Sat 8am–10:30pm, Sun 10am–8pm).

Visitor Information Network

There are more than 80 official visitor information centres in New Zealand, indicated by the green "i" logo. Most of them are open daily, with opening hours depending on the season. The centres offer free maps and help with information and bookings. Ask for the Visitor Information Network directory, which lists all centres and their contact details.

Most telephone numbers beginning 0800 are free within New Zealand.

Intercity Connections

Intercity Transport Fares
$ under NZ$30 $$ NZ$31–$50 $$$ NZ$51–$100 $$$$ over NZ$100

Domestic Flights

- **Air New Zealand** (tel: 0800 737 000 toll free; www.airnewzealand.com) is the country's international and main domestic airline, providing daily domestic connections between 26 destinations. The main hubs are Auckland, Wellington, Christchurch and Queenstown, and flights are available to most cities in New Zealand. Special fares are available on most sectors, usually involving advance booking and payment (three weeks prior to departure). These special fares can be booked only in New Zealand, but less expensive fares may be available in connection with an international flight (ask your travel agent for details).
- **Jetstar** (tel: 0800 800 995 toll free; www.jetstar.com) operates flights between Auckland, Wellington, Christchurch and Queenstown.
- **Pacific Blue** (tel: 0800 670 000 toll free; www.flypacificblue.co.nz) operates between Auckland, Hamilton, Wellington, Christchurch, Queenstown and Dunedin).
- **Soundsair** (tel: (03) 520 3080, 0800 505 005 toll free; www.soundsair.com) flies from Wellington to Picton, Blenheim and Nelson, and from Blenheim to Nelson.
- **Air2there.com** (tel: 0800 777 000 toll free; www.air2there.com) offers flights from Wellington to Blenheim, Nelson, New Plymouth, Palmerston North and Paraparaumu.

Buses

- Long-distance buses travel along all major routes ($–$$). The main company is **Intercity** (tel: (09) 583 5780; www.intercity.co.nz), which also operates **Newmans** (tel: (09) 583 5780; www.newmanscoach.co.nz). Both bus services offer a range of travel passes.

Trains

- New Zealand's train system, operated by **Tranz Rail** (tel: 0800 872 467 toll free; www.tranzscenic.co.nz), runs along the main trunk from Auckland to

Wellington and Picton to Christchurch, with the TranzAlpine branching to Greymouth (▶ 28–30).
■ Trains are comfortable and about as fast as buses, but more expensive.

Ferries
■ Tranz Rail also operates ferry services across Cook Strait (tel: 0800 802 802 toll free; www.interislander.co.nz). It has three car and passenger Interislander ferries; the trip takes three hours.
■ Bluebridge sails across the Cook Strait between Wellington and Picton four times daily (tel: 0800 844 844 toll free; www.bluebridge.co.nz).

Shuttles
■ Several small door-to-door shuttle bus companies offer useful **regional services**. Ask at a visitor information centre for details.

Driving
■ Highways (single or dual carriageway) link major cities; rural roads are usually single-carriageway links between smaller centres; and you'll find unsealed roads in remote areas. Distances are measured in kilometres.
■ Outside the main centres, **traffic is light** and driver courtesy is reasonable.
■ The usual minimum legal age to **hire a car** in New Zealand is 21, in some cases 25. Most companies require an international driver's licence. Because hire car accidents are common in New Zealand, insurance premiums are relatively high.
■ Check with your hire company whether any roads are excluded from your **insurance policy**. Most companies don't cover the road to Skippers Park (▶ 176), and don't allow you to drive on Ninety Mile Beach (▶ 67).
■ For up-to-date **road reports**, go to www.maps.aa.co.nz/traffic.
■ **Regular road signs** give the frequency for the local tourist radio station. Tune in to hear the hourly news bulletins, which usually end with a traffic and weather report for the area.
■ If you are a member of a motoring organization affiliated to the Alliance Internationale de Tourisme (AIT), then you are entitled, for a period up to six months, to reciprocal services from the **New Zealand Automobile Association (NZAA)**. If you break down, call 0800 500 222 toll free.

Road Rules
■ **Drive on the left**. On a motorway, keep left unless overtaking.
■ When **turning at a junction**, give way to traffic not turning, and to all traffic crossing or approaching from your right.
■ When turning left at a junction and a vehicle coming from the opposite direction is turning right, you must give way.
■ **Traffic signals** are red, amber and green, and you cannot turn left at a red light unless there is a green arrow pointing left.
■ All occupants, including passengers – adults and children – in the back seats, must wear **seatbelts**.
■ The normal **maximum speed** on the open road is 100kph (62mph); in urban areas 50kph (31mph); in a Limited Speed Zone (LSZ) it is 50kph (31mph) in adverse weather conditions, 100kph (62mph) in normal conditions.
■ **One-lane bridges** are common on rural roads. Approach cautiously and be prepared to give way. Watch for right-of-way signs before the bridge.
■ The **legal limit for alcohol** is 30mg alcohol per 100ml blood (blood alcohol content 0.03) for drivers under 20, and 80mg alcohol per 100ml blood (0.08) for drivers aged 20 and over. There is no insurance cover for drivers over the legal limit.
■ All **cyclists must wear helmets**.

Accommodation

Choose between luxurious country lodges, campsite chalets, bed and breakfast in a character villa, sharing life on a farm, the privacy of a self-catering apartment or the conviviality of a backpacker hostel.

Hotels

■ In smaller towns and rural areas, some pubs offer simple accommodation with lots of character, but they can be noisy.

■ Most **hotel chains** are represented in the main cities and resorts. Rooms are likely to have tea- and coffee-making facilities and some may also have hairdryers, irons and ironing boards. Most places offer non-smoking rooms.

■ **Rates in city hotels** range from around NZ$150 to $700 for a double room. In business areas, hotels may offer discounted rates at weekends.

■ Good hotel chains include: **InterContinental Hotels** (Crowne Plaza, InterContinental, Holiday Inn; tel: 0800 801 111 toll free; www.ichotelsgroup.com) and **Choice** (Comfort, Quality Hotels; tel: 0800 692 464 toll free; www.choicehotels.com.au).

Lodges

■ From heritage buildings furnished with antiques to exclusive sporting retreats with fishing, hunting or golf, lodges offer **top-class facilities** in beautiful surroundings, usually in the countryside and often with excellent food. They may cost from NZ$500 to $2,000 per person per night.

■ The best way to book accommodation at a lodge is through the New Zealand Lodge Association website: www.lodgesofnz.co.nz. This provides links to the websites of individual lodges.

Motels

■ Motels are popular with families and travellers who want to drive to the door of a self-contained unit and cater for themselves. They tend to be **designed for convenience** rather than charm, but are reasonably priced and generally well appointed, with telephone, television, ensuite bathroom and cooking facilities. Laundry facilities may be located in a separate block.

■ Most motels offer **breakfast**, delivered to the unit at an extra cost. Some complexes have swimming pools and children's playgrounds. Rates are around NZ$120 to $200 per double room, and most have spa pools.

■ Good motel chains include: **Best Western** (tel: 0800 237 893 toll free; www.bestwestern.co.nz) and **Golden Chain** (tel: 0800 80 465 336 toll free; www.goldenchain.co.nz).

Serviced Apartments

■ Self-catering apartments are increasingly popular in the larger cities. **Centrally situated**, they may be in converted offices or heritage buildings and range from studios to spacious suites, at prices to match. You can pay anything from NZ$100 to $350 per night, though prices are often reduced at weekends and for stays of several days.

■ Self-catering apartments usually have **fully equipped kitchens and laundry facilities**, and are serviced daily or according to your needs. They may also have a shared gym, spa, pool and sauna facilities.

■ Good companies for finding serviced apartments are: Quest (tel: 0800 944 400 toll free; www.questapartments.com.au); or, in Auckland, Gatehouse Management (tel: (09) 302 1458; www.gatehouse.co.nz).

Bed and Breakfast

■ This covers **hosted accommodation** from boutique hotels to guest houses, vineyard cottages and rooms in private homes ("homestays"). The proprietors live on the premises and you can expect a personal welcome.

■ Rooms may have **private or shared bathrooms**. There is usually a guest lounge. Some places offer evening meals as well as breakfast.

■ **Prices** range from NZ$80 to $200 or more, with dinner extra.

■ For more details contact: New Zealand Federation of Bed and Breakfast Hotels (tel: (06) 358 6928; www.nzbnbhotels.com) or Heritage and Character Inns of New Zealand (www.heritageinns.co.nz).

Home and Farm Stays

■ **Staying with a family** at their home or farm for a couple of days is a popular way to meet the locals. Guests share family meals and you can often join in the milking, mustering, shearing or crop harvesting.

■ The **cost** is likely to be around NZ$80 to $150 per double for bed and breakfast, with dinner extra.

■ These organizations can help: **Rural Holidays New Zealand** (tel: (03) 355 6218, 0800 883 355 toll free; www.ruralholidays.co.nz), **New Zealand Farm Holidays** (tel: (09) 412 9649; www.nzaccom.co.nz; or try the websites www.homestays.co.nz or www.homestays.net.nz).

Budget Accommodation

■ **Backpacker hostels** are booming in New Zealand, with about 450 purveyors offering anything from dormitories at NZ$15 per night to double rooms with private bathrooms at around $90. There are **communal** cooking facilities and a lounge. Bed linen may be provided at an extra charge.

■ **Campsites and holiday parks** are often in beautiful locations. Many have chalets, ranging from basic units with four bunks and little else at around NZ$50, to more comfortable ones with kitchens at around NZ$120 for a family of four.

■ Contact **Budget Backpacker Hostels** (www.bbh.co.nz – note bookings can only be made by phoning individual hostels listed on the website) or **YHA New Zealand** (tel: (03) 379 9970, 0800 278 299 toll free; www.yha.org.nz), **Holiday Accommodation Parks New Zealand** (tel: (04) 298 3283; www.holidayparks.co.nz).

Practical Tips

■ **Prices tend to be higher in the main cities** and may climb steeply in the main tourist resorts during the high season.

■ **Pre-book in peak season** (Dec to Apr), and in ski resorts in the winter.

■ **Tourism New Zealand's** website, www.newzealand.com, is useful. AA New Zealand Accommodation Guides (PO Box 101 001 North Shore Mail Centre, Auckland; www.aatravel.co.nz), published annually, include detailed accommodation directories, especially of motels and campsites.

■ The **Qualmark** rating and classification system, a joint venture by Tourism New Zealand and the NZAA, awards stars to hotels, motels, hostels and holiday parks, based on annual assessments.

Accommodation Prices

The following categories are used for hotels listed in this guide, based on two people sharing a double room per night:

$ under NZ$200 $$ NZ$200–$350 $$$ over NZ$350

Food and Drink

With a plentiful supply of fresh, local seafood, meat and vegetables, choices for eating out are endless. Dining tends to be casual compared with Europe, and award-winning chefs are as likely to be found in bustling brasseries and vineyard restaurants as they are in top hotels.

New Zealand Food

- New Zealand's **European heritage** is largely British, with a culinary tradition strong on roast meat, baking and hearty breakfasts. You may still get this sort of food at farm and homestays and country pubs, but nowadays a family meal is more likely to be a barbecue.
- **Modern New Zealand chefs** draw on influences from Asia, the Mediterranean and the Pacific, developing a cuisine that reflects the climate and New Zealand's position in the world, sometimes called "Pacific Rim" food. Menus often focus on regional products, such as beef, lamb, scallops, oysters, wines and cheeses. Many vineyards have restaurants offering food to match their wines.
- Although New Zealand is still largely a nation of meat eaters, most restaurants offer **vegetarian** options, and there are some specialist vegetarian establishments.

Fine Dining

Fine dining in a formal sense is not common in New Zealand. The surroundings may be spectacular and the food exquisitely presented, but Kiwis are an informal lot. Meals often cost less than NZ$100 per head.

Four of the Best

- The Grove, Auckland (➤ 71)
- Logan Brown, Wellington (➤ 115)
- Herzog's, Blenheim (➤ 134)
- Pescatore at The George Hotel, Christchurch (➤ 156)

Cafes

Stylish and quirky, often with deli bars and a reputation for excellent coffee, these are popular meeting places and offer good value. A main course usually costs less than NZ$20; a coffee around NZ$3.50.

Ethnic Restaurants and Takeaways

Informal ethnic restaurants offer some of the least expensive eating options. Japanese sushi bars and Thai, Chinese, Mexican and Indian restaurants are common, and often have takeaway services. Chinese yum cha (also known as dim sum) is popular at weekend lunchtimes – a range of Cantonese hors d'oeuvres, washed down with copious amounts of Chinese tea. The favourite takeaways are still meat pies, pizzas and fish and chips.

Hangi

Many places, especially in Rotorua, offer the opportunity to try a Maori *hangi*. Traditionally, this is a simple meal of meat and vegetables cooked over hot stones in an underground oven. Although a version can be tasted at some hotels, for a more authentic experience it's best to go to a *marae* (area around a meeting house) or other Maori venue, such as Tamaki Maori Village (➤ 91) or Te Puia (➤ 82–85). See also ➤ 86.

Bring Your Own (BYO)

Some restaurants still allow you to bring your own wine to drink with the meal. You save the restaurant's mark-up fee, but they charge corkage.

Pubs

Cheap, hearty meals are available in many country pubs. Pubs serve draught and bottled beer, spirits and a limited range of wine. Boutique breweries offering interesting local beers are increasingly popular, especially in the cities. Smoking is banned in all indoor public areas.

Practical Tips

- **Restaurant hours** are usually 12–2:30 for lunch, and 6:30–10:30 for dinner, although many **cafes** offer all-day dining, and **bar snacks** may be served until the early hours.
- **Service charges and government taxes** are included in menu prices. Tipping is not traditional, although it is becoming more widespread in tourist centres and upmarket restaurants.
- When travelling, **take a picnic** – there may be long distances between refreshments. Places in country towns close early and may not open at the weekend.

The Best for...

...**Location**: Dining Room, Duke of Marlborough Hotel, Russell (➤ 71–72)
...**View**: Panorama Restaurant at the Hermitage, Aoraki/Mount Cook (➤ 155)
...**Breakfast**: 50 on Park at The George Hotel, Christchurch (➤ 155)
...**Vineyard lunch**: Twelve Trees Restaurant, Blenheim (➤ 134–135)
...**Afternoon tea**: The Bathhouse, Queenstown (➤ 180)
...**Seafood**: Martin Bosley's Wellington (➤ 115)
...**West Coast tavern**: Lake Mahinapua Hotel, Hokitika (➤ 151)
...**Heritage building**: Chambers, County Hotel, Napier (➤ 96)
...**Country cafe**: Colenso Café, Coromandel Peninsula (➤ 72)

Kiwi Specialities

- **Kumara:** sweet potato.
- **Manuka honey:** distinctively flavoured from manuka tree blossom.
- **Feijoas:** an egg-shaped fruit with green skin and aromatic, cream-coloured flesh. You'll find it fresh, stewed, pickled or juiced.
- **Tamarillos (tree tomatoes):** egg-shaped fruit with gold or crimson skin and dark seeds. Eat fresh, as a sweet or savoury sauce, or as a chutney.
- **Greenshell mussels:** native New Zealand mussels, with green-lipped shells.
- **Bluff:** (deep sea) oysters, crayfish, rock lobster and Nelson scallops.
- **Kina:** sea urchins (also called sea eggs), usually eaten raw.
- **Whitebait:** juvenile freshwater fish, mixed with a batter and fried in fritters.
- **Paua:** abalone, with meaty black flesh, usually eaten as steaks or fritters.
- **Pavlova:** meringue and fruit dessert, the subject of much friendly rivalry between New Zealand and Australia as to which country invented it.
- **Hokey-pokey:** honeycomb toffee.
- **Milo:** a popular malted milk energy drink.

Restaurant Prices

The following categories are used for restaurants listed in this guide, based on the price per person for a three-course meal, excluding drinks:
$ under NZ$45 $$ NZ$45–$60 $$$ over NZ$60

Shopping

New Zealand is fast losing the sleepy hollow reputation that caused wits to quip that they had visited, but it was closed. Liberalized trading hours mean it's now possible to shop every day in many places. You can find a range of shopping, from chic boutiques and old-fashioned department stores to factory outlets, markets, craft co-operatives and fashion retailers. In the suburbs, traditional or individual shops are being replaced by undercover one-stop shopping centres. Goods posted to overseas destinations are free of the 15 per cent government tax normally imposed, and many stores offer mailing and shipping services.

Arts and Crafts

■ Everywhere you go, no matter how small the community, there's likely to be a **gallery** or **co-operative** selling paintings or pottery, woodcarving or jewellery. With ventures like the Nelson craft trail and Christchurch Arts Centre you can meet the artist and buy direct. In Northland, look out for items made from swamp kauri – wood up to 50,000 years old, buried after some ancient natural disaster, which is being unearthed and transformed into anything from tables to bookends.

■ **Pictures of native birds, flowers and woods** decorate souvenirs, from mugs to ashtrays, T-shirts and corkscrews to placemats. Paua (abalone) are used to cultivate iridescent pearls, which command top prices.

■ **Maori art** is unique to New Zealand: intricate wood carvings on canoes and meeting houses depict ancestors and tell traditional stories. Paua shell, used for the eyes of *tiki* (human figures), and greenstone (pounamu), used for weapons and symbolic gifts, are now turned into jewellery and ornaments in traditional and modern designs.

■ Also popular are **bone carvings** in fish-hook and symbolic designs – you can even carve your own. Rotorua is a good place to watch Maori artists and hear explanations of their work (➤ 82–83).

■ **Antiques shops** often turn up bargains for collectors, especially 19th-century furniture and silver brought over by early European settlers. Browse around High Street in Christchurch, Broadway in Dunedin, and Cuba Street in Wellington.

Sheep Products

■ With an estimated 10 sheep to every person, it's not surprising that sheepskin turns up in many guises, from hats, gloves and coats to rugs.

■ The wool is made into a remarkable range of garments: handspun jerseys, rugged Swanndri bush jackets, gossamer-soft merino underwear and trans-seasonal fashion knitwear by houses like Sabatini.

■ Lanolin is used in a range of skincare products.

Clothing

■ New Zealand's funky young **fashion designers** are making a splash on international catwalks with labels such as Karen Walker, Nom*D, Zambesi, Zana Feuchs and Kate Sylvester. Their designs are often available here at a fraction of the price you would pay overseas.

■ Some designers have their own outlets in Auckland, but each of the main centres has a fashion quarter worth exploring: High Street and Merivale in Christchurch, Lambton Quay and Willis Street in Wellington, High Street and Newmarket in Auckland.

■ **Dress Smart** operates multiple factory outlet shopping malls in Auckland, Hamilton, Wellington and Christchurch (www.dress-smart.co.nz).

■ **Outdoors enthusiasts** head for Christchurch, home to specialist

manufacturers and importers such as Macpac, Kathmandu and Bivouac, to stock up on high-tech sports and climbing gear. Christchurch is also home to the Canterbury brand of leisurewear, which has outlets in the main tourist centres.
- **All Blacks** rugby shirts and other paraphernalia associated with New Zealand's sporting heroes are available from most souvenir shops.

Wine
- New Zealand wines have a growing **international reputation**, particularly Marlborough's distinctive Sauvignon Blanc, but the range exported is limited, so wine lovers will enjoy the opportunity to discover labels and grape varieties produced by the more than 500 wineries dotted around the country.
- Marlborough and Hawke's Bay are the **main wine-producing areas**, but picturesque vineyards and fine wines can also be found in the Auckland region, Martinborough, Nelson, Canterbury and Otago.
- Many wineries are open for **tastings**.
- **Dessert wines**, affectionately known as "stickies", are particularly good value compared with prices in Europe.
- Supermarkets sell wine quite cheaply, but specialist shops such as Glengarry in Auckland and Wellington, and Vino Fino in Christchurch have a **wider selection of top labels**. A word of warning: many wines are made in such small quantities that they are available only from the winery itself or from certain restaurants.
- For descriptions of individual wines, ➤ 13.
- For more details on wine trails, ➤ 44. For tours in a particular region, see the relevant Where to... Be Entertained sections of this guide.

Food
- In country areas, **roadside stalls and farms** sell local produce, from organic fruit and vegetables to lavender, honey, cheese and salmon.
- **Native flower honeys** such as rata and manuka make attractive gifts. They are available prettily packaged at souvenir shops or more inexpensively at supermarkets.
- **Apricots, cherries, apples** and **kiwi fruit** are turned into fruit brandies, chocolates and preserves – even kiwi fruit wine.
- **Markets** are great sources of fresh food for picnics. Try Auckland's **Otara Market** for Polynesian specialities (Sat 6–noon), or the **Marlborough Farmer's Market** in Blenheim (Oct–Apr Sun 9–noon) for the best locally grown supplies.

Shopping Hours
- **Shopping hours** are generally 9am–5:30pm, with a late night, usually Friday, until 9pm.
- **In smaller towns**, shops may close at 1pm on Saturday and all day Sunday.
- **In large cities**, supermarkets are often open daily 8am–9pm, and sometimes operate longer hours.

Methods of Payment
Most city shops are geared up for EFTPOS (Electronic Funds Transfer at Point of Sale) and accept major credit cards. Be prepared to pay cash at markets and in some rural areas. Travellers' cheques can be exchanged at most banks.

Entertainment

Outdoor Activities

- New Zealanders love the great outdoors. All the major cities are at or near the sea – Auckland and Wellington spectacularly so – and unspoiled countryside is never far away. Local councils and the Department of Conservation maintain a range of footpaths, and guide maps are available from visitor centres.
- The most popular **swimming beaches** are manned by lifeguards during the summer.
- **Spectator sports**, especially rugby, netball and cricket, command a passionate following. All the main centres have large stadiums and host national matches and international tests.
- **Horse racing** is also a popular day out. Each racecourse has regular meetings: phone the local harness racing or jockey club for details.
- **Golf** is very popular, and many courses are in spectacular sites.
- Salmon and trout **fishing** are also popular, especially around Taupo and the South Island rivers, with guides who can supply equipment. Sea fishing trips are on offer at all seaside resorts.
- Surfing, windsurfing, sailing, parasailing, kayaking, kite surfing, water skiing, scuba diving – whatever **water sport** takes your fancy, someone will be offering to hire out the gear and teach you what to do.
- **Skiing** may be less glamorous in New Zealand than in Europe but, particularly in the South Island, it's accessible, as challenging as you want and relatively inexpensive. During the ski season, usually June to September, you can hire equipment on the field or from shops in town.

Adventure Sports

- To many travellers, New Zealand is synonymous with adventure sports such as bungy jumping, jet boating, sea kayaking, white-water rafting, zorbing, sky diving and ever more daring variations of such activities.
- Make sure the risks you take don't extend to your insurance – it's imperative that your policy is extended before you go to cover named "dangerous sports". The slight extra cost could save you thousands of dollars in medical bills. See also Insurance, ➤ 202.

Performing Arts

- New Zealand's national symphony **orchestra and ballet** company, both based in Wellington, perform regularly and there are plenty of theatres, opera companies, choirs and orchestras elsewhere.
- At festivals and in the long summer holidays, the **arts move outdoors**, with opera under the stars, theatre in the park, vineyard concerts, buskers in the street and free programmes of family entertainment.

Festivals and Shows

From art deco in Napier (February) to wild foods in Hokitika (March), New Zealanders love **any excuse** for a festival.

- In February, you could also catch the start of the month-long **International Festival of the Arts** in Wellington, and **wine and food** festivals in Marlborough, Hawke's Bay, Canterbury, Devonport and Whangarei. Nelson's Hooked on Seafood festival is held in March.
- Most of the main centres hold annual **arts, music and literary festivals** at different times of the year.

- **Pacific Island culture** is celebrated with Pasifika in March, held in Auckland. For many, the most significant national event is **Waitangi Day**, on 6 February, when the birth of the nation is celebrated in Waitangi and on *marae* all over the country.
- **Agricultural shows** are important events in each region, with funfairs and food stalls alongside the prize cattle, sheep-shearing and wood-chopping competitions. Auckland's Royal Easter Show (April), and Christchurch's Cup and Show Week (November) are among the most popular.
- New Zealand's major horticultural event, the **Ellerslie Flower Show**, is held at Christchurch's North Hagley Park in March.
- See also recommendations in the Where to... Be Entertained sections.

Wine Trails

- Going to a vineyard for a **wine tasting** or lunch is a popular pastime, especially in the warmer months. Many wineries welcome visitors and have built attractive cellar-door facilities, often with a restaurant.
- **There are eight main wine regions** and each has its distinctive personality but as a rough guide, Marlborough is the biggest, Nelson and Waiheke are the prettiest, Waipara and Martinborough are so compact that you can walk between some vineyards, Hawke's Bay has the best range of reds, and Central Otago has the most spectacular sites.
- **Wine trail maps** of most regions are available from wineries or visitor centres. Wine trail tours range from small, education-oriented groups to party buses. The local visitor centre should be able to advise.

Nightspots

- Apart from the nightclubs on Auckland's Karangahape Road (known as K Road, ➤ 74) and Wellington's Courtenay Place (➤ 118), nightlife in most New Zealand centres is focused on restaurants and bars.
- Several of the cities and resorts have **casinos** that stay open late, or even 24 hours. Some, like Sky City in Auckland, are large and purpose built, with restaurants, bars and several gaming rooms; others are boutique affairs in heritage buildings. Dress codes and age restrictions may apply.

Making Reservations

Many theatres, concert halls and sporting venues use booking agencies such as Ticketek (tel: 0800 842 538 toll free), which can advise on the availability of tickets and make the booking. Check the local phone book.

Gay Scene

New Zealand doesn't boast the outrageous nightlife you can find in some cities, but there are a lot of gay bars and clubs, especially in Auckland.
- The main area for bars and clubs in Auckland is on K Road. The busiest nightclub (on Fridays and Saturdays only) is Family Bar for a younger crowd. Naval & Family has two drag shows on Friday and Saturday nights, and Urge is mainly for older guys. Finale and Caluzzi are drag cabaret/restaurants.
- In Wellington visit Club Ivy. In Christchurch it's hoped that the quake-damaged Cruz will reopen soon, check online at http://cruz.co.nz

---

Admission Prices
The following categories are used to indicate the cost of admission to sights and attractions:
Inexpensive under NZ$10 **Moderate** NZ$10–$25 **Expensive** over NZ$25

Auckland and the Far North

Getting Your Bearings

Auckland is New Zealand's only truly big city, but size has not diminished its charms. The "City of Sails" is regularly voted one of the world's top 10 cities for its cosmopolitan lifestyle and exhilarating recreational opportunities.

Set between two harbours, Auckland's heart is the waterfront, with its busy wharf, attractive marinas and an inviting cafe scene. In the Maori language, Auckland is known as *Tamaki Makau Rau* – "the spouse of a hundred lovers" – and Aucklanders certainly are passionate about their city. More than a million people – almost a third of all New Zealanders – call Auckland home. Many can't understand why anybody would want to live south of the Bombay Hills, which form an imaginary boundary line south of the city.

Aucklanders have good reason for their local patriotism. Their metropolis blends modern city life with an easily accessible outdoor playground. Mountain ranges, rainforests and the glistening Hauraki Gulf with its myriad islands are all within reach – and even the bustling downtown breathes easily, courtesy of countless parks that cover the city's dramatic volcanic landscape.

Apart from its metropolitan and outdoor appeal, Auckland is also home to the world's largest concentration of Polynesian people, who add an eclectic mix of languages and

**Page 45:
Discover more about Maori culture at the War Memorial Museum**

traditions, and who make the city pulsate to the rhythm of the Pacific.

For those who want to escape from city life, Auckland is the ideal gateway to subtropical Northland and the Bay of Islands, or the rugged and romantic Coromandel peninsula.

The Bay of Islands is a popular sailing and boating destination

In Five Days

If you're not quite sure where to begin your travels, this itinerary recommends five practical and enjoyable days in and around Auckland, taking in some of the best places to see using the Getting Your Bearings map on the previous page. For more information see the main entries.

Day 1

Morning
From ❶ **Downtown**, get your bearings from the viewing platform of the **Sky Tower** (left and right, ➤ 50–51), with views over Auckland's skyline and its volcanic hills. Then stroll down **Queen Street** from **Aotea Square** (➤ 50) and explore downtown Auckland. Collect brochures and bus timetables at the visitor information centre at the Viaduct Basin (➤ 52), where you can also pick up a map for the Link bus (➤ 34), which runs a circular route past most of Auckland's attractions.

At the ❷ **Harbour** (above), Viaduct Basin is the site of New Zealand's America's Cup victory – and defeat (➤ 23) – as well as the **New Zealand National Maritime Museum** (➤ 52–53). Have lunch at its cafe.

Afternoon
Catch the free shuttle from Sky City or opposite the downtown ferry building to the **Kelly Tarlton's Antarctic Encounter and Underwater World** (right, ➤ 53) on the far side of town. Afterwards, take a short stroll along Tamaki Drive for vistas of Devonport and the ❹ **Hauraki Gulf** (➤ 58–59). Enjoy views of the **Harbour Bridge** (➤ 52–53) on the bus ride back to the city.

Evening
Return to the **Sky Tower** for night views of Auckland and to try Orbit, the revolving restaurant, for dinner (➤ 51). Ponsonby Road, to the southwest of the city centre, is another good place to eat – you will be spoiled for choice with its many small ethnic restaurants.

Day 2

Morning
Plan at least two hours to explore **3** **Auckland War Memorial Museum**
(▶ 55–57) and the Auckland Domain, then walk to the historic **Parnell village** (▶ 73) for lunch and shopping.

Afternoon
During the afternoon, explore the **4** **Hauraki Gulf** islands (▶ 58–59).
A "coffee cruise" will give you good views of many islands and, looking back as you leave Auckland Harbour, some of the best views of the city's skyline. If you are interested in natural history, go for a walk on **Rangitoto Island** (▶ 58). If your tastes are more for arts, fine food and wine, explore **Waiheke Island** (▶ 59). On your way back from the Hauraki Gulf, catch a ferry that stops at Devonport for a walk and your evening meal.

Day 3

Get up early to fly to Kerikeri. Then hire a car or catch a shuttle for the short distance to Paihia, to start your visit of the **5** **Bay of Islands** (▶ 60–62). Join a boat cruise to see or **12** **swim with dolphins** (▶ 66), and in the afternoon visit historic **Waitangi National Reserve** (▶ 61–62) and explore its historic grounds, the Treaty House and the meeting house.

Day 4

Take a day cruise of the sun-drenched Bay of Islands and the spectacular Hole in the Rock (▶ 60). Explore the historic township of **Russell** (▶ 61) in the afternoon and evening.

Day 5

Fly back to Auckland and then drive to the **6** **Coromandel peninsula** (▶ 63–64), where you can explore Hot Water Beach, Cathedral Cove, sandy bays, rugged hills and charming seaside towns.

❶ Downtown Auckland

Unlike the planned settlements of Wellington, Nelson, Christchurch and Dunedin, Auckland had a slow start. It was not long, however, before its mild climate and scenic maritime setting soon attracted thousands of new migrants. Their vibrant mix of cultures is still obvious as you walk along Queen Street, Auckland's main artery, to the harbour.

Start your downtown explorations in **Aotea Square**, the focal point for Auckland's performance venues and civic offices. In one corner is the triangular **Town Hall**, with its Oamaru limestone facade. On the other side of the square, the low **Aotea Centre** was built at the request of opera singer Kiri Te Kanawa, and is now the country's foremost concert hall.

Head in the Clouds
The **Sky Tower** dominates Auckland's skyline. Completed in 1997, it's part of a complex called **Sky City** that also includes a casino, restaurants, cafes, a hotel and a theatre. At 328m (1,076 feet), the Sky Tower is the highest structure in New Zealand, beating France's Eiffel Tower by almost 30m (100 feet). It was designed to survive once-in-a-millennium storms and a magnitude 8 earthquake 20km (12 miles) away.

The three public **observation decks** all offer stunning views of Auckland's urban sprawl. The map that comes with your entry ticket points out all the landmarks you can see from the top, and there are also explanation panels on the observation deck itself. Look for the Harbour Bridge (➤ 52–53) and

Auckland's Sky Tower is the country's tallest structure

LEAP FOR THE STARS

In 1998, AJ Hackett (► 25) used the Sky Tower to set a new height record for bungy jumping. Leaping from the observation deck, he fell 180m (590 feet) at 130kph (81mph), breaking his own record, set (illegally) in 1997 at the Eiffel Tower. Now you can do the same, with the SkyJump – a 192m (630 feet) freefall off the Sky Tower (tel: (09) 368 1835, 0800 759 586 toll free; www.skyjump.co.nz).

the Westhaven marina. Then survey Auckland's northern suburbs to Devonport, the Hauraki Gulf islands (► 58–59) and the Auckland War Memorial Museum (► 55–57) in the Auckland Domain. The distant ranges behind the Hauraki Gulf islands belong to the Coromandel peninsula (► 63–64).

Volcanoes on View

The top of the tower also offers views of some of the 48 extinct volcanoes in the area. **Mount Hobson**, named after New Zealand's first governor and Auckland's founder Captain William Hobson, looks like a giant armchair, and although **One Tree Hill** (► 65) has lost its lone pine tree, it is still easily recognized by the tall obelisk. All volcanic cones are reserve land, so they stand out like green pyramids amid the suburbs.

Back on terra firma, continue on Queen Street towards the harbour, wandering down the narrow side streets, such as **Vulcan Lane**, **High Street** and **O'Connell Street**, to window shop for gifts and fashion.

TAKING A BREAK

If, after your heady trip up the Sky Tower, you feel in need of refreshments, try the rotating **Orbit Restaurant** (tel: (09) 363 6000) or, for a lighter snack, the **Sky Lounge**.

➕ 204 B4

Visitor Information Centres

✉ Viaduct Basin, corner of Quay and Hobson streets ✉ Corner of Victoria and Federal streets ☎ (09) 367 6009, 0800 282 552 toll free; www.aucklandnz.com 🕐 For both centres: Nov–Apr daily 8:30–6:30; May–Oct daily 9–5 ℹ Also at the airport (► 33)

Sky Tower

➕ 204 A4 ✉ Corner of Victoria and Federal streets ☎ (09) 363 6000, 0800 759 2489 toll free; www.skycity.co.nz 🕐 Sun–Thu 8:30am–10:30pm, Fri–Sat 8:30am–11:30pm. Last lift leaves 30 mins before closing time 🚌 Link bus (► 34) 🎟 Moderate; Sky Deck (top public level): expensive

DOWNTOWN AUCKLAND: INSIDE INFO

Top tip The Sky Tower is open late into the evening and the **night views** are particularly spectacular.

Hidden gem Albert Park, accessible from Kitchener Street or Wellesley Street East, is an oasis of calm in the hustle and bustle of the city centre.

2 Auckland Harbour

One fifth of Aucklanders own a boat, so the waterfront is where it's all happening. Walk along Quay Street, between Queens Wharf and the Viaduct Basin, to see luxury yachts, tall ships, steamboats, ferries, fishing dinghies and enormous cruise liners all plying the waters of the Waitemata Harbour.

Flung across the narrow Tamaki isthmus, Auckland is surrounded by the sea: the Waitemata Harbour and Hauraki Gulf to the north and east, and the Manukau Harbour and Tasman Sea to the south and west. The largest of Auckland's six marinas, Westhaven marina, at the southern end of the Harbour Bridge, bobs with more than 2,000 masts, most metamorphosing into full sail every summer weekend.

A focal point of the waterfront is the **Viaduct Basin**, home to Auckland's fishing fleet since the 1930s but extensively rebuilt for New Zealand's defence of the America's Cup in 2000 (► 23). The basin is a short walk downhill from the Sky Tower (► 50–51), and only a few metres from the old ferry building opposite the harbour end of Queen Street.

Races on the Waves
The cup races brought the basin alive again in early 2003 but between races the **Viaduct Basin** comes to life in the evenings with bars and restaurants around the water's edge. But you can still get a taste of cup fever: as you walk towards the basin, you will see the *KZ1*, the New Zealand boat in the 1988 America's Cup challenge, strung up across the entrance. And you can book a two-hour turn around the harbour on the 1995 America's Cup boat *NZL-40* or a three-hour match race on *NZL-40* or *NZL-41*.

The history of New Zealand yachting and the country's America's Cup victories takes up a whole gallery in the **New**

This plexiglass tunnel in Kelly Tarlton's Antarctic Encounter and Underwater World enables visitors to get a closer look at marine life

Auckland Harbour Bridge

Zealand National Maritime Museum, with the winning yacht *NZL-32* (*Black Magic*) forming the centrepiece. You can see the darker side of the sea in the Edmiston Gallery, where there is an exhibition on the sinking of the HMS *Orpheus* on 7 February 1863. In what is still New Zealand's worst maritime disaster, 189 men and boys lost their lives after the ship struck a sandbar at the entrance to Manukau Harbour in fine conditions.

Stories of Discovery and Settlement

The Polynesian discovery of New Zealand is brought to life in a 10-minute video, *Te Waka: Our Great Journey*, while the Hawaiki gallery features a number of original vessels, from Pacific Island dugouts to a twin-masted outrigger canoe. These are fittingly installed in a room beautifully decorated with traditional Maori woven wall panels.

Even more impressive are the displays about early settlement. The 300,000 European immigrants who came during the first wave of settlement in the 1840s faced three to six months at sea, travelling in cramped quarters with no daylight and only a pint of drinking water per day. The museum has re-created one such gloomy bunk cabin, peopled with lifesize dummies; moving floors give an instant sensation of being at sea.

The museum is just beside the passenger terminals at **Princes Wharf**. You may see some of the world's largest cruise ships berthed here, but this area is also the starting point for ferries sailing across the harbour and to the islands of the Hauraki Gulf (➤ 58–59).

Exploring the Underwater World

Fronting the harbour about 6km (4 miles) east of Viaduct Basin is **Kelly Tarlton's Antarctic Encounter and Underwater World**, reached on a free shuttle from Sky City. Kelly Tarlton was an avid diver and treasure hunter, and his idea of showing marine life is the reverse of the usual aquarium experience: here animals get most of the space while humans watch from a confined hide. There are two main sections: in the Antarctic Experience, you can visit a re-creation of Captain Scott's 1911 South Pole hut then board a snowmobile to drive through a vast, authentic Antarctic landscape to see thriving colonies of king and gentoo penguins. Afterwards, you walk past Stringray Bay to reach the plexiglass tunnel where sharks roam freely overhead. Several marine habitats are represented, and you can see thousands of sea creatures that thrive in New Zealand's waters.

TAKING A BREAK

The **cafe at the maritime museum** offers a range of reasonably priced drinks and snacks, and there are several bars and restaurants on Princes Wharf.

Creatures large and small can be seen at Kelly Tarlton's marine attraction

➕ 204 B5

NZL-40 and *NZL-41*
➕ 204 B5 ✉ Booking booth next to maritime museum, Viaduct Basin
☎ (09) 359 5987, 0800 347 567 toll free; www.sailnz.co.nz 🕐 Daily; up to five two-hour sailings in peak season. Match races three times a week 💲 Expensive

New Zealand National
Maritime Museum
➕ 204 B5 ✉ Corner of Quay and Hobson streets, Viaduct Basin
☎ (09) 373 0800, 0800 725 897 toll free; www.maritimemuseum.co.nz 🕐 Daily 9–5
💲 Moderate

Kelly Tarlton's Antarctic Encounter and Underwater World
➕ 204 off C4 ✉ 23 Tamaki Drive, Orakei, Auckland ☎ (09) 528 0603, 0800 805 050 toll free; www.kellytarltons.co.nz 🕐 Daily 9–5:30; last entry an hour before closing time 🍴 Refreshment Kiosk ($) 🚌 746, 757, 767, 769 depart from bus terminal on Commerce Street. A free shuttle bus departs hourly from the Sky City foyer daily 9–4 and from 172 Quay Street 💲 Expensive

---

AUCKLAND HARBOUR: INSIDE INFO

Hidden gem Several **historic vessels** are berthed at the maritime museum's marina, including a 1926 steam floating crane and the *Ted Ashby*, a replica 19th-century scow that takes visitors on harbour cruises (Tue–Sun).

In more depth AJ Hackett (➤ 25) runs bungy jumps off the Auckland Harbour Bridge, as well as the Auckland Bridge Climb, which offers great city views (tel: (09) 361 2000, 0800 286 4958 toll free; www.bungy.co.nz).
■ Opened in 1985, Kelly Tarlton's Antarctic Encounter and Underwater World was built into **disused sewage holding tanks**. The interesting story behind its construction is detailed in a photographic display there.

3 Auckland War Memorial Museum

This superb museum houses one of the best collections of Maori treasures and ethnic crafts from the Pacific, and provides a compelling introduction to the country's history and culture. Built as a memorial to Aucklanders who died at war, the museum also chronicles New Zealand's involvement in global conflicts, from the 1800s to the present day.

The museum's atrium provides a complementary contrast to the building's original neo-classical design

Set in the Auckland Domain, one of the city's oldest volcanic cones, the Auckland War Memorial Museum Tamaki Paenga Hira is a landmark building with sweeping views across the waterfront. At the entrance a cenotaph, modelled on the one in Whitehall, London, is a reminder of the building's origins as a memorial to the country's war heroes. The museum's three architects, who had all served in World War I, chose a Greek neo-classical style to re-create the view of Greek temples they had seen from warships in the Mediterranean Sea.

Welcome to Maori Culture

Once you step inside, you will encounter a Maori warrior blowing a conch shell to draw people to the **exhibition of Maori treasures**. You could easily spend an hour in this part of the museum alone, and it's a good idea to allow two hours for your visit if you want to see other exhibitions.

The best way to start your museum visit, particularly if you're new to Maori culture, is by watching a 30-minute

cultural performance, which includes several Maori action songs, traditional stick games, weaponry displays and a haka, the fierce Maori war dance.

The **Maori treasures** are on display on the ground floor – the most impressive being the carved meeting house and the war canoe. Built around 1836 to transport people across Manukau Harbour, the canoe (known as T*e Toki a Tapiri* or "Tapiri's Battle Axe") is the **last of the great Maori war canoes**. One hundred warriors fit inside the 25m (82-foot) hull, which was carved by hand from a single totara tree.

Cultural perfomances are a highlight within the museum

Inside the Meeting House

The **meeting house** is a magnificent example of **traditional Maori carving and weaving crafts**, both ancient methods of story telling. Each carved beam and woven panel depicts the stories of a tribe or an ancestor, and was crafted to transmit history from generation to generation. The house on display was a wedding gift, exchanged when one tribal chief's daughter married into another chief's tribe. The building was completed in 1875 and you can see that Maori had already started combining traditional carvings with modern materials such as corrugated iron, paint and milled timber. Inside you will find elaborate carvings of Hotonui, the ancestor after whom the house was named, as well as other, mythical figures.

The building follows the typical architectural plan for meeting houses, or *whare nui* (meaning "big house"), which represent a god-like guardian who watches over the people gathered within. At the apex of the roof is the guardian's head, the ridgepole is the backbone, the bargeboards are the arms, outstretched in a welcoming gesture, and, inside, the rafters represent the guardian's ribs.

Other Exhibits

Right next door to the large meeting house is the much smaller, but equally intricately carved **storage house**. These were erected on stilts to stop animals and water from

An outrigger canoe in the Pacific Masterpieces gallery

damaging the precious food reserves inside. Take your time to explore the nearby collection of carved paddles, weapons and garments. There are also a number of objects used during rituals, notably some beautifully carved gourds intended to hold placentae.

Upstairs, the emphasis moves away from Maori culture. The **first floor** has displays on **natural history** and two discovery centres, while the **second floor** focuses on war-related exhibits.

TAKING A BREAK

Try the **Columbus Café** in the atrium (daily 10–5).

🕂 204 C3 ✉ The Domain, Auckland ☎ (09) 309 0443, 0800 256 7386 toll free, (09) 306 7067 recorded info; www.aucklandmuseum.com 🕐 Daily 10–5; closed 25 Apr (Anzac Day) morning. Maori cultural performance: daily 11, noon, 1:30 (also 2:30, Jan–Apr) 🚍 Link bus (➤ 34) 💰 Donation: inexpensive; temporary exhibitions may cost extra; cultural show moderate

---

AUCKLAND WAR MEMORIAL MUSEUM: INSIDE INFO

Top tip Focus on the Maori treasures and the war-related displays – the natural history exhibits are excellent, but you'll find similar ones in museums throughout the country.

Hidden gem The **Auckland Domain's Wintergardens and Fernery** are less than five minutes from the museum. The Domain is the city's oldest park and this is a beautiful spot in which to relax.

In more depth On the same floor as the Maori treasures, the **Pacific Lifeways and Pacific Masterpieces** exhibitions together form one of the most important collections of this kind in the world. Learn more about the art and culture of New Zealand's nearest neighbours.

❹Hauraki Gulf

The balmy seas and enchanting islands of the Hauraki Gulf are only 30 minutes from downtown Auckland. More than 50 islands provide a refuge for both endangered wildlife and city-weary humans.

The Hauraki Gulf is a protected marine area stretching from north of Auckland to the Coromandel peninsula (➤ 63–64). Several outer islands are nature reserves, off limits to people. However, the inner gulf islands are public reserves and visitors are free to explore. Ferry services leave Auckland's waterfront each day for Rangitoto and Waiheke, and there are sailings each week to other islands.

Top: Rangitoto Island as seen from One Tree Hill (➤ 65)

Above: Waiheke's small port Matiatia

Rangitoto Island

Rangitoto guards the entrance to the Waitemata Harbour and is Auckland's largest and youngest volcanic cone. Its last eruption was only 600 years ago, and its **volcanic landscape** is clearly unfinished, almost alien, with eerie lava caves, rugged rock formations and primeval vegetation. The hardened lava hasn't had time to break down into soil, and the lower reaches of the island are covered in pohutukawa trees, growing straight from the fissured rock. There are no rivers, no lakes and no fresh water; any rainfall trickles straight through to underground reservoirs.

The strange landscapes alone are worth the visit, but the island's summit offers **spectacular views** of the Hauraki Gulf, the Harbour Bridge and Auckland's skyline. Guided tours cover the entire island on a canopied trailer towed by a tractor, which takes you to the start of a boardwalk, 900m (980 yards) from the summit.

Waiheke Island

Waiheke is a complete contrast: perfect for relaxing on sandy beaches and enjoying fine food, wine, arts and crafts. Covering 93sq km (36sq miles), it is the second largest of the gulf islands after Great Barrier Island, and it is also the most accessible (by ferry, car ferry or helicopter). In the past, it attracted mostly alternative lifestylers, but has since developed into a genteel suburb of Auckland. During the summer the island's 8,000 population swells to more than 30,000.

As you arrive at Waiheke's small port of **Matiatia**, buses, taxis, shuttles and trikes will be waiting to take you uphill to the island's main settlement of **Oneroa**, 2km (1 mile) away. You can also hire a car or scooter at Matiatia, but make sure to book early during summer. On the way to Oneroa is the **Artworks centre**, with several galleries, businesses, a theatre, cinema and cafe, and the local visitor information centre. From there you can explore the white beaches between the Oneroa and Onetangi bays and the tidal southern coastline, visit the vineyards or join a tour of art galleries and studios.

TAKING A BREAK

A Fullers "**coffee cruise**" provides a commentated tour around Auckland Harbour.

➕ 210 C3

Fullers Cruise Centre
➕ 204 B5 ✉ Ferry Building, 99 Quay Street ☎ (09) 367 9111; www.fullers.co.nz ⏲ Office: daily 8–5:30; phone reservation line: Mon–Fri 7:30–6, Sat–Sun 8–5

Waiheke Visitor Information Centre
➕ 210 C3 ✉ 2 Korora Road, Oneroa ☎ (09) 372 1234; www.waihekenz.com ⏲ Daily 9–5

HAURAKI GULF: INSIDE INFO

Top tip If you are planning to visit **Rangitoto Island**, bring sturdy footwear, sun protection and drinking water.

Hidden gem Tiritiri Matangi Island is an open sanctuary where you can see endangered birds in their natural habitat.

In more depth Up to seven days a week in peak season, ferries and small planes depart for **Great Barrier Island**, a mountainous island 90km (55 miles) from Auckland. It's a popular destination for hiking, riding and water sports.
■ On the first floor of the **Auckland War Memorial Museum** (▶ 55–57), look for the footprints of an adult, child and dog made in the ash that fell during the last Rangitoto eruption and which have since hardened to a concrete.

5 Bay of Islands

The Bay of Islands is one of New Zealand's most popular destinations and a boat-lover's paradise. What you see from the beach is a mere hint of the turquoise and blue wonders further offshore. Sprinkled with almost 150 mostly uninhabited islands, the bay is a subtropical haven of secluded coves, forest-clad hills and unspoiled sandy beaches.

The area is historically significant, as it was here that Europeans first settled in New Zealand. **Paihia**, a small resort that grew from one of New Zealand's first Christian mission stations, established in 1823, is the base for most operators and is the hub for many tourist activities. It has plenty of amenities and is a good starting point for explorations.

Cruising the Island

The most popular cruises are the dolphin-watching trips (► 66) during which you may be able to swim with the marine mammals if conditions are suitable, or all-day excursions to the **Hole in the Rock**, an impressive natural arch at the tip of **Cape Brett**. The rugged tunnel cuts through **Piercy Island**, at the entrance to the Bay of Islands, and is just wide enough for a catamaran to travel through on a calm day. The cruise catamarans double as goods-delivery boats and make brief stops at most inhabited islands. Only the farm managers are permitted to build here, and the houses nestle in palm groves or pockets of native forest. It's often impossible to tell whether anybody lives there at all until an excited farm dog bursts forth to meet the boat at the jetty.

A bird's-eye view of the Bay of Islands

Beautiful and detailed carvings can be found in the meeting house, Whare Runanga at Waitangi

Sheltered **Otehei Bay**, on **Urupukapuka Island**, is a popular lunch stop for cruise ships and private yachts. American writer Zane Grey camped here in the 1920s and used the island for his fishing expeditions, but today people come to swim in the clear water or to explore the numerous Maori archaeological sites found here. Urupukapuka is the largest island in the bay and from its summit, about 15 minutes from the beach, there are panoramic views of the surrounding islands and the deeply fissured coastline leading to Cape Brett. The bumpy ride through the Hole in the Rock is an imposing finale, within view of the cape's lighthouse and with the entire bay unfolding before you.

On your return, you can disembark at **Russell**, the first European settlement in the area. Today, it's a small seaside town with whitewashed weatherboard houses enclosed by white picket fences and cottage gardens. The waterfront is dotted with cafes and restaurants, which spill out onto the sunny promenade. The town's present tranquillity belies its turbulent past as the "hell-hole of the Pacific". It started out as a destination for 19th-century sailors, whalers and traders looking for provisions, rum and fun after months at sea. The first Europeans to settle were not usually idealists hoping for a new life but largely ship deserters and time-expired convicts from New South Wales, who did nothing to enhance the town's reputation.

Birthplace of the Treaty

It's a short ferry ride back to the bustle of Paihia and from there to one of New Zealand's most significant historic sites. It was in the Bay of Islands that 45 Maori chiefs gathered in February 1840 to discuss and sign the **Treaty of Waitangi**, a document that remains the lynchpin of race relations in New Zealand (► 10). So you shouldn't miss the **Waitangi National Reserve**, about 2km (1 mile) from Paihia.

The Waitangi grounds include the **Georgian-style Treaty House**, originally built as the home of James Busby, whose job it was to protect British commerce in the embryonic colony, and a magnificent **Maori meeting house**, Whare Runanga. Completed in 1940 to commemorate the centenary of the treaty, 14 carved panels in the meeting house represent the major Maori tribes. This symbolizes the unity of the tribes under the treaty, as meeting houses usually show carvings that relate only to a particular tribe or region. Walk across the sweeping lawns to see two war canoes, launched every year on 6 February for the Waitangi Day celebrations.

TAKING A BREAK

If you want to avoid the buzzing activity of Paihia, there are several cafes along the waterfront at Russell. The **Waikokopu Café** at Waitangi is also a good option.

Most day cruises will include a trip to the Hole in the Rock

➕ 210 B4

Bay of Islands Visitor Information Centre
✉ The Maritime Building, Paihia
☎ (09) 402 7345;
www.visitnorthland.co.nz
🕐 Dec–Feb daily 8–8; Mar 8–7;
Apr 8–6; May–Oct 8–5

Fullers Bay of Islands
✉ The Maritime Building, waterfront,
Paihia ☎ (09) 402 7421;
www.dolphincruises.co.nz
🕐 Nov–Mar daily 7am–8pm; Apr–Oct
7am–10pm for phone reservations

Waitangi National Reserve
✉ 1 Tau Henare Drive, Paihia
☎ (09) 402 7437; www.waitangi.
net.nz 🕐 Nov–Mar daily 9–6;
Apr–Oct 9–5 🍴 Waikokopu Café ($)
💵 Inexpensive–expensive

Pompallier
✉ The Strand, Russell ☎ (09) 403 9015; www.pompallier.co.nz
🕐 Nov–Apr continuous tours daily 10–5, rest of year hourly tours 10–4
💵 Inexpensive

BAY OF ISLANDS: INSIDE INFO

Hidden gems Kerikeri, a charming town surrounded by citrus orchards, is worth exploring for its historic buildings and replica Maori village.
■ When in Russell, wander through the 19th-century graveyard around **Christ Church**, the country's oldest, still scarred with bullet holes – legacies of a clash between a group of Maori and the British navy in 1844.

In more depth Explore the Bay of Islands by kayak, underwater or on a tall ship. To **hire a kayak** or join a guided kayaking tour, contact Coastal Kayakers in Waitangi (Te Karuwha Parade, tel: (09) 402 8105, 0800 334 661 toll free; www.coastalkayakers.co.nz). Dive the wreck of the *Rainbow Warrior* (▶ 20), the Greenpeace flagship sunk in 1995, or the HMNZS *Canterbury* with Paihia Dive HQ (tel: 09 402 7551; www.divenz.com). Or cruise in style on board the tall ship the *R. Tucker Thompson* (tel: 09 402 8430, 0800 882 537 toll free; www.tucker.co.nz), which departs for day trips from Russell.

6 Coromandel

Escape from the city to the Coromandel peninsula, with its dramatic coastline and forested mountains. With a history of relentless logging and gold mining, the peninsula has become the cradle of New Zealand's environmental movement, and inspires those seeking an alternative lifestyle.

On a clear day, you can see the Coromandel's mountains from the Hauraki Gulf islands (► 58–59). Much of the peninsula's spine is covered with pockets of regenerating bush and remnants of kauri trees, which were logged almost to extinction during the pioneer period. Its rugged interior is fringed with fine surfing beaches, sheltered inlets and estuaries, and impressive coastal scenery.

Natural Beauty and Gold Mines

The gateway to the Coromandel is its main town, **Thames**, on the shallow Firth of Thames about 90 minutes from Auckland, where rich saltwater shallows and mud flats provide a habitat for migratory and wading birds. Thames is small and sleepy, with old wooden houses, some built in the town's 19th-century gold rush heyday. Its main attraction is the **Goldmine Experience**, a tour of a gold mine and the rock-crushing stamper battery at its northern end.

Pretty bays and golden beaches line the Coromandel peninsula

The road between Thames and **Coromandel town** hugs the coastline, offering exquisite views over pretty bays and calm beaches. The 55km (34-mile) journey is particularly scenic during December and January when the pohutukawa trees are in flower. Coromandel town also showcases its gold-mining history – it was just north of here, at **Driving Creek**, that New Zealand's first gold discovery was made in 1852.

From Coromandel, you can cross to the east coast by either taking the longer (41km/25-mile) but more scenic SH25, or the 32km (20-mile) unsealed "309 Road", which passes a waterfall and a grove of kauri trees. The state highway winds around estuaries, through holiday towns and past beaches, offering great views of the **Mercury Islands** before it reaches **Whitianga**. This is the peninsula's main holiday resort and a pleasant town from which to explore **Mercury Bay**.

The peninsula's most popular beaches are south of Whitianga, near **Hahei**. Just north of Hahei is **Cathedral Cove**, a gigantic, arched limestone cavern that connects two sandy beaches but is accessible only at low tide; it appears in the film *The Chronicles of Narnia: Prince Caspian* (➤ 18–19). To the south of Hahei is **Hot Water Beach**, where thermal waters boil up just below the surface and people gather at low tide to dig their own natural spa pools.

Natural thermal waters lie just beneath the sand at Hot Water Beach

TAKING A BREAK

Café Nina (20 Victoria Street, Whitianga, tel: (07) 866 5440) offers home-cooked food in a 100-year-old miner's cottage.

✚ 210 C3

Thames Visitor Information Centre
✉ 206 Pollen Street, Thames ☎ (07) 868 7284; www.thamesinfo.co.nz
🕐 Mon–Fri 9–5, Sat–Sun 12–4

Coromandel Information Centre
✉ 355 Kapanga Road, Coromandel ☎ (07) 866 8598;
www.coromandeltown.co.nz 🕐 Mon 9–5, Sun 10–2

Whitianga Information Centre
✉ 66 Albert Street, Whitianga ☎ (07) 866 5555; www.whitianga.co.nz
🕐 26 Dec–end Jan daily 8–6; rest of year Mon–Fri 9–5, Sat 9–4, Sun 9–4

Goldmine Experience
✉ Main Road (SH25), Thames ☎ (07) 868 8514; www.goldmine-experience.
co.nz 🕐 Daily 10–4 (phone in winter as hours may be limited) 💰 Inexpensive

---

COROMANDEL: INSIDE INFO

Top tip Be careful if you want to take a cooling swim in the ocean at Hot Water Beach. There are **dangerous currents** and several tourists have drowned.

Hidden gem At Driving Creek, local potter Barry Brickell has built a 2.5km (1.5-mile) **narrow-gauge railway**, originally to transport clay from one end of his property to his kiln. The railway travels up steep grades, across trestle bridges, along two spirals and through two tunnels.

At Your Leisure

7 Auckland Art Gallery

The Auckland Art Gallery has the most comprehensive collection of New Zealand and international art in the country. Its main gallery is currently undergoing a major development, due for completion in 2011. In the meantime, changing displays of the collection and temporary exhibitions, including works by prominent artists, are on show at the New Gallery across the road.

🔁 204 B4 ✉ Corner of Wellesley and Lorne streets ☎ (09) 379 1349 (24-hour info line); www.aucklandartgallery.com 🕐 Daily 10–5; free tours daily 2pm 🍴 Cafe ($) 🚌 Link bus 💷 Free; exhibitions: inexpensive

8 One Tree Hill

This (along with Mount Eden, ► 66) is the place to come for fantastic views of Auckland, but it also has an eventful history. Many of the volcanic cones around Auckland were once occupied by Maori, and One Tree Hill has remnants of a *pa*, or fortified village. The eponymous tree, however, is gone (see panel) and only the obelisk remains atop. On the fringe of the hill is the Stardome Observatory and Planetarium, which has a 360° digital dome theatre.

🔁 204 off C1

THE STORY OF ONE TREE HILL

The summit of One Tree Hill (also known by its Maori name Maunga-kiekie) was once marked by its single sacred totara tree. After settler vandals cut it down in 1852, Sir John Logan Campbell (a founder and mayor of Auckland) planted a pine to make amends. However, his choice of an exotic tree over a native totara proved to be controversial and provoked some local Maori to attack it with a chainsaw in the early 1990s. The tree has now been removed.

StarDome Observatory and Planetarium

✉ Near gates to One Tree Hill Domain, 670 Manukau Road ☎ (09) 624 1246; www.stardome.org.nz 🕐 Mon 9–5, Tue–Fri 9am–9:30pm, Sat, Sun 1–9:30. Evening shows: Tue–Thu, Sun 7pm, 8pm, 9pm, Fri–Sat 7pm, 8pm, 9pm, 10pm 🚌 302, 304, 305, 312 from mid-city 💷 Free; evening shows: moderate

One Tree Hill offers stunning views over Auckland

Views of Auckland from Mount Eden

9 Mount Eden

Mount Eden (Maungawhau) is Auckland's highest volcanic scoria cone, and from its 196m (643-foot) summit there are panoramic views of Auckland. Several quarries once produced dressed stone from here for the city's older buildings and the basalt kerbstones that line its streets. One quarry on the flanks of Mount Eden has since been rehabilitated as Eden Garden, known for its camellias and rhododendrons. July and August are the best times to see the flowers in bloom.

🞣 204 B1 ✉ 24 Omana Avenue. Road access to a car park near the summit off Mount Eden Road; pedestrian access from Clive Road and Owens Road (steep path). Access to Eden Garden is via Mountain Road to Omana Avenue ☎ (09) 638 8395; www.edengarden.co.nz 🕐 Garden: Sep–Apr daily 9–4:30; May–Aug 9–4 🍽 Cafe ($) daily 10–4 🚌 274, 275 from Commerce Street 🎫 Inexpensive

10 Piha Beach

About an hour's drive from central Auckland, the city's western coastline is dramatic and rugged, with many iron-sand beaches. Piha Beach is one of the most popular black beaches and comes alive in summer with surf competitions, horse races and beach parties. Jutting several metres into the ocean is windswept Lion Rock, which has a short, steep track leading to its 101m (331-foot) summit (a one-hour return trip). Beware: west coast beaches have powerful currents and you should always stay between the flags. Keep children under supervision and if in doubt, ask a lifeguard.

🞣 210 C3 ☎ www.piha.co.nz

11 Gannet Colony at Muriwai Beach

The colony of Australasian gannets was once confined to a small rock stack offshore, but has now spilled over to several cliffs along Muriwai Beach. An easy walking track skirts the cliffs, providing views of elegant seabirds as they nest on the rocks or dive for fish (binoculars are useful here). The first birds begin nesting in late July and their numbers peak by mid-November. Chicks fly when they are 15 weeks old and migrate to the east and south coasts of Australia. Several years later they return to Muriwai Beach to breed. The road to Muriwai Beach is signposted from Waimauku on SH16.

🞣 210 B3

12 Swimming with Dolphins

The experience of seeing hundreds of dolphins swirling in the water with you is unforgettable, particularly as the water in the Bay of Islands is relatively warm, reaching 23°C (73°F) in January and February. Operators supply wetsuits, masks, snorkels and fins, and will generally take you on another free trip if you don't see any dolphins or whales. Visitor information centres in Auckland and Paihia list operators, but two reputable companies are detailed below.

Dolphin Discoveries

🞣 210 B4 ✉ Corner of Marsden and Williams roads, Paihia ☎ (09) 402 8234, 0800 397 567 toll free; www.dolphinz.co.nz 🌊 Nature tours, snorkelling, swimming with dolphins

Fullers Great Sights

🞣 210 B4 ✉ The Maritime Building, Paihia ☎ (09) 402 7421, 0800 653 339 toll free; www.dolphincruises.co.nz 🌊 Cruises, swimming with dolphins, dolphin and whale watching

⓭ Ninety Mile Beach

If you want to go north as far as Cape Reinga (see right) and Ninety Mile Beach, take a morning flight from Auckland to Kaitaia, and set aside a day to drive to the country's northern tip. Ninety Mile Beach is the western portal through which sands have been blown to create the Aupouri peninsula, a skein of land connecting Kaitaia with North Cape and Cape Reinga, which were once islands. The sand originates from the volcanic eruptions of the central North Island; the rock created was worn down and carried north by the Waikato River, ocean currents and the wind. Much of the dune landscapes are now covered by forests, but almost the entire western coast is flanked by Ninety Mile Beach (actually 90km/56 miles long). The beach is so hardened that you can drive on it, but most hire cars aren't insured for this. Three roads lead from the main road to the beach, sometimes negotiable only by 4WD vehicles. Daily bus tours and scenic flights are available or simply take a beach walk.

✚ 210 A5

Information Far North
✉ Centennial Park, South Road, Kaitaia
☎ (09) 408 0879; www.visitnorthland.co.nz
🕘 Daily 8:30–5

⓮ Cape Reinga

In Maori legend, Cape Reinga is the departure point for spirits of the dead, which travel from here to the mythical homeland of Hawaiki. The gnarled branches of an 800-year-old pohutukawa tree, seen hanging off the cliff-face at Cape Reinga, form the entrance to the underworld.

The cape is often referred to as New Zealand's northernmost point, but that title is actually taken by a cliff face at North Cape, 30km (20 miles) to the east. Nevertheless, it's invigorating to walk on windswept Cape Reinga. It's the convergence zone of the Tasman Sea and the Pacific Ocean, and on a stormy day 10m (30-foot) waves swirl around Columbia Bank below Cape Reinga lighthouse. Tracks lead to the beaches on either side of Cape Reinga and to Cape Maria van Diemen.

✚ 210 A5

⓯ Te Paki Sand Dunes

Most of the northern sand dunes are now covered with forests, but where the wind blows unfettered, the sand has formed landscapes of rare elemental beauty, such as the giant, shifting dunelands that have built up at Te Paki stream. The turn-off to Te Paki stream is about 15km (9 miles) from Cape Reinga. A picnic area is set

Ninety Mile Beach – despite its name the beach is actually only 56 miles long

BEST FOR KIDS
- Feeding times at **Kelly Tarlton's Antarctic Encounter and Underwater World** (▶ 53). Divers jump into the water with the sharks at 1:30pm on Tuesday and Thursday to feed them by hand, and in the Oceanarium daily at 2pm. Other feeding times are at Fish Alley daily at noon, Stingray Encounter at 11am and 3pm, and a surface feed at the Oceanarium daily at 4pm.
- Both **Kelly Tarlton's** and the **Auckland War Memorial Museum** (▶ 55–57) have excellent hands-on discovery centres for children.

aside at the road end, immediately below towering 30m (100-foot) sand hills. A brief walk into the dunes seems to take you to the middle of a sandy desert. Watch out for signs warning about areas of quicksand in the stream.

✚ 210 A5

16 Waipoua Forest and Tane Mahuta

Waipoua Forest is the largest remaining tract of native kauri forest in Northland, which was once dominated by these giant trees. Most were felled for their timber during early settlement. However, pockets of kauri, such as Waipoua Forest, remain along the western coast.

It's not so much the height of kauri trees that is impressive as their girth and age. Tane Mahuta is the largest living kauri tree, a "mere" 52m (170 feet) tall but with a girth of more than 13m (43 feet) and an estimated age of 1,250 years. It stands in the northern reaches of Waipoua Forest (look for the road signs), and is only a short walk from SH12, which runs through the forest and along the

west coast of Northland. About 2km (1 mile) further south is another turn-off and car park; a track leads to The Four Sisters, a rare stand of four tall trees. Watch out for kauri trees whenever you turn a corner along SH12. No kauri was felled when the road was cut through the forest, so it has to wind its way around the giant trees.

✚ 210 B4

The native kauri are ancient giants; the oldest is estimated to be 1,250 years old

Where to...
Stay

Prices
Expect to pay for two people sharing a double room per night:
$ under NZ$200　　**$$** NZ$200–$350　　**$$$** over NZ$350

AUCKLAND

The Great Ponsonby Art Hotel $$

This restored 1898 villa lies down a quiet street in the lively district of Ponsonby. Near by are Auckland Zoo, Eden Park and the waterfront. Bed-and-breakfast accommodation ranges from standard ensuite rooms with private balcony to luxury garden studios. The house is furnished with Turkish carpets, leather sofas and New Zealand Pacific artworks. Make sure you have enough time to savour the freshly cooked-to-order breakfasts.

🚹 204 off A4 🖂 30 Ponsonby Terrace 📞 (09) 376 5989; www.greatpons.co.nz

The Heritage $–$$$

Formerly an art deco department store, The Heritage is in a downtown location. It has 467 rooms and suites straddling two sites. The complex has a tennis court, ballroom, swimming pools, health clubs, restaurants, bar and shops. Suites have a bedroom, living and dining area, and full kitchen and there are options for guests with disabilities.

🚹 204 B4 🖂 35 Hobson Street 📞 (09) 379 8553; www.heritagehotels.co.nz

The Langham Auckland $$–$$$

This five-star luxury hotel has convenient access by car but is also an easy walk to the Auckland Domain and War Memorial Museum. Its spa, Chuan Spa, is one of the most luxurious in the country. High tea is served daily (with or without champagne) from midday to 4:30pm in The Winery. Barolo restaurant opened in 2009 and takes its inspiration from the home of the Slow Food movement, Northern Italy's Piedmont region.

🚹 204 B3 🖂 83 Symonds Street 📞 (09) 379 5132; www.auckland.langhamhotels.co.nz

Sky City Hotel $–$$$

Part of the downtown Sky City complex, this hotel's 306 deluxe rooms and 38 suites all have super-king beds or double twins and many boast harbour views. There are also 17 restaurants and bars on site, two casinos, a heated rooftop pool, a sauna and a gym. The Sky City Grand Hotel is even more luxurious and home to the award-winning Dine by Peter Gordon restaurant.

🚹 204 B4 🖂 Corner of Victoria and Federal streets 📞 (09) 363 6000, 0800 759 2489 toll free; www.skycity.co.nz

WAIHEKE ISLAND

Vineyard Guesthouse $$–$$$

At the edge of Kennedy Point Vineyard on Waiheke Island's southwestern coast (▶ 59), and with views across the Hauraki Gulf to Rangitoto Island, this beautifully furnished guesthouse offers a variety of accommodation. You can rent just one bedroom with lounge and kitchen, a two-bedroom unit with lounge and minibar, or if you have a larger party the whole three-bedroom house. The vineyard itself produces quality red wines and a Sauvignon Blanc, as well as olive oil. Also available is a cosy two-bedroom beachside cottage on Great Barrier Island.

+ 210 C3 ⊠ Kennedy Point Vineyard, 44 Donald Bruce Road, Waiheke Island ☎ (09) 372 5600; www.kennedypointvineyard.com

Bay of Islands Lodge $$$

This luxury bed and breakfast sits above an unmilled coastal rainforest surrounded by a native bush reserve with views to the Russell peninsula and beyond. Four spacious guest bedrooms on two floors ensure this lodge remains a hideaway, yet is only minutes from Paihia. Evening meals can also be booked and are served at a large table with fellow guests.

+ 210 B4 ⊠ SH 11, Port Opua, Bay of Islands ☎ (09) 402 6075; www.bayofislandslodge.co.nz

Copthorne Hotel and Resort Bay of Islands $–$$

Although this sprawling complex is part of a chain, it has an attractive waterfront location and landscaped gardens, and is conveniently set adjacent to the Waitangi National Reserve (▶ 61). The 180 rooms and suites are fairly standard, but the freeform rock swimming pools will appeal to children in particular. There is also a spa, massage studio and tennis courts, a restaurant and a bar, and next door is an 18-hole golf course (▶ 74). The resort offers very reasonable last-minute and off-season rates making it more affordable for families – see the website for details.

+ 210 B4 ⊠ Tau Henare Drive, Paihia ☎ (09) 402 7411; www.copthornebayofislands.co.nz

Ludbrook House $$

Ludbrook house is set on a 420ha (1,037-acre) sheep and cattle property, halfway between Paihia and the Kauri Coast. The Ludbrook family has been farming here since the mid-19th century. The homestead, built in the 1920s, has commanding views and is surrounded by mature gardens. Decorated in period style, it is a gallery for work by local artists. Although there's a lounge, owner Christine Ludbrook finds that most guests gravitate to the kitchen to chat. The four guest rooms are simply but comfortably furnished and have private bathrooms. Dinners are also provided.

+ 210 B4 ⊠ 7491 SH1, Ohaeawai, RD2, Kaikohe ☎ (09) 405 9846; www.ludbrook.co.nz

The Summer House $$

Christine and Rod Brown have built their French-inspired bed and breakfast in a former citrus orchard on the outskirts of Kerikeri. Though some trees have been replaced with a lush subtropical garden, there are still plenty to provide juice for breakfast. Lodgings include one "queen" room, another with an antique French bed, and a self-contained super-king suite with a Pacific theme. All are ensuite.

+ 210 B4 ⊠ 424 Kerikeri Road, Kerikeri ☎ (09) 407 4294; www.thesummerhouse.co.nz

Kuaotunu Bay Lodge $–$$

This purpose-built lodge is set in 5ha (12 acres) of pasture and native bush overlooking Kuaotunu beach, with views of the Coromandel peninsula and nearby islands. Guest rooms have private bathrooms and French windows leading onto a private deck. Light evening meals are available by arrangement.

+ 210 C3 ⊠ SH25, RD2, Whitianga ☎ (07) 866 4396; www.kuaotunubay.co.nz

Villa Toscana $$–$$$

Giorgio and Margherita Allemano built a grand Tuscan villa in the hills above Whitianga, with spectacular views. The lower level is a lavish, self-contained, two-bedroom suite. Breakfast is provided and you can choose to dine with the Allemanos, who are lovers of gourmet Italian food. They also own a game-fishing boat, which guests can charter.

+ 210 C3 ⊠ Ohuka Park, Whitianga ☎ (07) 866 2293; www.villatoscana.co.nz

Where to...
Eat and Drink

Prices

Expect to pay per person for a three-course meal, excluding drinks:

$ under NZ$45 $$ NZ$45–$60 $$$ over NZ$60

AUCKLAND

The Grove $$$

Crowned Auckland's best restaurant in 2010 by *Metro* magazine, owner and award-winning sommalier Michael Dearth and his wife Annette hire some of the best chefs in New Zealand – who in turn go on to open their own acclaimed restaurants.

Wine matching to every course is The Grove's speciality. Try the perfect Hans Herzog with a starter of tuna sashimi and the velvety Mt Difficulty Pinot Noir with their superb pork belly and loin with petit pois dotted with edible flowers.

✛ 204 B4 ✉ St Patrick's Square, Wyndham Street, Auckland ☎ (09) 368 4129; www.thegroverestaurant.co.nz ◷ Mon–Fri 12–late, Sat 6pm–late

Kermadec $$–$$$

Seafood is the theme of this first-floor complex in the Viaduct Basin. It has a casual brasserie and bar, which spills out onto a balcony. The upmarket restaurant next door carries the sea theme into its dramatic decor, with bright tapa-cloth sails slung from the ceiling and Japanese tatami rooms with a water wall and stone garden. As well as traditional Japanese sashimi, you can order seafood platters to share as well as delicious fusion dishes like seared tuna steak on soba noodles in shiitake and oyster mushroom broth.

✛ 204 B5 ✉ Viaduct Quay ☎ (09) 304 0454; www.kermadec.co.nz ◷ Brasserie: daily 10–8; restaurant: Mon–Fri 12–3, 6pm–late, Sat–Sun 6pm–late

Prego $

One of the longest-standing restaurants on Ponsonby Road's "munchy mile", this stylish Italian cafe offers good food at reasonable prices. Dine alfresco in the enclosed front courtyard or inside the busy bistro-style restaurant. Pizzas and pasta are on offer, including lamb and whole fish, cooked in the wood-fired oven. They don't take bookings, but you can always drink at the bar while you wait for a table.

✛ 204 off A4 ✉ 226 Ponsonby Road ☎ (09) 376 3095; www.prego.co.nz ◷ Daily 12–late; closed 25 and 26 Dec

WAIHEKE ISLAND

Mudbrick Vineyard and Restaurant $$$

Built in French provincial style from handmade earth bricks, Mudbrick Vineyard has spectacular views over the Hauraki Gulf. The upmarket restaurant offers an à la carte menu of French and rural vineyard dishes, with wafer-thin slices of seared venison fillet, and roast leg of lamb stuffed with pistachios, brandy, garlic and shallots among the choices. Vegetables come from the vineyard's own gardens. Tours and tastings are also available.

✛ 210 C3 ✉ 126 Church Bay Road, Oneroa, Waiheke Island ☎ (09) 372 9050; www.mudbrick.co.nz ◷ Daily 12–3, 6–9

BAY OF ISLANDS

The Dining Room and Bistro, Duke of Marlborough Hotel $–$$

It's hard to think of a more romantic place than this old waterfront hotel in Russell. The site of so many dramatic goings-on in New Zealand history (▲ 61), it's now a peaceful spot, looking onto the sparkling water and bobbing boats of the bay. The more formal Dining Room, which has a weatherproof veranda, is open for dinner only, while the Bistro serves lighter meals all day. Burgers, steaks and chicken are on offer as well as fresh local fish.

♿ 210 B4 ⊠ 35 The Strand, Russell ☎ (09) 403 7829; www.theduke.co.nz ⏰ Dining Room: daily 6pm–10pm; bistro: daily 11–9

Kamakura $$

This renowned waterfront restaurant is in the historic town of Russell. There are lovely views of the bay through wide glass windows, and in summer you can sit outside watching yachts swing on their moorings. Chef de Cuisine David Hull brings his experience in France and Australia by combining Mediterranean and Pacific Rim flavours with the local cuisine. Try the chargrilled gamefish with cannellini beans. Be sure to leave room for one of the tempting desserts – the bay espresso crème brûlée is particularly good. Reservations are recommended.

♿ 210 B4 ⊠ 29 The Strand, Russell ☎ (09) 403 7771; www.kamakura.co.nz ⏰ Oct–Apr daily 9–3, 5–late, May–Sep 5–late

Marsden Estate $$

Named after Reverend Samuel Marsden, who planted New Zealand's first grapevines in Kerikeri in 1819, Marsden Estate is one of several vineyards that are bringing wine making back to Northland. There's seating inside the informal restaurant, where wine tasting takes place, and outdoors on a patio overlooking the vines. The menu ranges from antipasto platters to main courses such as chargrilled lamb. There is also a range of desserts from which to choose.

♿ 210 B4 ⊠ Wiroa Road, Kerikeri ☎ (09) 407 9398; www.mardenestate.co.nz ⏰ Aug–May daily 10–5, Jun–Jul 10–4

Only Seafood $

Seafood is an obvious choice in the Bay of Islands, an area famous for its game fishing. At Only Seafood, housed in a weatherboard building on the Paihia waterfront, you don't only get seafood – you also get a view. Oysters farmed locally at Orongo Bay are one of the specialities here. So is gamefish, served lightly seared with Asian seasonings, and hapuka.

♿ 210 B4 ⊠ 40 Marsden Road, Paihia ☎ (09) 402 6066 ⏰ Daily from 5pm; closed 25 Dec

COROMANDEL PENINSULA

Colenso Café $

This cafe and country shop on the main highway between Whitianga and Tairua is a delightful place to stop for lunch or a snack. Set in an old-fashioned herb garden, it has shady verandas where you can sit and relax among the flowers, and also tables indoors, where the rooms are crammed with goods made by local craftspeople. The blackboard menu includes home-baked lunch dishes, seasoned with herbs from the garden. There's also a selection of New Zealand wines, plus teas and coffees. Freshly squeezed citrus juice from the café's organic orchard is a speciality.

♿ 210 C3 ⊠ Main Road, Whenuakite ☎ (07) 866 3725 ⏰ Daily 10–5; closed Aug, 25 Dec

The Fireplace $$

A massive fireplace greets visitors to this rustic restaurant and bar on the waterfront overlooking Whitianga inlet, and the theme is carried on inside. The varied menu includes traditional pizzas from the wood-fired oven, baked flounder, rack of lamb and venison cutlet. There is also a selection of chef's specials, including pasta, curry and Coromandel oysters.

♿ 210 C3 ⊠ 9 The Esplanade, Whitianga ☎ (07) 866 4828; www.thefireplace-restaurant.com ⏰ Daily 11–2, 5–11

Where to...
Shop

Shopping Centres

Near the waterfront, the **Downtown Shopping Centre** (11–19 Customs Street, tel: 0800 166 245 toll free) has 70 speciality shops. **DFS Galleria**, in the restored 1880s Customhouse (corner of Customs and Albert streets, tel: (09) 308 0700, 0800 388 937 toll free) specializes in designer fashions.

Botany Town Centre has 150 shops (corner of Ti Rakau and Te Irirangi drives, Botany Downs, tel: (09) 272 3888). **Newmarket** has upmarket fashion and high street stores. **Sylvia Park** is the newest shopping centre with 200 stores (286 Mt Wellington Hwy, tel: (09) 570 3777). Factory outlets are found at **Dress Smart** (151 Arthur Street, Onehunga, tel: (09) 622 2400).

Fashion

Head for High Street, with designers such as **Kate Sylvester** (47 High Street, tel: (09) 307 3282) and **Karen Walker** (15 O'Connell Street, tel: (09) 309 6299), or to Parnell for clothing by **Trelise Cooper** (536 Parnell Road, tel: (09) 366 1962). Other chic stores are **Zambesi** (cnr Vulcan Lane and O'Connell Street, tel: (09) 303 1701), **Workshop** (18 Morrow Street, tel: (09) 524 6844) and **Saks** (254 Broadway, tel: (09) 520 7630).

Parnell

A cluster of heritage villas is now a village of boutiques, galleries and cafes. For crafts, browse at **The Elephant House** (237 Parnell Road, tel: (09) 309 8740).

Markets

La Cigale Market sells French products (cheese, charcuterie and bread), antiques and clothing on Saturdays 8–1 (69 St Georges Bay Road, Parnell, tel: (09) 366 9361). Also on Saturday mornings is the **Otara Market** in Newbury Street, good for for Pacific Island crafts.

Food and Wine

The **New Zealand Winemakers Centre** (National Bank Centre, corner of Elliott and Victoria streets, tel: (09) 379 5858) offers wine tasting, retail, and travel advice. In Newmarket, gather a picnic at **Zarbo** deli-cafe (24 Morrow Street, tel: (09) 520 2721).

The Cabbage Tree has two shops in Paihia (Williams Road and Maritime Building, tel: (09) 402 7318) selling crafts and leisure wear. Pick up a guide to Kerikeri's **Art and Craft Trail** from the Paihia visitor centre (Paihia Wharf, tel: (09) 402 7345). **Living Nature** (SH10, Kerikeri, tel: (09) 407 7895) sells natural skincare goods. Buy cheese from **Mahoe Farm-house Cheese** (SH10, Oromahoe, tel: (09) 405 9681) or chocolates from **Makana Confections** (504 Kerikeri Road, tel: (09) 407 6800), and visit Kerikeri's Sunday farmer's market (9–noon, Books and More car park). At the **Ancient Kauri Kingdom** (229 SH1, RD1, Awanui, tel: (09) 406 7172), ancient logs are converted into furniture.

Pick up a copy of the **Coromandel Craft Trail** leaflet from an information centre. Choose from the cheeses at **Matatoki Farm** (12km (7.5 miles) north of Thames, tel: (07) 868 1284).

Where to...
Be Entertained

Information on events, clubs, cinema and theatre listings can be found on www.viewauckland.co.nz.

Nightspots

Karangahape Road ("K Road") is the centre of Auckland's club scene. Tune in to Radio95 bFM's gig guide for what's on. **Sky City Casino** (corner of Federal and Victoria streets, tel: 0800 759 2489 toll free) is open 24 hours.

Performing Arts

The **Aotea Centre** (Mayoral Drive, tel: (09) 309 2677) is Auckland's premier classical concert venue. The Auckland Theatre Company performs at several venues including the University's **Maidment Theatre** (8 Alfred Street, tel: (09) 308 2383).

Sports

Boat charters in Waitemata Harbour are offered by almost 100 companies. There are popular **windsurfing** beaches at Bayswater, Mission Bay, Takapuna and Point Chevalier. Over 20 golf courses are near by, including New Zealand's longest, the **Formosa Country Club** (110 Jack Lachlan Drive, Beachlands, tel: 0800 842 538 toll free). Auckland has three stadiums, hosting rugby union, rugby league or test cricket. Call **Ticketek**, tel: 0800 842 538 toll free. Watch the tennis at the **ASB Bank Tennis Centre** (1 Tennis Lane, Parnell, tel: (09) 373 3623), or have a bet at **Ellerslie Race Course** (80 Ascot Avenue, Remuera, tel: (09) 524 4069).

Wine Trail

The Auckland visitor centre produces a brochure listing wineries in the region and can book tours (Viaduct Basin, tel: (09) 979 2333).

Festivals

Pasifika festival (March) showcases Pacific Islands arts, ▲ 43–44.

Sports

The Bay of Islands offers great game fishing; charter operators are found at Paihia Wharf. The region also has golf courses. Try the **Waitangi Golf Club** (tel: (09) 402 7713).

Wine Trail

Get a **wine trail map** from the information centre in Paihia (The Wharf, Marsden Road, tel: (09) 402 7345).

Festivals

The region's most famous celebration is **Waitangi Day** (▲ 44). The **Whangarei Jazz and Blues Festival** is held in October, while November heralds the **Taste Bay of Islands** wine and food festival and the **Bay of Islands A & P show** in Waimate North, and January the **Waipu Highland Games**.

Sports

Whangamata has a famous surfing beach, and charter operators offer water activities. Take a wilderness walk with **Kiwi Dundee Adventures** (tel: (07) 865 8809). Golf courses include **Mercury Bay Golf Club** (12 Golf Road, Whitianga, tel: (07) 866 5479).

Festivals

The crimson-flowered **pohutukawa tree** is celebrated in December. January brings the well-attended **Keltic Fair**.

Central Plateau

Getting Your Bearings

The volcanic plateau in the central North Island is New Zealand's hotspot of angry natural forces – one of the world's most active geothermal areas. Towering geysers, hissing steam, boiling mud and evil smells are constant companions as you travel along the Thermal Explorer Highway from Rotorua to Taupo, exploring New Zealand's contribution to the Pacific Ring of Fire.

The Taupo Volcanic Zone stretches 250km (155 miles), right through the central North Island. This band of thermal activity varies in width from 30km (20 miles) to 80km (50 miles), anchored by White Island in the north and the three Tongariro volcanoes in the south. These four active volcanoes enclose a huge field of dormant cones and vast craters formed by earlier eruptions.

In this area, the earth is constantly on the move, spewing fiery bad breath wherever toxic fumes find an escape route through the thin crust. Nature is at her rawest – her face pockmarked with festering boils and oozing craters – but also at her most impressive and beautiful.

The region's original inhabitants, Maori belonging to the Te Arawa tribe, learned to harness the region's tremendous natural energy, cooking their food in hot springs and relaxing in mineral-rich warm pools. They were also the country's first tour guides,

back in the 1870s, as the area gained a reputation for its natural spectacles and began drawing British visitors, inspiring New Zealand's first commercial tourism ventures.

But in 1886 Mount Tarawera erupted, destroying several villages and popular tourist attractions. The region recovered only slowly. Rotorua finally rediscovered its heritage as a spa town and several of the original mock-Tudor buildings have been restored to their former glory, adding charm and contrast to the city. Today, many of the modern tourist guides are young Maori, proudly continuing their ancestors' tradition of hospitality.

Tihiroa

Waitomo Caves [10]

Te Kuiti

Piopio

Maungatupoto

Ohura

Taumarunui

Raetihi

★ Don't Miss

Page 75: The central plateau is full of geothermal craters

Opposite: The sun sets over the hills and valleys surrounding Te Mata Peak

Below: A Maori warrior in challenge pose

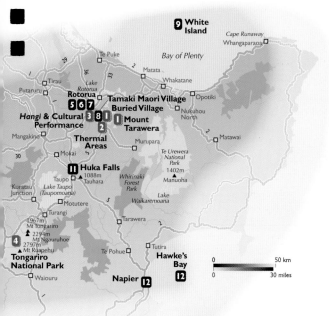

At Your Leisure

In Four Days

If you're not quite sure where to begin your travels, this itinerary recommends four practical and enjoyable days in the Central Plateau, taking in some of the best places to see using the Getting Your Bearings map on the previous page. For more information see the main entries.

Day 1

Morning

Check out the visitor information centre in downtown Rotorua to make bookings for Day 2's ❸ *Hangi* **and cultural performance** (above, ➤ 86). Walk to the Government Gardens on the shores of Lake Rotorua and take your time to explore the ❺ **Rotorua Museum of Art and History** (➤ 90), which has

excellent exhibits about the eruption of **Mount Tarawera** (left). Have lunch in town (➤ 95–96), or drive 20km (12 miles) on to Lake Tarawera.

Afternoon

Walk along the shore of Lake Tarawera or join a cruise on Lake Rotomahana past the former site of the Pink and White Terraces. Then drive back 1km (0.5 miles) to visit the fascinating ❶ **Te Wairoa, the Buried Village** (➤ 80–81), which was devastated by the volcanic explosion. Return to Rotorua to relax in the hot pools at the ❻ **Polynesian Spa** (➤ 91).

Day 2

Morning
Spend another day in Rotorua, this time exploring **2 Whakarewarewa** (▶ 82–83), where most of the survivors from the Buried Village moved after the eruption. This thermal resort also offers excellent performances of Maori culture and is next to the **New Zealand Maori Arts and Crafts Institute**.

Afternoon
Return to Lake Rotorua's western shore on the other side of the city and take a ride on the **7 Skyline Skyrides** (▶ 91) for sweeping views across Rotorua, the lake, Mount Tarawera and the steaming thermal areas in between. Spend the rest of the day exploring the **Agrodome** or **Rainbow Springs** animal park (▶ 98), and enjoy a traditional **8** *hangi* **and cultural performance** (▶ 86) in the evening.

Day 3

Morning
Drive 19km (12 miles) south along SH5 to the stunning **Waimangu Valley 2 thermal area** (above, ▶ 83–84), which was created by Mount Tarawera's eruption. Spend the morning exploring the startling landscapes and springs, and take lunch at the coffee shop.

Afternoon
Continue for another 10km (6 miles) further south to visit the **Wai-o-tapu 2 thermal area** (▶ 84–85) to see its rainbow-coloured silica terraces and hot pools. Detour to Waikite (▶ 85) for a soak in the hot springs, then continue south towards Taupo (▶ 87). You can take a detour to **11 Huka Falls** (▶ 92) and enjoy a meal at the Huka Prawn Park (▶ 98).

Day 4

For your last day, stroll along the shores of **Lake Taupo** or explore any of the water-based activities on offer. Then drive along the lake towards Turangi and Whakapapa in the magnificent **4 Tongariro National Park** (▶ 87–89). Take the chair lift up Mount Ruapehu for a view across the other two volcanoes, then take a short walk from the visitor centre in Whakapapa (▶ 89). Alternatively, drive 139km (86 miles) from Taupo to **12 Napier and Hawke's Bay** (▶ 93) along SH5. Soak up the city's art deco architecture on a walk or visit some of the local wineries.

☐ Mount Tarawera and the Buried Village

Mount Tarawera is sacred to the Maori tribe that first settled this area. It isn't one of New Zealand's highest mountains, but its many jagged peaks and long, deep crater are reminders that it is one of the most volatile. One winter's night in 1886, the volcano exploded, burying the surrounding area under a layer of mud and obliterating its famous silica terraces.

The violence of the 1886 eruption is still evident even from a distance. One of the best places for a good view of Mount Tarawera is the **Landing Café at Lake Tarawera** (➤ 95). The mountain's summit is non-existent – instead it has a giant, gaping crater. When it blew, the mountain opened and ripped a 17km (11-mile) fissure creating a new lake and the thermal Waimangu Valley (➤ 83–85), and ejecting enough material to blanket 16,000sq km (6,000sq miles) around it.

Tarawera's jagged and vast crater

Boat cruises are available on Lake Tarawera, and 4WD vehicles or helicopters can take you to Mount Tarawera's crater rim (at a price) to see the eruption's effect on the landscape. However, the most haunting sight of the mayhem that followed the eruption can be found at **Te Wairoa, the Buried Village**, about 1km (0.5 miles) from Lake Tarawera.

Village Life

The village was the hub of tourism and home to several guides who took visitors to the famous **Pink and White Terraces** during the 1870s, the biggest tourist attraction of the time. Hot water once poured over these huge, silica terraces into nearby Lake Rotomahana, which was less than half its current size before the eruption.

A **small museum** at the entrance to the Buried Village provides an excellent introduction to the area. Photographs

THE PRICE OF WISDOM

An eerie atmosphere surrounds Tuhoto Ariki's house. He had warned villagers that they would be punished for their greed in encouraging tourism. When his predictions came true, villagers blamed him for the disaster and refused to dig him out. The sage was finally rescued four days later but died within a week.

recount the development of Te Wairoa from a quiet settlement to a thriving staging post. Eyewitness accounts describe the chaos and tragedy of the rescue effort and there is also the chilling story of the warnings that preceded it. According to several witnesses, shortly before the eruption a group of tourists was crossing Lake Tarawera with Guide Sophia, one of the most popular guides, when they saw a phantom Maori waka (canoe); the warriors paddling towards the mountain had the faces of dogs. The village sage, Tuhoto Ariki, interpreted the sight as a warning of imminent destruction. Soon after, the village was destroyed and more than 150 people were killed.

Revealing Artefacts

Excavations of Te Wairoa have revealed a number of small dwellings, accessible to visitors, and hundreds of artefacts, among them the blacksmith's tools, millstones from the village mill, the baker's large oven and full bottles from the tavern.

TAKING A BREAK

There are **tea rooms** at the entrance to the Buried Village, but if the weather's good, have a **picnic** under the tall aspen poplars that have grown from the original fence posts.

✚ 209 E4

Visitor Information Centre
✉ 1167 Fenton Street, Rotorua ☎ (07) 348 5179; www.rotoruanz.com
🕐 Nov–Mar daily 8–6; Apr–Oct 8–5:30

Te Wairoa – the Buried Village
✉ 1180 Tarawera Road, RD5, Rotorua ☎ (07) 362 8287; www.buriedvillage.co.nz 🕐 Nov–Mar daily 9–5; Apr–Oct 9–4:30 💲 Expensive

Clearwater Cruises
✉ The Tarawera Landing, Lake Tarawera ☎ (07) 345 6688; www.clearwater.co.nz 🕐 Lake Tarawera Experience (3 hours): daily 9am 💲 Expensive

---

MOUNT TARAWERA AND THE BURIED VILLAGE: INSIDE INFO

Top tip Join a **guided tour** through the museum and the excavation sites. Some of Guide Sophia's descendants now work as guides and their personal connection with the area brings the stories to life.

Hidden gem Traditional Maori villages used to have communal storehouses to keep food for winter. During excavations of the storehouse at Te Wairoa, archaeologists discovered some rare **Maori stone carvings**, and two of these precious relics are now on display at the storehouse entrance.

2 Thermal Areas

Rotorua is the centre of a thermal wonderland of bubbling mud pools, kaleidoscopic silica terraces and spouting geysers. The odour of hydrogen sulphide pervades the city day and night, and has earned it the nickname Sulphur City.

Three of the most stunning spectacles are along the Thermal Explorer Highway (State Highway 5) between Rotorua and Taupo. Although they're all within 30km (20 miles) of Rotorua, plan to spend at least two hours at Whakarewarewa Thermal Valley and a day at Waimangu Valley and the Wai-o-tapu thermal area.

Whakarewarewa Thermal Valley

Whakarewarewa Thermal Valley is closest to downtown Rotorua, at the southern end of the city, and is part of the **Te Puia complex**. Uniquely, this combines an extensive **geothermal park** with a centre of **Maori culture** and a kiwi house, where you can catch a rare glimpse of these nocturnal birds. Whakarewarewa village became the new home for those displaced by the 1886 eruption of Mount Tarawera (➤ 80–81). Villagers still use the hot pools for bathing and cooking – try a cob of corn cooked in one of the mineral pools if you can.

Champagne
Pool in
Wai-o-tapu

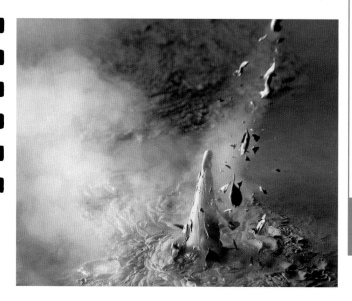

Bubbling mud pools

Whakarewarewa's main attraction is the **geyser flat**, a moonscape silica terrace of about 1ha (2.5 acres) pierced by seven active geysers. Two are very reliable: the **Prince of Wales Feathers geyser** regularly spouts hot fountains about 12m (40 feet) high and heralds the awakening of **Pohutu** ("**Big Splash**") **geyser**, at around 30m (100 feet), New Zealand's highest. It erupts every hour or so, and while you wait you can stroll through a bizarre landscape of burping mud puddles, bubbling hot pools and steaming vents.

Cultural Exhibits

Most people come to see the earth forces, but you shouldn't miss the **meeting house** and the **New Zealand Maori Arts and Crafts Institute**, established in 1963 to preserve Maori heritage and now a respected training school for carvers and weavers. You can watch Maori artisans instructing young craftspeople, and browse the galleries for souvenirs. The ornately sculpted meeting house nearby is used for daily cultural concerts, which are included in the entrance fee.

Waimangu Valley

South of Whakarewarewa, 14km (9 miles) along SH5, you'll see a sign for **Waimangu Valley**, about 6km (4 miles) from the turn-off. This narrow valley was created by the eruption of Mount Tarawera, which tore a gash into the land around its base. The valley has since filled with regenerating bush, creating splendid landscapes. Before you enter the valley, browse through the photographs taken before and after Mount Tarawera exploded, and pick up a trail map.

Just a few metres from the start of the walkway, the valley opens up for a panoramic view. From here the path winds its way past cool, algae-covered **Emerald Pool** to **Frying Pan**

Lake. This is the world's largest hot spring, fed by boiling water and toxic fumes, and producing incredibly eerie sounds. Continue past smaller fizzing pools and a steaming rock stream and a barren basin, whose rim is marked with a white cross. Here, in 1903, four people were killed by the **Waimangu geyser**, the largest known hot fountain. For a short time in the early 20th century, the geyser used to spit scalding muddy water high into the air, but it is dormant at the moment.

A few minutes further into the valley, the constantly gurgling **Inferno Crater Lake** gives a performance that befits its name every month or so. Closer still to **Lake Rotomahana**, the magnificent **Marble and Warbrick terraces** channel hot water down a maze of scalloped sinter flats and cascading buttresses. The lake cruise is a very tranquil journey, past scarred and steaming cliffs and smaller geysers to the former site of the Pink and White Terraces.

Wai-o-tapu

From the Waimangu turn-off, it's another 13km (8 miles) along SH5 to the awesome thermal wonders of **Wai-o-tapu**. Here, the water flows over landscapes rich in silica. As it cools, the mineral forms sinter. This thermal area is most notable for the mineral-encrusted **Champagne Pool**, delicately tinged with all the colours of the spectrum, and the **Primrose Terraces**, which have formed over more than 900 years and are the largest in the southern hemisphere. There are also several large caves, whose overhanging ceilings are decorated with filigreed formations of crystallized sulphur.

> **BUBBLING OVER**
> Wai-o-tapu is home to the Lady Knox Geyser, which erupts at 10:15am daily – with a little help. As the story goes, prisoners were brought here in the 1900s to wash their clothes in the hot pools. A warden noticed that the water started boiling as it became soapy, so he had the prisoners build a rock cairn over the pool to confine the water and drive up a fountain. Today, silica has coated the cairn and it acts as a natural geyser, but the eruption still has to be triggered with soap.

Opposite: Lady Knox Geyser blows her top on a daily basis

Below: The mud pools of Hell's Gate

TAKING A BREAK

Both Waimangu Valley and Wai-o-tapu have excellent **coffee shops**, which offer a range of light meals and refreshments.

➕ 209 D4

Whakarewarewa Thermal Valley
✉ Hemo Road, Rotorua ☎ (07) 348 9047, 0800 837 842 toll free; www.tepuia.com ⏰ Daily 8–5. Guided tours: 9–5 on the hour. Daytime Maori concerts: daily 10:15, 12:15, 3:15 💷 Expensive

Waimangu Volcanic Valley
✉ 587 Waimangu Road, Rotorua ☎ (07) 366 6137; www.waimangu.co.nz ⏰ Daily 8:30–5 (last entry 3:45) 💷 Expensive

Wai-o-tapu Thermal Wonderland
✉ 201 Wai-o-tapu Loop Road, off SH5, Rotorua ☎ (07) 366 6333; www.geyserland.co.nz ⏰ Daily 8:30–5 (summer later) 💷 Expensive

THERMAL AREAS: INSIDE INFO

Top tips You'll need at least an hour to walk to the end of the Waimangu Valley at the shore of Lake Rotomahana, where you can join a cruise to view volcanic features inaccessible from the paths. Alternatively, a shuttle bus makes a regular loop around the valley's thermal sites to the lake.
■ Don't dress up – the odour of sulphur tends to stick to clothes for some time.

Hidden gems Visit **Waikite**, a forested thermal valley with a small public pool fed by a hot stream. There are also private baths and a cafe. Turn into Waikite Valley Road at the Wai-o-tapu Tavern on SH5 (tel: (07) 333 1861; www.hotpools.co.nz; open daily 10–9 (cafe: 12–7:30); admission: moderate).
■ Te Puia's **kiwi house** allows visitors to see these rare birds close up. The nocturnal kiwis are kept in a dimly lit environment, and are viewed through a glass wall.

In more depth If you want to see more fumaroles and mud pools, **Hell's Gate** is about 15 minutes from Rotorua. Travel north on SH30 past Rotorua Airport, continuing right towards Whakatane. After about 4km (2.5 miles) you will come to Tikitere and Hell's Gate, on the left (tel: (07) 345 3151; www.hellsgate.co.nz).

③ *Hangi* and Cultural Performance

After decades of assimilation, Maori language, culture and crafts are experiencing a renaissance among both Maori and Pakeha (New Zealanders descended from European settlers). Enjoying traditionally cooked food and a live performance are unmissable experiences.

The best way to experience Maori culture is to attend a performance at a venue such as Tamaki Maori Village (► 91) or Te Puia (► 82). Both sites include a traditional Maori village with a *whare nui* (large meeting house), smaller dwellings and storehouses, and combine a *hangi* with a performance of action songs and dances.

Hospitality is essential to Maori culture. You will receive a traditional welcome, when a warrior will perform mock attacks and lay out a small branch as a challenge. The elected "chief" of your group picks up the branch to signal a peaceful visit. The women will then call you onto the *marae* (area outside the meeting house), where hosts and guests exchange speeches and songs. Maori songs and dances are an integral part of oral history and are accompanied by actions to illustrate the story. A *hangi* is traditionally prepared in an earth oven by steaming vegetables and a range of meats together over hot rocks.

Rituals, songs and dances form a traditional Maori welcome

Tamaki Tours
✉ 1220 Hinemaru Street, Rotorua
☎ (07) 349 2999;
www.maoriculture.co.nz ⏰ Daily, booking required
💷 Expensive

HANGI AND CULTURAL PERFORMANCE: INSIDE INFO

Top tips Catch the **courtesy bus** to your venue rather than driving there yourself. The bus drivers often use the journey to explain the protocol of visiting a *marae*.

■ Be prepared to **exchange songs** with your Maori hosts. It doesn't have to be anything elaborate – a popular song will do. It's better to sing something badly than to sing nothing at all!

4 Tongariro National Park

Few views are as striking as the first glimpse of the three volcanoes of the Tongariro National Park. Rising starkly from a surrounding plateau of tussocklands and near-desert, the peaks mark one of the country's most popular national parks.

A view across Lake Taupo

Tongariro was New Zealand's first national park, the vision of a Maori tribal chief who gave the mountains to the nation to ensure their protection (▶ 10). Volcanic forces and weather continue to mould this area, which is one of a handful of places worldwide with dual World Heritage status in recognition of its natural and cultural value. It's also a magnet for outdoor enthusiasts, who come to walk its tracks in summer and to ski the slopes of **Mount Ruapehu** (at 2,797m/9,174 feet the North Island's highest mountain) in winter.

Calm Waters

The most scenic approach is from **Taupo**, at the northern end of **Lake Taupo**. The huddled peaks first come into view across the water as you drive along the lakefront. The lake's calm, deep blue water belies its violent creation from one of the world's biggest volcanic eruptions. The Taupo explosion in AD186 is believed to have darkened skies and caused blood-red sunsets as far away as Italy and China, and pumice now forms a thick layer over much of the North Island. The lake, which fills several of the craters carved by the eruption, is the country's largest and is a trout-angler's paradise. Rainbow trout

The peaks of Mount Ngauruhoe, Tongariro and Ruapehu

are hooked by the tonne each day and you are likely to spot lines of anglers sitting on the lake's banks as you drive south for about 50km (30 miles) along its eastern shores.

Still Active
Even from a distance, it is clear that the volcanoes of Tongariro National Park are anything but dormant. **Mount Ngauruhoe**, an almost perfect cone with a clearly recognizable volcanic crater at the 2,291m (7,514-foot) summit, smoulders and occasionally belches steam and gas into the sky. **Mount Tongariro**, at 1,967m (6,451 feet) the lowest of the volcanic trio, is a maze of volcanic craters and spouts the cascading Ketetahi hot spring from one of its flanks. **Mount Ruapehu**, the only peak that is constantly snow-capped, erupts every few years. During the last eruption, in September 2007, Ruapehu spewed out a cloud of steam and ash and several lahars (mud flows), one of the latter engulfing a mountain hut and seriously injuring a climber.

Introducing the Park
The national park's main access is through the small settlement called **Whakapapa**, itself worth a visit, not least to see one of New Zealand's best known hotels, the **Bayview Chateau** (▶ 94). The Department of Conservation, which administers all protected lands, runs a **visitor centre** at Whakapapa with excellent displays on the region's geology and history, as well as information about walks and weather forecasts. At the entrance, you are greeted by a bust of **Horonuku Te Heuheu Tukino IV** (▶ 10), the far-sighted paramount chief of the local Ngati Tuwharetoa people, who realized in 1887 that the only way to preserve an area of cultural significance was to give it away. Just outside the centre, a commemorative rock is a reminder of the peaks' continuing importance for Maori.

To explore the park, you can take the ski field chair lift and on a clear day the views from the top terminal are stunning – just sit outside and take in the majestic atmosphere. Scenic plane and helicopter flights are available from a small airfield a few minutes from Whakapapa, and there are myriad short walks and nature trails starting from the village.

TAKING A BREAK

Take tea at the **Bayview Chateau** (► 94) or eat at **Knoll Ridge Café** (open 7:30am–11pm), which, at about 2,000m (6,500 feet) above sea level, is New Zealand's highest restaurant. Knoll Ridge Café closes in bad weather, but nearby **Lorenz's Bar and Café** (open 8:30am–4:30pm) at Top o' the Bruce always stays open.

✚ 209 D3

The landscape surrounding Mount Ruapehu; its peaks are always covered with snow

Whakapapa Visitor Information Centre
✉ SH48, Whakapapa; mailing address: Private Bag, Mount Ruapehu 2650 ☎ (07) 892 3729; www.doc.govt.nz ◷ Nov–Mar daily 8–6; Apr–Oct 8–5

Mount Ruapehu
✉ Guided walks and chair lift from Top o' the Bruce, road end SH48, Whakapapa ski area ☎ (07) 892 4000; www.mtruapehu.com ◷ Chair lift services to Whakapapa ski field (weather dependent): Mid Jan–Oct, mid Dec–Easter daily 8:30–4. Closed Sep–mid Dec, Easter–mid Jan ▓ Moderate

Mountain Air
☎ (07) 892 2812, 0800 922 812 toll free; www.mountainair.co.nz

Helistar Helicopters Limited
☎ (07) 374 8405, 0800 435 478 toll free; www.helistar.co.nz

TONGARIRO NATIONAL PARK: INSIDE INFO

Top tips Explore the **Whakapapa Visitor Information Centre** and its audiovisual displays on the national park's volcanoes, biodiversity and conservation.
■ Be aware that out of the **skiing season** (approximately November to March), most of Whakapapa's amenities are likely to be closed.

One to miss It is possible to **climb to the top of Mount Ruapehu**, but the track is not well marked and a return trip can take up to six hours, so it is only for experienced walkers with a guide who knows the area. The weather can change very quickly and clouds can close in around the peaks within a few minutes, so if you're not a confident hiker save your energy and stay close to the top station of the chair lift to enjoy the views.

In more depth The 18.5km (11.5-mile) **Tongariro Crossing** is one of the most popular day walks in New Zealand. The track makes its way over the saddle between mounts Ngauruhoe and Tongariro through volcanic landscapes of craters, steaming valleys, hot springs, and the tantalizingly named Emerald and Blue lakes. It takes about eight hours, and hikers should be prepared for changeable weather. Buy maps from the Whakapapa Visitor Centre.

At Your Leisure

Once a government-run spa, the Bath House is now home to the Rotorua Museum

5 Rotorua Museum of Art and History

Come here for more on Rotorua's thermal activity, the area's significance to local Maori tribes, and the town's past as a spa resort. The museum itself is housed in the Bath House, a Tudor-style building surrounded by the Government Gardens. The Bath House was the government's first major commitment to the region's tourist industry, which was thriving by the time the "Great South Seas Spa" opened in 1908. The rich and famous came to soak in the hot mineral waters that still bubble up near Lake Rotorua. They even took baths in tubs connected to electrical currents. The old treatment rooms and bathtubs have been restored and are now permanent exhibits at the museum. Another display features ancient carvings of the Te Arawa, the local Maori tribe. You can witness the violent eruption of Mount Tarawera (➤ 80–81) in a brief film, before exploring the museum's display on the tragedy. Next to the museum are the Blue Baths, designed during the 1930s for recreational rather than medicinal bathing and one of the first public pools to allow mixed bathing.

➕ 209 D4 ✉ Queens Drive, Government Gardens, Rotorua ☎ (07) 349 4350; www.rotoruamuseum.co.nz ⏰ Oct–Mar daily 9–8; Apr–Sep 9–5 🍴 Bath House Café ($) 💰 Moderate

HAPPILY EVER AFTER

The love story of Hinemoa and Tutanekai is retold in the popular Maori song "Pokarekare Ana". Both lovers were of high birth in their respective subtribes, but as Tutanekai was an illegitimate son, Hinemoa's family was not in favour of a marriage. Hinemoa lived on the western shore of Lake Rotorua, while Tutanekai lived on the lake's Mokoia Island, where he liked to play his flute. The wind would carry the music to Hinemoa – until one night she couldn't resist and swam across to him. When the families heard of her feat, they celebrated the couple's union. You can see the lovers embracing at the main gates to the Whakarewarewa Thermal Valley.

6 Polynesian Spa

After a hard day's sightseeing, treat yourself to an evening soak in the hot mineral pools and elegant atmosphere of the Polynesian Spa. The facility has integrated elements of a spa house built on the same site during the 1930s. You can choose between warm, invigorating acidic pools, set in rocks at a sheltered part of Lake Rotorua's shoreline, and soothing alkaline pools that are fed by a boiling spring beside the complex. Follow up your soak with massages, skin treatments and mud baths – all with a view out to the lake. If you're looking for privacy, there are 13 small, enclosed pools that can be locked.

🚩 209 D4 ⊠ Hinemoa Street, Government Gardens, Rotorua ☎ (07) 348 1328; www.polynesianspa.co.nz 🕐 Daily 8am–11pm; therapies and treatments: 9–8 💰 Treatments: expensive; pools: moderate–expensive

7 Skyline Skyrides

For those with energy to spare, this family entertainment area combines a gondola ride with several luge tracks and bush walks. The gondola climbs the side of Mount Ngongotaha to almost 500m (1,500 feet) above sea level, opening up panoramic views of Rotorua, the lake and the surrounding district. At the top you can choose different activities, including the Sky Swing and luge tracks, ranging from scenic to advanced. You can also walk downhill following easy footpaths.

🚩 209 D4 ⊠ Fairy Springs Road, Rotorua ☎ (07) 347 0027; www.skylineskyrides.co.nz 🕐 Daily 9am–late 🍴 Licensed restaurant ($$), Terraces Café ($) 💰 Moderate

8 Tamaki Maori Village

If you want to see how Maori people lived before Europeans arrived in New Zealand, visit this re-created village on an evening tour. It was built into a sheltered forest, complete with a market place, meeting house, sleeping houses, storehouses and a fortified entrance. Maori performers bring the village alive as they go about their daily business, such as weaving and carving. A highlight is the cultural performance and *hangi* feast (▶ 86). Visitors receive a formal welcome and then enjoy a traditional concert and a dinner cooked in an earth oven over hot boulders.

🚩 209 D4 ⊠ 14km (9 miles) south on SH5 towards Taupo. Tamaki Tours: 1220 Hinemaru Street, Rotorua ☎ (07) 349 2999; www.maoriculture.co.nz 🕐 Daily tours at 5:30pm, 6:30pm, 7:30pm. Free pickup is one hour before start time 🚌 Courtesy transport from and to accommodation, with introduction to Maori protocol 💰 Expensive

9 White Island

The plume of smoke rising from White Island can be seen from the coastline of the Bay of Plenty. New Zealand's most active cone volcano is about 50km (30 miles) offshore from the towns of Whakatane and Opotiki, and is accessible only by pre-booked boat or helicopter. The volcano had a sulphur mine within its crater in the late 19th and early 20th centuries, until an eruption in 1914 killed all 11 of the miners who were working there. The island's wide crater floor is littered with fumaroles, and hot water and steam constantly escape from these sulphur-encrusted vents. Trips are dependent on the weather and also demand a reasonable level of fitness.

🚩 209 E5 ⊠ 15 The Strand, Whakatane ☎ (07) 308 9588, 0800 733 529 toll free; www.whiteisland.co.nz 💰 Expensive

10 Waitomo Caves

Waitomo is a sleepy settlement famous for its limestone caves. The region is riddled with more than 50km (30 miles) of cave passages, part of a karst limestone landscape that has been sculpted by water into blind valleys, sinkholes, arches and fluted outcrops. About three hours' drive west of Rotorua, the village is 8km (5 miles) off SH3, between the towns of Te Kuiti and Otorohanga. Though comprising little more than a main road, over half a million visitors come every year to see the caves. You could easily

Aranui Cave, part of the warren of passages and openings in the Waitomo Caves

spend a day exploring the activities on offer. Most people come to walk through the glow-worm caves and to see the stalactites and stalagmites; other options range from three-hour blackwater rafting expeditions (navigating an underground river on a tyre inner tube) to all-day abseiling and climbing. A shuttle bus runs daily return trips between Rotorua and Waitomo (tel: (0508) 926 337 toll free).

🗙 208 C4

Visitor Information Centre
✉ 21 Waitomo Caves Road
☎ (07) 878 7640, 0800 474 839 toll free;
www.waitomo-museum.co.nz ⊕ Oct–24
Dec daily 8:45–5:30; 26 Dec–Feb 8:45–7:30;
Mar–Sep 8:45–5

🚻 Huka Falls

Just a few minutes north of Taupo, the Waikato, New Zealand's longest, and normally 100m (300 feet) wide and 4m (13 foot) deep river, is forced through a narrow cleft only 15m (50 feet) wide and 10m (30 feet) deep. The blue water surges through the channel and bursts out in a foaming waterfall, plunging over

an 11m (36-foot) shelf. There is a footbridge across the channel and a walking track to the falls, but you can also take a jetboat or a cruise boat to view them from the water.

From Huka Falls it's a short drive to Aratiatia Rapids. The rapids and the beautiful narrow gorge here dried up after a dam was installed on the Waikato, but the dam is opened for half an hour several times a day so that people can still see the majesty of the rapids.

🗙 209 D4

Aratiatia Rapids
⊙ Rapids: Oct–Mar daily 10am, 12,
2pm, 4pm; Apr–Sep 10am, 12, 2pm
💲 Free

Huka Falls River Cruise
✉ Departs from Aratiatia dam ☎ 0800
278 336 toll free; www.hukafallscruise.co.nz
⊙ Daily 10:30, 12:30, 2:30 (plus 4:30
26 Dec–end Jan) 💲 Expensive

Hukafalls Jet
✉ Wairakei Park, SH1, 6km (4 miles)
north of Taupo ☎ (07) 374 8572;
www.hukafallsjet.com ⊙ Booking
recommended 💲 Expensive

12 Napier and Hawke's Bay

With a Mediterranean-like climate and fertile soil, Hawke's Bay is New Zealand's prime wine-growing and fruit-producing area. Aside from the wineries, its main appeal is the art deco buildings in the city of Napier.

On 3 February 1931, a massive 7.9-rated earthquake struck Hawke's Bay. Virtually every building in Napier and Hastings collapsed, and subsequent fires destroyed the city's commercial heart. Aftershocks continued for 10 days and more than 250 people were killed. But locals refused to be beaten: the city was rebuilt in the styles fashionable at the time – Spanish Mission, Stripped Classical and, above all, art deco. Today, Napier has one of the world's highest concentrations of art deco architecture. The best examples of this pastel-coloured, geometric style are on Emerson, Dalton and Tennyson streets, all within the inner city and close to Marine Parade.

Take at least half a day to stroll through the city centre and along Marine Parade, with its trademark palms and angular Norfolk pines.

The annual Art Deco Weekend in February draws hundreds of people dressed in 1930s regalia.

✚ 209 E3

Visitor Information Centre
✉ 100 Marine Parade, Napier
☎ (06) 834 1911, 0800 847 488 toll free; www.hawksbaynz.com ⏲ Daily 9–5

Art Deco Shop
✉ Deco Centre, 163 Tennyson Street, Napier
☎ (06) 835 0022; www.artdeconapier.com
⏲ Daily 9–5

Napier has a fine selection of art deco buildings all built after the 1931 earthquake

Where to...
Stay

ROTORUA

Regent of Rotorua $

This former 1960s motel is now a chic boutique hotel within easy walking distance of the heart of the restaurant district. A new restaurant, cocktail bar and one- and two-bedroom suites have been added. Enjoy the 30°C (86°F) geothermally heated pool or the indoor mineral pool, or sit beside the indoor/outdoor fireplace in winter with a glass of wine.

🚑 209 D4 ⬚ 1191 Pukaki Street
📞 (07) 348 4079, 0508 734 368 toll free;
www.regentrotorua.co.nz

The Springs Fine Accommodation $$$

Colleen and Murray Ward have designed this luxury B&B to blend in with the 1930s bungalows in their quiet residential street. Plump sofas and objets d'art decorate the library, where guests are offered refreshments on arrival.

The four ensuite bedrooms have king-size beds, walk-in wardrobes and access to the tranquil private terrace. The hearty breakfasts include pancakes, smoked salmon and scrambled eggs.

🚑 209 D4 ⬚ 16 Devon Street, Rotorua
📞 (07) 348 9922; www.thesprings.co.nz

Treetops $$$

Set in 1,000ha (2,500 acres) of native New Zealand bush, this luxury lodge is a secluded retreat. The main lodge has been built over a natural stream with hunting trophies standing elegantly over the enormous fireplace in the Great Room. There are four lodge rooms attached to the main building and eight villas in separate buildings, each with their own lake or bush views. Activities include trout fishing, hunting, horseback riding, clay shooting and hiking on some of the 70km (43 miles) of trails that meander past lakes, glow-worm caves, streams and waterfalls.

🚑 209 E4 ⬚ 351 Kearoa Road, Horohoro, Rotorua 📞 (07) 333 2066;
www.treetops.co.nz

TONGARIRO NATIONAL PARK

Bayview Chateau Tongariro $–$$

Perched on the slopes of Mount Ruapehu, the Bayview Chateau was built in 1929 for skiers. The refurbished hotel retains an elegant atmosphere and there are spectacular views. The most appealing rooms look directly onto Ngauruhoe's volcanic cone, and there are also family units and a top-floor suite.

The hotel has seasonal packages for walkers and skiers, a golf course, gym and sauna, billiards table and tennis courts. There's a choice of dining, from à la carte in the elegant restaurant to casual in the café.

🚑 209 D3 ⬚ SH48, Mount Ruapehu, Tongariro National Park 📞 (07) 892 3809, 0800 242 832 toll free; www.chateau.co.nz

Ruapehu Golf and Country Lodge $–$$$

This welcoming lodge overlooks the third tee of the Waimarino Golf Course just outside Ohakune, with views of both the greens or mountains. Vivienne Pitman has decorated the four bedrooms in French country style, and welcomes guests with pre-dinner drinks in the comfortable lounge. Her husband, a PGA professional, advises on golf – there are five courses within an hour's drive, plus a golf school. Non-golfers, meanwhile, can enjoy hiking, canoeing or skiing.

⊞ 209 D3 ⊠ Ohakune-Raetihi Road, Ohakune ☎ (06) 385 9594; www.ruapehucountrylodge.co.nz

HAWKE'S BAY

Cobden Garden Homestay $–$$

This boutique bed-and-breakfast homestay has three king-size rooms, each with ensuite, in an 1880s Victorian villa. Run by fourth-generation New Zealanders, Phillip and Rayma Jenkins, you'll get to sample locally grown food and wine, and enjoy the free pre-dinner drinks and canapés before heading down the hill into Napier for dinner.

⊞ 209 E31 ⊠ Cobden Crescent, Bluff Hill, Napier ☎ (06) 834 2090, 0800 426 233 toll free; www.cobden.co.nz

Hawthorne House $$

This elegant Edwardian villa has four luxurious rooms with private bathrooms. Located at the end of an avenue of 100-year-old plane trees in a beautiful garden setting, Hawthorne is a blend of calming period features and modern comforts. It has the benefit of being a short drive from both Hastings and Havelock North, and just a 20-minute drive from the city of Napier.

Upon arrival, a homemade afternoon tea is on offer. When the sun starts to set, join the owners for a pre-dinner glass of wine with accompanying canapés. In the morning, you can choose to take breakfast in the breakfast room, on your private verandah, or even on the old train platform overlooking the duck pond. The menu features local organic produce and free-range eggs from their own hens.

⊞ 209 E3 ⊠ 1420 Railway Road South, Hastings ☎ (06) 878 0035; www.hawthorne.co.nz

Where to...
Eat and Drink

Prices
Expect to pay per person for a three-course meal, excluding drinks:
$ under NZ$45 $$ NZ$45–$60 $$$ over NZ$60

ROTORUA

Bistro 1284 $$$

The atmosphere is welcoming and the decor is simple but elegant, with dining on two levels. The menu offers modern New Zealand dishes. Try the ostrich carpaccio and goats' cheese followed by the boneless lamb shank wrapped in prosciutto. Home-churned ice cream is a speciality. There's a largely New Zealand wine list, but you can also bring your own.

⊞ 209 D4 ⊠ 1284 Eruera Street, Rotorua ☎ (07) 346 1284; www.bistro1284.co.nz
⊕ Daily 6pm–late

The Landing Café $–$$

An idyllic location overlooking Lake Tarawera makes this simple cafe worth a trip. Have a drink in the Garden Bar, or eat on the veranda (but mind the sandflies). Breakfasts include pancakes and Eggs Benedict, while lunches range from seafood chowder to tasty open sandwiches. Dinner is more sophisticated – try the spiced lamb rump or pan-fried fish of the day.

⊞ 209 E4 ⊠ The Landing, Lake Tarawera ☎ (07) 362 8595; www.thelandinglaketarawera.co.nz
⊕ May–Nov Wed, Sun 9:30–5:30, Thu–Sat 9:30am–late

Lime Cafeteria $

Located at the lake end of Fenton Street, you can sit outside in the sun with a peep of the lake or cosy up indoors and people watch through the large windows. This is a popular place with a huge selection of magazines, delicious breakfast and lunch menu, and wine by the glass. Try the signature creamy vanilla risotto topped with berries for brunch or in winter their excellent Boston beans.

✛ 209 D4 ⊠ Corner of Fenton and Whakaue streets, Rotorua ☎ (07) 350 2033 ◷ Daily 7:30am – 4:30pm

The Pig and Whistle City Bar $

Housed in an imposing 1940s building that used to be the police station, this bar has a lot of fun exploiting the joke. Micro-brewed beers have names like Swine Lager. The bar menu ranges from burgers to fish and chips to seafood chowder and beef and chorizo hotpot, and live bands play Thursday, Friday and Saturday nights.

✛ 209 D4 ⊠ Corner of Haupapa and Tutanekai streets, Rotorua ☎ (07) 347 3025; www.pigandwhistle.co.nz ◷ Daily 11:30–10 ⓟ Note that children are not welcome after 5:30pm on Fridays and 7:30pm on Saturdays

TAUPO

Replete Café $

A combined cafe, kitchenware shop and catering service, Replete is a local institution. The cafe serves breakfast, brunch and lunch, with good coffee. Dishes range from toasted muesli with fruit compote and yogurt to Thai beef salad. It's a casual place where you can browse through the magazines or pick up that vital kitchen gadget.

✛ 209 D4 ⊠ 45 Heu Heu Street, Taupo ☎ (07) 378 0606; www.replete.co.nz ◷ Mon–Fri 8–5, Sat–Sun 8:30–4

HAWKE'S BAY

Chambers $$$

This elegantly furnished dining room is in Napier's County Hotel, itself housed in the beautifully restored 1909 Edwardian-style Hawke's Bay County Council building, one of only two significant structures to have survived the 1931 earthquake. Despite the restaurant's formal decor, its menu consists of modern Pacific dishes, including such popular choices as crab ravioli in a coconut, lime and chilli sauce, lamb shanks, and espresso brûlée. Chambers also offers a wide selection of excellent Hawke's Bay wines.

✛ 209 E3 ⊠ County Hotel, 12 Browning Street, Napier ☎ (06) 835 7800; www.countyhotel.co.nz ◷ Daily 7:30am–10am, 6pm–late

Clearview Estate Winery $-$$

This vineyard, on the coast east of Hastings at Te Awanga, has been winning awards for its wines for nearly 20 years. Its restaurant uses fresh herbs, olives, citrus fruits and avocados from the estate's gardens, along with other local produce, to create delicious brunch and lunch dishes. Try the tasting plate, with gravlax, cheeses and cured meats. You can sit at long tables under the vines, in the shaded courtyard or by the seaside children's playground.

✛ 209 E3 ⊠ 194 Clifton Road, Te Awanga, RD2, Hastings ☎ (06) 875 0150: www. clearviewestate.co.nz ◷ Labour weekend– Easter daily 10–5; rest of year Thu–Mon 10–5

Shed 2 $-$$$

Shed 2 is a cleverly converted 19th-century wool store on the Ahuriri quayside. Head for the cafe and bar, with its harbourside tables during the day, or retreat to the restaurant at night, where the atmosphere is less casual and the food more sophisticated. The cafe menu ranges from wood-fired pizza to Asian and Middle Eastern-inspired dishes, as well as seasonal offerings. Hawke's Bay produce features strongly on the wine list. Booking is necessary for the restaurant.

✛ 209 E3 ⊠ West Quay, Ahuriri, Napier ☎ (06) 835 2202 ◷ Cafe and bar: daily 11:30–late; restaurant: daily 6pm–late

Where to...
Shop

In Rotorua, speciality shops are clustered around Tutanekai Street. The **Outdoorsman Headquarters** (6 Tarawera Road, tel: (07) 345 9333) has outdoor clothes and equipment, while **Finns** (1281 Tutanekai Street, tel: (07) 348 7682), sells womenswear. For menswear, try **Pollards** (1191 Tutanekai Street, tel: (07) 347 7139).

The government-owned **New Zealand Maori Arts and Crafts Institute** at Whakarewarewa (tel: (07) 348 9047) preserves the arts of wood carving (*whakairo*) and weaving (*raranga*). At the **Tribal Marketplace** in Tamaki Maori Village (tel: (07) 349 2999), artists make and sell wood-, bone- and greenstone-carvings, flax-weavings, foods, Maori medicines and tribal clothing. The **Buried Village**

(tel: (07) 362 8287) has Maori crafts not available elsewhere.

Downtown, at the **Jade Factory** (1280 Fenton Street, tel: (07) 349 3968), carvers produce jewellery, sculptures and bowls. The gift shop at **Rotorua Museum** (tel: (07) 349 4350) is also a good place to find crafts, cards, posters, and books on local history. The **Redwoods Gift Shop and Visitor Centre** (Long Mile Road, tel: (07) 350 0110), in Whakarewarewa Forest, sells giftware including items made by local woodturners.

In Taupo, crafts can be found along the **Lake Taupo Arts and Crafts Trail** – leaflets from the visitor centre. The town also has a major independent wine merchant, **Scenic Cellars** (32 Roberts Street, tel: (07) 378 5704).

Where to...
Be Entertained

ROTORUA AND TAUPO

ThermalAir, the weekly visitors' guide published in Rotorua on Fridays, lists concerts, exhibitions, and sporting fixtures.

Arts and Culture

Maori concert parties perform daily in Rotorua at the **Te Puia** complex (▶ 82), **Tamaki Maori Village** (▶ 86, 91), local *marae* and in many hotels. To hear bands, check out **the Pig and Whistle** (corner of Haupapa and Tutanekai streets, tel: (07) 347 3025) on Friday and Saturday nights. Rotorua also hosts several musical events, including **Opera in the Pa** in January at Rotowhio Marae. There are regular exhibitions at the Rotorua Museum of Art and History (▶ 90).

Adventure and Water Sports

You can swim in all the lakes in the Rotorua region except the Green Lake, which is sacred to Maori.

Whether you want to go jet boating, kayaking, white-water rafting, parasailing or water skiing, operators abound. From sky diving to aerial acrobatics, bungy jumping and luging to off-road driving, the region can satisfy most thrill seekers. Zorbing is a local invention – you roll downhill in an inflated ball, either harnessed inside the Dry Zorb or loose in the Wet Zorb. Mountain biking is popular in Whakarewarewa Forest, and horse treks can be taken over farmland or forest trails. **Paradise Valley Ventures** (tel: (07) 348 3300) and **Peka Horse Trekking** (tel: (07) 346 1755) are reputable centres.

Fishing

Hamill's (1271 Fenton Street, tel: (07) 348 3147) stocks brochures and guidebooks to trout fishing in the area, and also sells licences and tackle. **Tourism Rotorua** (1167 Fenton Street, tel: (07) 348 5179), has details of guides who can supply boats, rods and tackle.

Lake Cruises

Clearwater Cruises (tel: (07) 345 6688) offers three-hour luxury cruises, fishing trips and self-drive, charters on Lake Tarawera. On Lake Rotorua the paddleboat *Lakeland Queen* (tel: (07) 348 0265, 0800 572 784 toll free) offers breakfast, lunch and dinner cruises. *The Ernest Kemp* (tel: (07) 378 3444) is a replica steamboat giving trips on Lake Taupo, including an evening barbecue cruise in summer.

Walking

Well-maintained walking tracks explore native forest in the Rotorua lakes region and the volcanic terrain of Tongariro National Park. In addition to the 18.5km (11.5-mile) **Tongariro Crossing** (▶ 89) shorter walks like the two-hour **Taranaki Falls Track** or **Silica Rapids Track** from Whakapapa Village also take in spectacular sights. For maps contact the DOC **Whakapapa Visitor Centre** (tel: (07) 892 3729) or **Tourism Rotorua** (1167 Fenton Street, Rotorua, tel: (07) 348 5179).

Skiing

Two of New Zealand's largest ski areas are on the slopes of Mount Ruapehu: **Whakapapa** (tel: (07) 892 3738) and **Turoa** (tel: (06) 385 8456). Equipment can be hired.

Golf

There are eight golf courses within 30 minutes' drive of Taupo, and four around Rotorua. **The Rotorua Golf Club** (399 Fenton Street, tel: (07) 348 4051) promises unusual hazards – sulphur pits, boiling mud pools and steaming lakes.

Country Life

The show at the **Agrodome** (Western Road, Ngongotaha, tel: (07) 357 1050), near Rotorua, involves 19 breeds of sheep, shearing and dog handling. Try your hand at milking a cow and feeding lambs, or take a tour of a working farm and orchard. The complex also includes a souvenir shop, cafe and adventure park. At **Rainbow Springs** (Fairy Springs Road, Rotorua, tel: (07) 350 0440) you can feed four species of trout, see kiwis in the kiwi house and take walks through native bush. In Taupo, you can do a tour of the geothermal **Huka Prawn Park** (Huka Falls Road, Wairakei Park, tel: (07) 374 8474), then eat the prawns at the restaurant afterwards.

Wine and Food Trails

New Zealand's oldest winery, **Mission Estate** (198 Church Road, Taradale, tel: (06) 845 9350) was established in Hawke's Bay by French missionaries in 1851. The region is now one of the country's leading producers, with nearly 40 wineries that are open to visitors. **Church Road Winery** (150 Church Road, Taradale, tel: (06) 844 2053), for example, runs daily tours and has a winemaker's museum, restaurant and gift shop. Get a wine trail leaflet from the **Napier Visitor Centre** (100 Marine Parade, Napier, tel: (06) 834 1911), or enquire about wine tours there. The annual wine festival, **Harvest Hawke's Bay**, is held in February.

You can also follow the food trail, produced by Food Hawke's Bay (tel: (06) 974 8931), which includes farms, wineries, orchards, artisans, markets, cafes and restaurants. **Sileni Estates Epicurean Centre and Cellar** (2016 Maraekakaho Road, RD1, Hastings, tel: (06) 879 8768) runs on-site winery tours, wine courses, a culinary school, a restaurant, a tapas bar and a food store.

Wellington
and Around

Getting Your Bearings

By international standards Wellington is a small capital city, but its embassies and visitors endow it with a cosmopolitan atmosphere. A vibrant cultural scene is heightened by its attractive coastal location, buzzing cafes and good restaurants.

Defined by a magnificent harbour and hemmed in by steep forested hills, Wellington's downtown stretches across a narrow lip of flat land. Tall wooden houses cling to the hillsides, beyond the green belt of parks and reserves around the central core. The inner city is linked to the suburbs by steps, walkways and New Zealand's only public "cable car" (actually a funicular railway).

Wellington is only about a third of the size of Auckland, but in attitude, atmosphere and scenic appeal the two cities are equals. Their friendly rivalry for the title of New Zealand's best place to live keeps city planners on their toes. Redevelopment of Wellington's centre and waterfront has spruced up arts and performance venues and confirmed the city's reputation as New Zealand's cultural capital. This is epitomized by the national museum, Te Papa, whose mix of traditional and interactive exhibits draws more than a million visitors each year.

Page 99: Wellington city and harbour

The capital's main function is the business of government, and the beautifully restored Parliament complex makes for a fascinating visit. Away from urban development, the North Island's southernmost city is just a hop from the vineyards of Martinborough and the bird life of Kapiti Island.

Opposite: A detailed wood carving from the Te Papa museum

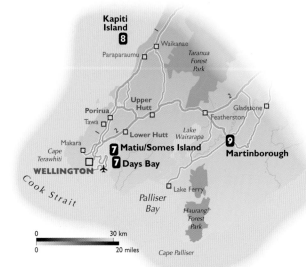

Kapiti Island **8**

Waikanae
Paraparaumu
Taranua Forest Park

Upper Hutt
Porirua
Tawa
Lower Hutt
Lake Wairarapa
Gladstone
Featherston

Makara
7 Matiu/Somes Island
Cape Terawhiti
WELLINGTON
7 Days Bay

9 Martinborough

Cook Strait

Lake Ferry
Palliser Bay
Haurangi Forest Park

0   30 km
0   20 miles   Cape Palliser

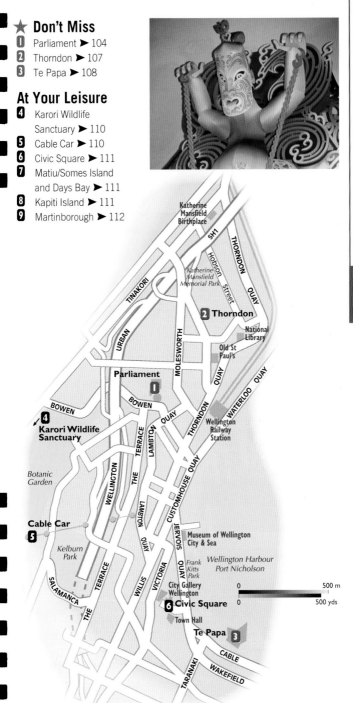

★ Don't Miss

At Your Leisure

Katherine
Mansfield
Birthplace

SH1

THORNDON

TINAKORI

URBAN

Hobson Street

Katherine
Mansfield
Memorial Park

THORNDON QUAY

2 **Thorndon**

National
Library

MOLESWORTH

Old St
Paul's

QUAY

WATERLOO QUAY

Parliament
1

BOWEN

BOWEN

THORNDON QUAY

THE TERRACE

LAMBTON QUAY

4 **Karori Wildlife
Sanctuary**

Wellington
Railway
Station

WELLINGTON

*Botanic
Garden*

LAMBTON

CUSTOMHOUSE QUAY

Cable Car
5

QUAY

JERVOIS

*Kelburn
Park*

THE TERRACE

WILLIS

VICTORIA

QUAY

Museum of Wellington
City & Sea

*Frank
Kitts
Park*

*Wellington Harbour
Port Nicholson*

SALAMANCA

City Gallery
Wellington

6 **Civic Square**

0   500 m

0   500 yds

THE

Town Hall

Te Papa
3

TARANAKI

CABLE

WAKEFIELD

In Four Days

If you're not quite sure where to begin your travels, this itinerary recommends four practical and enjoyable days in and around Wellington, taking in some of the best places to see using the Getting Your Bearings map on the previous page. For more information see the main entries.

Day 1

Morning

Pick up bus timetables and an events calendar at the **visitor information centre** (➤ 106) to check for any performances and exhibitions you may wish to see during your visit. Wellington is the site of New Zealand's government, so the best way to start your visit is to explore the refurbished **❶ Parliament complex** (above, ➤ 104–106), including the Beehive and Parliament House, and watch the politicians debate. From Parliament, head north to wander through the historic suburb of **❷ Thorndon** (➤ 107) and have lunch at one of the cafes there.

Afternoon

Stroll along **Tinakori Road** (➤ 107), one of the capital's oldest thoroughfares, and explore some of the charming galleries, boutiques and second-hand shops. At the northern end of the road, you'll find the **Katherine Mansfield Birthplace** (➤ 107) and its gardens.

Evening

Have dinner in town (➤ 115–116), then catch a performance at one of Wellington's many venues (➤ 118); choose from theatre, dance, opera, or classical, pop or jazz music.

Day 2

Morning

Spend the morning at **3 Te Papa national museum** (➤ 108–109), then walk to **8 Civic Square** (➤ 111, the sculpture pictured right is suspended above the square). If you are travelling with children, explore the shows and activities at Capital E. You can also check out the art exhibitions at the City Gallery Wellington.

Have lunch at the gallery's cafe or one of the many restaurants in the inner city.

Afternoon

Head back to the waterfront and stroll past the boat sheds here to the **7 Matiu/Somes Island** (➤ 111) ferry terminal. Catch the afternoon boat to the island for a walk around this scientific and historic reserve, or all the way to Days Bay, on the other side of Wellington's harbour, with one of the city's best swimming beaches. Return to have dinner in the city.

Day 3

Morning

Ride the **5 Cable Car** (➤ 110) from central Wellington up to the top terminal. Take in the views over the city, then have a look at the **Cable Car Museum**. At the nearby **Carter Observatory**, learn more about the southern hemisphere's night sky in a planetarium show. Walk downhill through the **Botanic Gardens** (left, ➤ 184–186) to have lunch in its Picnic Café.

Afternoon

Pick up a map of the Botanic Gardens and wander through them, exiting at Bolton Street (➤ 184) to walk back down to the city. Alternatively, leave via Glenmore Street and catch bus 21 to **4 Karori Wildlife Sanctuary** (➤ 110), where you can join a guided tour to see some of the endangered birds and animals that live there.

Day 4

If you want to see rare birds, get up early to take a day trip to **8 Kapiti Island** (➤ 111), one of the most accessible of New Zealand's many offshore wildlife sanctuaries. If your tastes are more for fine food and wine, visit charming **9 Martinborough** (➤ 112) in the Wairarapa wine-growing region, where you can indulge in some wine tasting and eat at one of the vineyards here.

❶ Parliament

It's the architecture of New Zealand's Parliament that grabs the attention. Of the three buildings in the complex at the northern end of Wellington's centre, the most distinctive is the modern Executive Wing – known as the Beehive. Beside it, the older, beautifully refurbished Parliament House and its library embody national heritage and pride.

The **Beehive** lives up to its name. Its dome rises from a broad base through layers of increasingly smaller circles of offices. A feature of Wellington since the 1970s, the building certainly stands out, some would say like a sore thumb, but others see it as a powerful example of modern architecture.

The rings of ministerial windows certainly suggest a hive of coordinated activity, but it is the imposing **Parliament House**, next to the Beehive, where politicians convene for debates. The current Parliament House was built in an Edwardian neoclassical style from granite and marble between 1911 and 1922. The original wooden General Assembly, which had been built when the city was declared the captial in 1865, was destroyed in a fire in 1907.

Loved and loathed, the Beehive stands alongside the neoclassical Parliament House

Protecting Parliament

If you want to see more than a live performance of politics, take a guided tour of the complex. Your first stop will be in the basement of Parliament House, where part of its foundations have been exposed to demonstrate its **earthquake protection**. Wellington straddles one of the South Pacific's most threatening fault lines, and masonry buildings with only minimal lateral movement, such as this one, can be at risk from collapse. So when the complex underwent a major facelift during a three-year refurbishment project in 1992, making the building earthquake-proof was a priority. The

POLITICAL DRAMA

Parliament House debates are open: you can watch them from the public gallery above the debating chamber. Sessions start with formal opening ceremonies, including the placing of a golden mace on the central table and the recital of a prayer by the Speaker of the House; then they often turn into heated arguments. Members of the governing and opposition parties sit about four musket-lengths apart, and like politicians elsewhere, frequently fire salvoes of insults at each other.

The debating chamber inside Parliament House

entire building now sits on 417 round rubber bearings, isolators that allow the building to sway and roll should the earth move below. The same technology – invented by a Wellington engineer – protects the national museum Te Papa (➤ 108–109).

Tour Highlights

A highlight of the tour is the ornately decorated **Maori Affairs Select Committee Room**, where Members of Parliament meet to discuss proposed law changes relating to Maori issues and race relations. The walls are covered with woven panels and intricate carvings recalling Maori legends.

A stunning suspended three-dimensional **multimedia installation** graces the **Galleria**, a glass-covered open space, formerly an open courtyard in the original Parliament House, which was roofed over during the refurbishment. To match the Edwardian style of the original, later extensions to the building had to be faced in the same materials: some of the quarries that had supplied the marble 80 years earlier were reopened especially.

One of the most beautiful areas within the Parliament complex is the Victorian Gothic **Parliamentary Library**. Thanks to the knowledge and skill of 19th-century architects, who included in their designs an early version of fire-resistant doors, the library's collection survived two fires, including the 1907 disaster. For the most part, the library's resources are available only to students and political researchers but it's worth having a look at its halls and corridors, which are exquisitely decorated with plaster mouldings and stained-glass windows and doors.

The **National Library,** just around the corner, is available to the public. By law, a copy of everything published in New Zealand is sent here, and it also contains numerous periodicals and documents, some dating back to the 18th century.

TAKING A BREAK

Word of Mouth cafe (100 Molesworth Street, tel: (04) 472 7202) is a hidden gem near Parliament for light meals. The **Single File Café** in the foyer of Archives New Zealand (10 Mulgrave Street, tel: (04) 495 6216) has a good selection of coffees, and its high ceilings make a welcome change from cramped downtown bars. While at the Archives take a look at the original Treaty of Waitangi (➤ 10) which is on display.

Beautiful architectural detailing can be found throughout the Parliament complex

➕ 205 B4

Visitor Information Centre
➕ 205 B2 ✉ Corner of Victoria and Wakefield streets, Civic Square ☎ (04) 802 4860; www.wellingtonnz.com ◉ Wed–Sun 8:30–5, Tue 9–5

Parliament Visitor Centre
➕ 205 B4 ✉ Ground-floor foyer of Parliament House, left and below the main stairs leading up to the entrance ☎ (04) 817 9503; www.parliament.govt.nz ◉ Mon–Fri 10–4, Sat 10–3, Sun 11–3, school holidays and Christmas period has extra tours; closed 1 and 2 Jan, 6 Feb, Good Friday, 25 and 26 Dec. Tours leave on the hour and take about an hour. Last tour Mon–Fri 4pm, Sat–Sun, public holidays 3pm 💲 Free

National Library
➕ 205 B4 ✉ 77 Thorndon Quay, Pipitea ☎ (04) 474 3000; www.natlib.govt.nz ◉ Mon–Fri 9–5, Sat 9–1 💲 Free

PARLIAMENT: INSIDE INFO

Top tip Parliament usually sits on **Tuesdays**, **Wednesdays** and **Thursdays** when in session. The most heated and entertaining debates occur during question time (2pm–3pm). Check schedules with the visitor centre at Parliament.

Hidden gem The **grounds** surrounding the Parliament complex are beautifully maintained and include several tranquil corners.

In more depth Opposite the Beehive you'll find the **Old Government Building**, the second-largest wooden building in the world. You'll have to look twice to convince yourself that the building is not made of stone.

② Thorndon

Thorndon is one of Wellington's oldest suburbs, first settled by Europeans in the 1840s and subsequently home to an arty set that included the likes of writer Katherine Mansfield and painter Rita Angus. Today, the area's lovely wooden villas – many of which retain their original features – are home to boutiques, galleries, lively cafes and attractive B&Bs.

The historic district of **Thorndon** extends from the Parliament complex to Hobson Street and Tinakori Road, and can be explored on a three-hour self-guided walk – pick up a brochure from the information centre (➤ 106). A highlight is **Old St Paul's** at 34 Mulgrave Street, a lovely church secluded in a small park, with a beautiful Gothic Revival interior in native timber: rimu, matai, totara and kauri. It was built in 1866 as a temporary cathedral, but maintained this role for a century until the Anglican Cathedral was erected.

At the far end of Tinakori Road is the **Katherine Mansfield Birthplace**, the childhood home of the country's most distinguished author (1888–1923), known internationally for her short stories and letters. The house (built in 1888) and the surrounding suburbs feature in many of Mansfield's stories, and extracts from her work are displayed alongside photographs in the restored house. There's a **video portrait** of the writer and a **doll's house** has been built using details in her short story of the same name. Her famous **garden** has also been restored to its late 19th-century appearance with the help of photographs.

Katherine Mansfield's childhood home

UPLIFTING EXPERIENCE
The earthquake that hit Wellington on 23 January 1855 measured 8.2 on the Richter scale and was the biggest ever recorded in New Zealand. It raised the beach at Thorndon by up to 1.5m (5 feet) and caused a tsunami in the Cook Strait.

TAKING A BREAK
For lunch or a coffee, try one of the cafes along Tinakori Road, such as **Aubergine** (No. 322, tel: (04) 471 2500).

➕ 205 B5

Old St Paul's
➕ 205 C4 ✉ 34 Mulgrave Street ☎ (04) 473 6722; www.oldstpauls.co.nz 🕐 Daily 9:30–5 or by special arrangement; access subject to functions 🎟 Free

Katherine Mansfield Birthplace
➕ 205 off B5 ✉ 25 Tinakori Road ☎ (04) 473 7268; www.katherinemansfield.com 🕐 Tue–Sun 10–4 🚌 14 to Wilton stops at nearby Park Street 🎟 Inexpensive

③ Te Papa

Te Papa's full name is Museum of New Zealand – Te Papa Tongarewa; the Maori words mean "a treasure trove" in free translation. Bold, sometimes provocative and often imaginative, it houses national treasures of all kinds that chart the special character of New Zealand and its people.

The museum is New Zealand's most ambitious cultural project, built at a cost of NZ\$317 million to tell the stories of the country's environment, arts, history and culture. Its intriguing mix of conventional museum exhibits with interactive virtual experiences can be overwhelming at first, but it's a hit with millions of visitors (see panel opposite). You will need at least two hours to see the main galleries, but you could easily spend a whole day here.

The building itself covers the space of three rugby fields and contains enough steel to stretch from Wellington to Sydney. Set on the waterfront, it's a prominent and enticing landmark: two wings stretch from the glass facade of its entrance lobby as if welcoming visitors with an embrace.

Exploring the Museum

Start on **Level 4** with the undoubted highlight of the museum – a modern *marae* (Maori meeting place). The Maori master carver Dr Cliff Whiting has created a magnificent *whare nui* (meeting house), whose symbols encompass New Zealand's ethnic groups, conveying a sense of peace and unity between cultures. The inside walls are decorated with colourful carvings symbolizing historic events that set New Zealand apart. From the floor design to the wall decorations and a painted glass door, every element in this hall tells a story.

Top: The impressive entrance to Te Papa

Above: Dr Cliff Whiting created the modern *marae*

A NATIONAL WINNER

When Te Papa opened in February 1998, it received a fair amount of criticism for its interactive displays and focus on learning through fun rather than scholarly discourse, but its success in attracting first-time museum visitors has since silenced many of the critics. It drew 3.5 million visitors in its first two years, and Wellington residents are said to make three to four visits each year.

The popular **Golden Days** object theatre is also on Level 4. Instead of displaying photographs and artefacts, the gallery is set up as a walk-in theatre. The stage is a junk shop full of Kiwiana (everyday things that describe national identity). The audience, seated in old armchairs and garden seats, watches a film portraying nationally significant moments as well as ordinary events: New Zealanders at work and play, but also images of larger events such as Kiwi soldiers returning home from war. As the film screens a particular event, items in the junk shop move or make noises. Though it's most evocative for native New Zealanders, this is an opportunity for visitors from overseas to grasp something of the national pysche.

Move downwards through **temporary exhibitions** to more interactive exhibits on Level 2. The best, **Awesome Forces** and **Mountains to Sea**, cover natural history. The latter includes a realistic "tree" large enough for children to climb to see birds and animals.

TAKING A BREAK

The **Te Papa Café** on Level 1 and the **Espresso** coffee shop on Level 4 are good places to stop and recharge your batteries before taking in the next exhibit.

Every element of the marae *– including its ceiling – tells a story*

🕂 205 C2 ✉ Cable Street ☎ (04) 381 7000; www.tepapa.govt.nz
🕙 Fri–Wed 10–6, Thu 10–9 💵 Free; Time Warp and short-term exhibitions: inexpensive

---

TE PAPA: INSIDE INFO

Top tips If you are overwhelmed or lost, ask the museum's hosts (in uniforms with Te Papa's fingerprint logo) for directions, or pick up the **Te Papa Explorer brochure** at the information desk on Level 2. It suggests tracks grouping permanent exhibitions in themes such as nature, arts, Maori or "Te Papa for kids".

■ If you are short of time, join one of the hour-long guided tours of the main galleries (Nov–Mar daily 10:15, 11, 12, 1, 2, 3 (also 7pm Thu) Apr–Oct 10:15, 2 (also 7pm Thu); moderate).

■ Children in particular will enjoy **Our Space** (free), a multimedia experience opened in 2008. This includes a huge interactive video wall, an interactive floor map of New Zealand, and two virtual rides (both inexpensive) – **Deep Ride**, into the ocean depths; and **High Ride**.

Hidden gem On Level 4 you'll find a **touchstone**, an enormous boulder of greenstone that has been polished on one side by the sheer number of hands touching it over time.

At Your Leisure

The endemic kiwi is just one of the endangered species that has been helped by reserves such as Karori and Kapiti

🕐 Daily 10–5 (last entry 4pm) 🚌 3, 17, 18, 21, 22, 23 ✋ Inexpensive; tours: moderate–expensive

5 Cable Car

The bright red Cable Car is a Wellington icon and the fastest way of getting from downtown to the Botanic Garden (➤ 184–186), Victoria University or the suburb of Kelburn. The Cable Car opened in 1902, linking the new hill-hugging suburbs to the city centre, and was immediately popular.

In the 1970s the track was reconstructed and new Swiss-made cars introduced. Near the top terminal you'll find the Cable Car Museum and the Carter Observatory, which offers planetarium shows, telescope viewing and astronomy displays, though the view down over the city is also worth the ride.

✚ 205 A3 ☎ (04) 472 2199; www.wellingtoncablecar.co.nz 🕐 Every 10 minutes, Mon–Fri 7am–10pm, Sat 8:30am–10pm, Sun and public holidays 9am–9pm ✋ Inexpensive

Cable Car Museum
✚ 205 A3 ✉ Upland Road, Kelburn ☎ (04) 475 3578; www.cablecarmuseum.co.nz 🕐 Nov–Apr daily 9:30–5:30; May–Oct 10–5 ✋ Free

Carter Observatory
✚ 205 A3 ✉ 40 Salamanca Road, Kelburn ☎ (04) 472 8167; www.carterobservatory.org 🕐 Nov–Feb Sun–Tue 10–5, Wed–Sat 10–late; Mar–Oct Mon–Thu 11–4, Fri–Sat 11–late ✋ Inexpensive–moderate

4 Karori Wildlife Sanctuary

Just 2km (1 mile) from downtown Wellington is one of New Zealand's most ambitious private conservation projects, established in 1995 when a group of Wellingtonians decided to reclaim a pocket of bush near the inner city and return it to its original state. First, the 225ha (556-acre) valley around the former Karori water reservoir was surrounded by a fence, specially designed to keep out predators. Then all pests inside the sanctuary were eradicated and, finally, endangered wildlife reintroduced. It's been a great success: the kiwi population produced chicks during the first season and other native birds are flocking here. A variety of guided walks, including a nocturnal tour (book in advance), allows visitors to appreciate the evolution of the sanctuary.

✚ 205 off A4 ✉ 31 Waiapu Road, Karori ☎ (04) 920 9200; www.sanctuary.org.nz

Wellington's Civic Square is a cultural and social centre

6 Civic Square

Some of the capital's premier cultural centres surround the square: as you face the visitor information centre, to your left are the Michael Fowler Centre and the Edwardian Town Hall, both magnificent settings for concerts. Opposite these is the Wellington public library and behind you is the City Gallery. Walk up to the gallery to Sea Bridge, which connects the square with the waterfront across Jervois Quay, and look back to see the visitor information centre and Wellington City Council building. Below the bridge is the entrance to Capital E, a children's activity centre with a theatre, television and sound studios, and a playground. At the lagoon end of the bridge you can hire paddle boats; walk south along the waterfront towards Te Papa (► 108–109) for inline skates or north to Queens Wharf for kayaks.
🚼 205 B2

City Gallery Wellington
🚼 205 B3 ☎ (04) 801 3021;
www.citygallery.org.nz 🕐 Daily 10–5
🎟 Donation; charges for exhibitions

Capital E
🚼 205 B2 ☎ (04) 913 3740;
www.capitale.org.nz 🕐 Mon–Fri 9–5,
Sat–Sun 10–4; phone for events schedule
🎟 Inexpensive; charges for exhibitions

7 Matiu/Somes Island and Days Bay

Matiu/Somes Island is a former quarantine station now administered by the Department of Conservation, which has turned it into a wildlife sanctuary. Lying in Wellington Harbour 8km (5 miles) from the city centre, it is one of the most accessible of New Zealand's predator-free islands and one of the few places where people can see tuatara in the wild. (Tuatara are the last representatives of reptiles that appeared 200 million years ago.) Matiu/Somes Island has a network of footpaths and there are great views from the summit.

Departing from Queens Wharf, ferries continue on their 20-minute journey to Days Bay, on the eastern side of the harbour, or to Petone at its northern tip.
🚼 208 C2 ✉ Ferries from Queens Wharf, waterfront off Jervois Quay ☎ (04) 499 1282; www.eastbywest.co.nz 🕐 Up to 16 sailings daily to Days Bay; at least three daily trips to Matiu/Somes Island 🎟 Moderate

8 Kapiti Island

Kapiti Island is another pest-free wildlife reserve near the capital, 5km (3 miles) offshore. The 1,965ha (4,854-acre) island dominates the coast off Paraparaumu, about 50km (30 miles) north of Wellington. It is a sanctuary for kiwi, kaka, takahe

The Voss Estate is just one of the vineyards near Martinborough

and saddlebacks, and offshore the waters are a feeding ground for birds and a nursery for fish. Kapiti Island is open to the public, but visitors are limited to 68 per day. You'll need to get a permit from the DOC's Wellington office, and book the boat trip separately from the Kapiti Coast. There are a number of walking tracks, some leading to the summit of Tuteremoana (521m/1,709 feet), but there are no shops or cafes so bring provisions with you.

✚ 208 C2

Department of Conservation
✚ 205 B2 ✉ 18 Manners Street, Wellington
☎ (04) 384 7770; www.doc.govt.nz
🕐 Mon–Fri 9–5, Sat 10–3:30
✋ Permits: moderate

Kapiti Marine Charter
✚ 208 C2 ✉ Paraparaumu ☎ (04) 297
2585; www.kapitimarinecharter.co.nz
🕐 Departs Paraparaumu daily 9 or 9:30am,
returning 3–4pm ✋ Expensive

9 Martinborough
Martinborough is an ideal stopover for a vineyard visit. A popular weekend destination for Wellingtonians, it is an hour's drive from the city, at the end of SH53. The main draw is the town's status as the centre of the Wairarapa

vine-growing region, and most wineries give tours. November sees the Toast Martinborough Festival.

✚ 209 D2

Visitor Information Centre
✉ 18 Kitchener Street, Martinborough
☎ (06) 306 5010;
www.wairarapanz.com 🕐 Mon–Fri 9–5,
Sat–Sun and holidays 10–4

BEST FOR KIDS
- Discovery centres and StoryPlace at Te Papa (▶ 108–109).
- Capital E on Civic Square (▶ 111).
- Play area or rollerblading on the waterfront.
- Seeing stars at the Planetarium in the Carter Observatory (▶ 110).

WALKING IN WELLINGTON
Wellington is hilly but compact and best explored on foot. Heritage trails take in suburbs such as Thorndon (▶ 107), historic streets and the waterfront, or you can try longer walks like the four-hour City to Sea route (▶ 184–186). Pick up a leaflet from the information centre.

Where to...
Stay

Prices

Expect to pay for two people sharing a double room per night:

$ under NZ$200 **$$** NZ$200–350 **$$$** over NZ$350

Booklovers B&B $–$$

Host Jane Tolerton is a published writer who enjoys sharing her love of books with her guests. Every room in this bed and breakfast has shelves of books you can read or take away with you, including works by local author Katherine Mansfield (▶ 107). There are three guest rooms, each with a queen-size bed, ensuite bathroom, television and CD player – and, of course, plenty of reading material. From here you can catch a bus or stroll down into the city – it is only a 15-minute walk from Te Papa – or explore the walking tracks on Mount Victoria.

➕ 205 C1 ☒ 123 Pirie Street, Mount Victoria ☎ (04) 384 2714; www.booklovers.co.nz

Duxton Hotel Wellington $$–$$$

Just across the road from Te Papa (▶ 108–109) is this large luxury hotel, whose rooms all have views of Wellington's famous harbour. The rooms range from singles to doubles, twins and suites, all comfortable and stylishly decorated, and with the usual facilities expected of a modern hotel. Downstairs is a restaurant and bar (although there are plenty of other excellent options near by if you fancy dining out), and there is also a gym. Check out the website for excellent-value internet deals.

➕ 205 C4 ☒ 170 Wakefield Street ☎ (04) 473 3900; www.duxtonhotels.co.nz

Holiday Inn $$

This newly built 16-floor hotel is the new-look Holiday Inn being rolled out across the world. Located at the Westpac Stadium/Parliament end of the city, it's a great spot for attending games. The luxurious leisure centre includes a 17m (50-foot) lap pool, spa pool and sauna. The lobby bar and restaurant, Plate, offers buffet breakfast and à la carte lunch and dinner. Rooms each have small kitchenettes and large bathrooms with modern decor and unique artwork throughout the hotel.

➕ 205 B4 ☒ 75 Featherston Street ☎ (04) 499 8686; www.holidayinn.com

Hotel InterContinental Wellington $$–$$$

Centrally situated, this striking, bronze-coloured building is a city landmark. Formerly the ParkRoyal, it is close to the Lambton Quay shops, cafes, Parliament, the waterfront and the Westpac Stadium. You're welcomed by a top-hatted doorman and the lobby gleams with marble. The 231 rooms include luxury suites, executive club level and standard rooms. There is a restaurant, a bar and grill, and a health and fitness centre with a gym, spa, sauna and heated pool. It's worth checking for the less expensive weekend rates.

➕ 205 B3 ☒ 2 Grey Street ☎ (04) 472 2722; www.intercontinental.com/wellington

Museum Hotel $–$$$

The luxurious Museum Hotel actually started life on the site of Te Papa (▶ 108–109), but the massive building was moved in an amazing engineering feat to its current site before the museum was built in

1993. Aside from being extremely handy for Te Papa and Wellington waterfront's other attractions, the hotel has rooms, ranging from the standard option with queen-size bed, through to two-bedroom suites with harbour views. There are also seven suites specially designed to be wheelchair accessible. In addition, the hotel has a restaurant, bar and cafe, a heated lap pool and spa pool, and a gym, spa and sauna.

205 C2 ⊠ **90 Cable Street**
☎ **(04) 809 8900, 0800 994 335 toll free;**
www.museumhotel.co.nz

Ohtel $$

This small four-storey boutique hotel is located in the exclusive neighbourhood of Oriental Bay across the road from the sea and just a short walk from Te Papa. It was designed by architect and owner Alan Blundell, who wanted something very different, and a place to showcase his furniture collection. His designs are based on Danish Modern and 1960s retro.

The focal point in each individually furnished room is the oversized bathroom with two-person bathtubs and large glass panels with New Zealand scenes behind them.

208 C1 ⊠ **66 Oriental Parade** ☎ **(04) 803 0600; www.ohtel.com**

Shepherds Arms Hotel $

Built in the 1870s and located in the historic Thorndon district (▶ 107), the Shepherds Arms is a convenient, good-value option in the heart of the city. There are 14 guest rooms, ranging from singles with a shared bathroom, to queen rooms and the King Suite, which has a four-poster king-size bed. Each room has the usual facilities, including Sky TV and a complimentary newspaper delivered each morning. Downstairs, the Speight's Ale House restaurant ($) serves hearty pub lunches and dinners.

205 B5 ⊠ **285 Tinakori Road, Thorndon**
☎ **(04) 472 1320, 0800 393 782 toll free;**
www.shepherds.co.nz

The Terrace Villas $$–$$$

Accommodation at The Terrace Villas is in eight 19th-century villas on The Terrace, close to the Cable Car and the Lambton Quay shopping district. The villas are divided into elegant self-contained serviced apartments, ranging in size from studios to three large bedrooms. Furnished with a mix of modern and character fittings, all have cable TV and laundry and kitchen facilities. A light breakfast is provided.

205 B3 ⊠ **202 The Terrace** ☎ **(04) 920 2020; www.terracevillas.co.nz**

MARTINBOROUGH

The Old Manse $–$$

Sandra and John Hargrave have restored an old Presbyterian ministers' house that overlooks the local vineyards. There are six guest rooms, five with queen-size beds and one twin, each of which has an ensuite bathroom. The gardens around the house are also beautifully laid out, and contain a petanque court and croquet lawn. In addition, there is a billiards table, Sky TV and a spa pool.

209 D2 ⊠ **19 Grey Street, Martinborough**
☎ **(06) 306 8599, 0800 399 229 toll free;**
www.oldmanse.co.nz

Tirohana Estate $$

This Martinborough winery has several accommodation options for visitors. Tirohana House, styled on a traditional French farmhouse, lies within the vineyard's grounds and sleeps up to 12 in four suites. It has two bathrooms, a kitchen and all modern conveniences, and the vineyard has a restaurant and cafe. In Martinborough itself is the lovingly restored Duckback Cottage, sleeping up to eight. And last but not least is Greytown's 1905 Heritage Cottage, which sleeps up to eight and has its own fruit and vegetable garden.

209 D2 ⊠ **Puruatanga Road, Martinborough** ☎ **(06) 306 9933; www.tirohanaestate.com**

Where to...
Eat and Drink

Prices

Expect to pay per person for a three-course meal, excluding drinks:

$ under NZ$45 $$ NZ$45–$60 $$$ over NZ$60

WELLINGTON

Caffe L'affare $

Enzo Laffare is credited with introducing Wellingtonians to espresso. A roaster roars at this relaxed cafe in a side street off Cambridge Terrace, and L'affare coffee appears on many restaurant menus. The cafe is a popular meeting place, serving snacks and all-day breakfast. There's even a children's play area.

✚ 205 C1 ⊠ 27 College Street, Wellington
☎ (04) 385 9748; www.caffelaffare.co.nz
⏱ Mon–Fri 7–4:30, Sat, Sun 8–4; closed public holidays

Logan Brown $–$$$

Logan Brown has taken a grand 1920s Grecian banking chamber and turned it into a gracious restaurant in the French style, with booth seating and a wine bar. It's a frequent winner of Wellington's best restaurant award. Its menu, which changes weekly, has a contemporary with a seafood focus. Look for dishes like paua ravioli, and pan-roasted hapuku (fish) with tuatua (shellfish) fritters. The three-course bistro menu, available at lunchtime and pre-theatre, is excellent value. On some Fridays there's live jazz. Booking recommended.

cafe where the atmosphere is casual but the food top-notch. Bread baked freshly every day and butter churned on site are indicative of the chef's attention to detail. Dishes to try include an excellent butternut squash risotto for lunch, tasty crab ravioli for dinner, roast mushrooms on toast for brunch, or there is always a great-value roast on Sundays, which you can wash down with one of the 320-plus wines. It also attracts a trendy crowd for its live music on Thu–Sun nights.

✚ 205 B1 ⊠ 192 Cuba Street, Wellington
☎ (04) 801 5114; www.loganbrown.co.nz
⏱ Mon–Fri 12–2, daily 5:30pm–late

Martin Bosley's $$$

Chef Martin Bosley has deservedly earned a reputation as one of the best in New Zealand, and his eponymous restaurant at the Royal Port Nicholson Yacht Club proves this point. The restaurant focuses on seafood, producing eye-catching dishes using seasonal, local ingredients. For starters, select from the likes of a trio of fish tartars, then move on to the fish of the day, grilled, roasted or poached to perfection. If you can't choose a dessert, opt for the tasting plate so that you can sample several.

✚ 205 off C2 ⊠ 103 Oriental Parade, Wellington ☎ (04) 920 8302; www.martin-bosley.com ⏱ Lunch: Mon–Fri 12–2:30; dinner: Tue–Sun 6–late

Matterhorn $$

Matterhorn is a Wellington institution: a restaurant, bar and

✚ 205 B2 ⊠ 106 Cuba Street, Wellington
☎ (04) 384 3359; www.matterhorn.co.nz
⏱ Daily 10am–late

One Red Dog $

This lively restaurant in the centre of Wellington is just around the corner from buzzing Courtenay Place, hub of the city's nightlife district. Most people come here for the gourmet pizzas – the Shawshank has New Zealand flavours of lamb shank, caramelized onion and roasted pumpkin, or there's the basic Red Dog Margherita among the other choices. Also on offer are antipasto starters and pasta and salad mains. The atmosphere is very relaxed, and it's also a great place to come if you have kids. You can find another branch on the waterfront at North Queens Wharf (tel: (04) 918 4723).

🕀 **205 C2** ⊠ **9–11 Blair Street, Wellington**
☎ **(04) 384 9777; www.onereddog.co.nz**
🕑 **Daily 10am–late**

Shed 5 $$$

Built in 1888 as a wool store on the wharf, Shed 5 is now an elegant restaurant and bar. The menu focuses on seafood and changes daily. It's also a pleasant place to have a coffee or a glass of wine, especially if you sit outside on the water's edge. It can get crowded and noisy inside, especially at lunchtime and in the early evening. Reservations are recommended.

🕀 **205 C3** ⊠ **Queens Wharf, Wellington**
☎ **(04) 499 9069; www.shed5.co.nz**
🕑 **Mon–Fri 12–late, Sat–Sun 10am–late**

Wagamama $

The popular Wagamama franchise is now on Wellington's waterfront, with views out across the harbour. Fans will find all their favourite Japanese noodle dishes on the menu, including seafood ramen noodle soup, ginger chicken fried udon noodles, and teriyaki salmon. The food is cooked fresh to order, and is great value if you are looking for an inexpensive yet tasty meal during a day's sightseeing.

🕀 **205 B3** ⊠ **Meridien Building, 33 Customhouse Quay, Wellington** ☎ **(04) 473 7999; www.wagamama.co.nz** 🕑 **Daily 11:30am–late**

The White House Restaurant $$$

Offering wonderful harbour views, this hotel offers first-rate food and service – a standard that has been maintained for more than 15 years. Dishes are made with the best seasonal ingredients; choose off the à la carte menu or opt for a fixed-price set meal. Starters include ravioli stuffed with local crab, while for your main course there is grilled salmon with wasabi mash or seared loin of hare. Save room for the excellent cheese platter, or why not try the passion-fruit soufflé?

🕀 **205 off C2** ⊠ **232 Oriental Parade, Wellington** ☎ **(04) 385 8555; www.whr.co.nz** 🕑 **Lunch: Fri 12–2; dinner: daily 6–late**

MARTINBOROUGH

The French Bistro $$

This small restaurant in the heart of the Wairarapa wine region is run by a husband-and-wife team who are passionate about French provincial cooking and the region's wine. Like the bistro itself, the menu is small but is changed regularly depending on the availability of local produce. Chef Wendy Campbell is Cordon Bleu trained, and produces divine dishes such as Normandy-style pork with an apple and Calvados sauce, and fresh fish with an anchovy and caper sauce. Because of the restaurant's proximity to Wellington and its popularity, booking is essential.

🕀 **209 D2** ⊠ **3 Kitchener Street, Martinborough** ☎ **(06) 306 8863** 🕑 **Wed–Sun 6pm–late**

Saluté $$

Wellingtonians flock here for the modern Middle Eastern and Mediterranean cuisine, which can be enjoyed in the casual dining room or outside in the shaded courtyard. At weekends, brunch is served until 3pm and includes mainly egg-based dishes served with grilled Turkish bread. The lunch selections are fairly light, with dishes such as double-baked spinach and feta soufflé and freshly baked bread filled with falafels. Dinner is more substantial, although you can still order mezze dishes such as spiced lamb and pork dumplings, fried haloumi and chickpea-battered mussels.

🕀 **209 D2** ⊠ **83 Main Street, Greytown** ☎ **(06) 304 9825; www.salute.net.nz** 🕑 **Wed–Sat 12–late, Sun 12–3.30**

Where to...
Shop

Shopping Centres

Wellington is a compact city, with most shopping districts close together. There are several centres on Lambton Quay, including **Capital on the Quay** (No. 226–262, tel: (04) 474 9865), with 25 shops and eateries. Or visit the country's oldest department store, **Kirkcaldie and Stains** (No. 165–177, tel: (04) 472 5899), founded in 1863.

Fashion

The **Old Bank Arcade** (233–237 Lambton Quay, tel: (04) 922 0600) houses some top NZ designers. For avant-garde labels, try **Zambesi** (107 Customhouse Quay, tel: (04) 472 3638) and **Spacesuit** (164 Cuba Street, tel: (04) 382 8786). Also along Cuba Street you can find designers **Frutti** (No. 176, tel: (04) 384 6965) and **Mandatory** (No. 108, tel: (04) 384 6107) for men. Get a **Fashion Map** from the Wellington Visitor Centre (corner of Victoria and Wakefield streets, tel: (04) 802 4860).

Arts and Crafts

For fine and applied art, try **Emerge Gallery** (corner of Wakefield and Chaffers streets, tel: (04) 385 2766) and **Avid** (48 Victoria Street, tel: (04) 472 7703). For souvenirs, try **Sommerfields** (296 Lambton Quay, tel: (04) 499 4847), or the museum stores at **Te Papa** (▶ 108–109) and the **Museum of Wellington City and Sea** (Bond Store, Queens Wharf, tel: (04) 472 8904).

Food and Drink

The **Dixon Street Deli** (45–47 Dixon Street, tel: (04) 384 2436) bakes its own bread and pastries and has a selection of cheeses and other deli items. Other downtown delis include **Caffe' Italiano** (229 Cuba Street, tel: (04) 385 2703), which sells coffee machines as well as food, and **Truffle** (22 Garrett Street, tel: (04) 385 2802), the largest importer of truffle-based products in New Zealand.

For sweet treats, check out **Butlers Chocolate Café** (103 Willis Street, tel: (04) 472 7630). **Ciocco Chocolaterie and Espresso Bar** (11 Tory Street, tel: (04) 382 8907), and **Tempt** (Old Bank Arcade, Lambton Quay, tel: 0800 868 367 toll free), with its delectable cakes.

To buy delicious fresh produce, visit the **City Market** (Chaffers Dock, Waterfront, tel: (04) 801 8380) or **Harbourside Market** (Waitangi Park, Cable Street, tel: (04) 495 7895). Both are held on Sunday mornings.

Children

The **Baby's Room** in Old Bank Arcade on Lambton Quay (tel: (04) 386 1171) is a specialist baby boutique. **Kids' Store** on Level 2 at Te Papa (▶ 108–109), stocks toys that are both educational and fun. Teenagers, meanwhile, should check out **Real Groovy** (250 Cuba Street, tel: (04) 385 2020) for music, DVDs, games, posters and T-shirts.

Sports and Outdoor Gear

For outdoor supplies try **Bivouac Outdoor** (39 Mercer Street, tel: (04) 473 2587) or **Kathmandu** (57 Willis Street, tel: (04) 472 0113). For water and winter sports, head to **Rip Curl** (82 Willis Street, tel: (04) 473 2298) or **Surf n Snow** (45 Cuba Street, tel: (04) 473 3371).

The **Lindale Centre** (SH1, Paraparaumu, tel: (04) 297 0916) has agricultural shops selling cheese, honey and olive products.

Where to...
Be Entertained

For what's on, see the Thursday and Saturday editions of the *Dominion Post*. **Cuba Street** and **Courtenay Place** are the nightlife centres – bars, clubs, cinemas, theatres and cafes stay open until late.

Performing Arts

Wellington calls itself the cultural capital of New Zealand. The large, modern **Michael Fowler Centre**, Wakefield Street, is home to the New Zealand Symphony Orchestra (tel: (04) 801 3890). The **town hall**, next door, hosts more intimate concerts. The New Zealand String Quartet, Chamber Music New Zealand and the Wellington Sinfonia also give regular concerts. The Royal New Zealand Ballet

(tel: (04) 381 9000) is based at the **Westpac St James Theatre** (77–83 Courtenay Place, tel: (04) 381 9000), also the venue for musical shows and the NBR New Zealand Opera (tel: (04) 384 4434).

For professional theatre, try **Downstage** (corner of Courtenay Place and Cambridge Terrace, tel: (04) 801 6946) or **Circa** (1 Taranaki Street, tel: (04) 801 7992). Alternative performers appear at **Bats** (1 Kent Terrace, tel: (04) 802 4175). Get an **Arts Map** from the visitor information centre (corner of Victoria and Wakefield streets, tel: (04) 802 4860).

Nightlife

Live music venues include the trendy **Matterhorn** (▶ 115), as well as the **Bodega bar** (101

Ghuznee Street, tel: (04) 384 8212), a Wellington favourite that showcases up-and-coming New Zealand bands. For live jazz, try **Blondini's Jazz Lounge and Café** on the first floor of the Embassy Theatre (see below), or on Wednesday nights **Sandwiches** bar and restaurant (corner of Majoribanks Street and Kent Terrace, tel: (04) 385 7698). The latter also hosts national and international club DJs on Friday and Saturday nights, and has soul/funk/disco nights on Thursdays.

Cinemas

The 1924 **Embassy Theatre** in Courtenay Place (10 Kent Terrace, tel: (04) 384 7657) has been refurbished in grand style, making it an atmospheric place to catch a movie. Near by are the **Paramount Theatre** (25 Courtenay Place, tel: (04) 384 4080), Wellington's longest established cinema, and the **Rialto** (corner of Cable and Jervois streets, tel: (04) 385 1864).

Sports

Wellington's Westpac Stadium (Waterloo Quay, tel: (04) 473 3881) is the capital's main venue for major sporting events, including international soccer, cricket and rugby tournaments.

Festivals

The **New Zealand International Arts Festival** is held in March in even years, overlapping with the annual **Wellington Fringe Festival**. A **Jazz Festival** is held in November. The **Montana World of Wearable Art Show** takes place in September.

The region celebrates its wine in the annual **Toast Martinborough** festival in November. For wine tasting throughout the year join a tour with **Martinborough Wine Tours** (tel: (06) 306 8032), or pick up a map of the vineyards at the visitor information centre (▶ 112).

Top of the
South Island

Getting Your Bearings

The Top of the South Island is a microcosm of New Zealand, where all the natural features for which the country is renowned can be found in a relatively small area. Here, you can ski down alpine peaks, soak in natural hot springs, sip wine among the vines, kayak past golden beaches, hike through remote forests and see at close quarters nature's most impressive marine mammals – all in the space of a few days.

The region was fairly heavily populated by Maori in early times, and the first ever encounter between Europeans and the *tangata whenua* (native people) took place in Golden Bay in 1642 when Dutch explorer Abel Tasman anchored here. Unfortunately, the meeting was not a happy one, ending with the deaths of four of the Dutch sailors.

Some 130 years later, Captain James Cook also sailed along this coast, spending time in Ship Cove in the Marlborough Sounds, mapping the region and naming many of its features. Following on Cook's heels in the 1820s came whalers, who set up stations in the Marlborough Sounds and at Kaikoura, and then the New Zealand Company, which bought land off local Maori in the early 1840s to establish the city of Nelson.

Today, European immigrants and holidaymakers are still attracted to the region in large numbers, drawn to its sunny climate, beautiful scenery and vibrant arts and crafts scene. Visitors stepping off the ferry in Picton can choose either to spend some time locally, exploring the Marlborough Sounds and nearby vineyards around Blenheim; travel west to historic Nelson and the beaches of the Abel Tasman National Park and Golden Bay; or head south to go whale watching off Kaikoura and relax in the hot pools of Hanmer Springs. Whether your interests lie in such active pursuits as hiking, skiing and kayaking, or in the more sybaritic pleasures of wine tasting, good food and fine art, the Top of the South will not disappoint.

Page 119: The Abel Tasman Coastal Track is popular with hikers

Left: Tourists board a water taxi to explore the coastline of Abel Tasman National Park

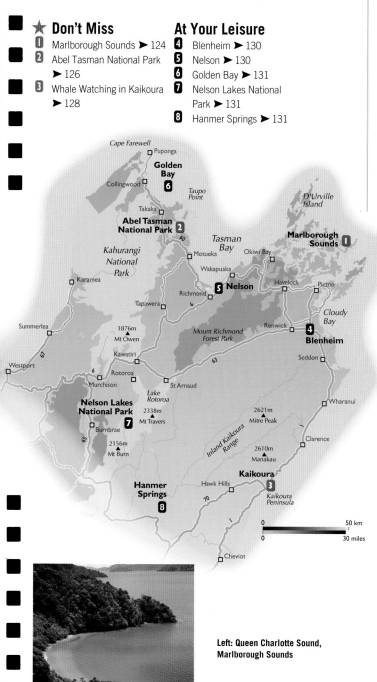

Left: Queen Charlotte Sound, Marlborough Sounds

In Four Days

If you're not quite sure where to begin your travels, this itinerary recommends four practical and enjoyable days taking in some of the best places to see around the Top of the South Island using the Getting Your Bearings map on the previous page. For more information see the main entries.

Day 1

Morning
Join a half-day cruise in the ❶ **Marlborough Sounds** (above, ➤ 124–125), either to Motuara Island to go birdwatching or to historic Ship Cove, keeping an eye out for dolphins along the way.

Afternoon and Evening
On your return to Picton, have lunch in a local cafe and take a look at the *Edwin Fox* exhibition. Drive to nearby ❹ **Blenheim** (28km/17 miles) and join a guided tour of the surrounding **vineyards**, or pick up a map from the visitor centre and create your own itinerary.

Book dinner at one of the excellent **winery restaurants**, such as Twelve Trees or Herzog's (➤ 134).

Day 2

Morning
Drive the 112km (70 miles) to ❺ **Nelson** (➤ 130), stopping off in the city for a coffee or early lunch at one of the many cafes there (➤ 135). If you are visiting on a Saturday, be sure to check out the funky craft stalls in the **Montgomery Square market**.

Afternoon and Evening
Continue 50km (31 miles) west along the coast to the town of Motueka to join a half-day guided **kayak tour** of the beautiful coves and golden beaches of the ❷ **Abel Tasman National Park** (➤ 126–127). Alternatively, catch a

water taxi to Awaroa Lodge (► 132), where you can go for a walk, kayak or relax on the beach before staying the night.

If you are not staying in the park, head back to Nelson for the night. Dine on the fine seafood for which the area is renowned (► 135).

Day 3

Morning
Pick up a picnic in Nelson before driving 117km (73 miles) inland to Lake Rotoiti in the heart of the **7 Nelson Lakes National Park** (► 131). Enjoy your lunch on the lakeshore, surrounded by bush-covered mountains, then go for a nature walk or rent a boat for a paddle on the calm waters.

Afternoon and Evening
From Lake Rotoiti, continue 233km (145 miles) through the spectacular mountain scenery surrounding Murchison, Springs Junction and the Lewis Pass to **8 Hanmer Springs** (► 131). Stretch your limbs on arrival – literally – by making a bungy jump, or hiring a mountain bike and cycling along the forest tracks around the town.

Soak away the dust of the day in the alpine resort's hot pools (below), before enjoying a meal in one of the restaurants here (► 135).

Day 4

Morning
After an early morning dip in Hanmer's rejuvenating springs, head off for Kaikoura (124km/77 miles) via the scenic SH70 Waiau road, to join a pre-booked **9 whale-watching tour** (► 128–129). Don't forget your camera, so that you can take pictures of the magnificent sperm whales' tails rising up as the creatures dive.

Afternoon and Evening
See more of the marine wildlife by **swimming with dolphins** or from above on a **whale-spotting plane tour**, or join a **cultural tour** to learn more about the customs and history of the local Maori.

Before dinner, take a drive out to the **seal colony** to watch the sun set behind the mountains, then literally *kai koura* ("eat crayfish") at one of the restaurants back in town (► 134).

⓪ Marlborough Sounds

For many visitors, the Marlborough Sounds are their first sight of the South Island. The tranquil waterways are ideal for a relaxing stop-off, where you can potter about in boats, wander along the Queen Charlotte Track or fish for snapper.

Many travellers strike out further afield as soon as they get off the inter-island ferry from Wellington, but Marlborough Sounds are worth an exploration in their own right. Here, at the South Island's northeastern tip, the rise in sea-level after the last ice age created a labyrinth of islands, peninsulas and coves.

Cook Strait

The ferry crossing of Cook Strait is itself a rewarding and scenic journey. There are two inter-island services available from Wellington: Tranz Rail's **Interislander ferries** and **Bluebridge ferries**, both of which carry cars and foot passengers. They leave daily at varying frequencies (see opposite), the journey to Picton taking three hours with Interislander and slightly longer with Bluebridge.

For the longest part of the journey the ferry travels through the narrow passages of the Marlborough Sounds, passing dramatic scenery. The sea calms down once you pass the tight entrance to **Tory Channel**, which stretches between a narrow tongue of the South Island mainland and Arapawa

KUPE AND THE OCTOPUS
A Maori legend tells of the Polynesian explorer Kupe, who was being pestered by a giant octopus that was eating his harvest of fish. Kupe decided to kill it, but the creature fled and Kupe had to chase it across the ocean to the southern Pacific, where he discovered New Zealand. He finally caught the octopus at Arapawa Island in the Marlborough Sounds.

Island. It was here that 18th-century explorer Captain Cook first spotted the strait now named after him, and also here that the Polynesian explorer Kupe finally caught up with the giant octopus that led him to discover New Zealand (see box).

Exploring Queen Charlotte Sound

Once the boat passes the island, the channel opens into **Queen Charlotte Sound**, at whose head is the small port of **Picton**, where passengers can transfer to buses or trains. The town makes a good base from which to explore the sounds. Picton's wharf, a short walk from the ferry terminal, is the departure point for cruise boats and water taxis.

Cruise options range from short journeys around the inner Queen Charlotte Sound to full-day trips to the neighbouring **Kenepuru** or **Pelorus sounds.**

Another popular stop for visitors is **Ship Cove**, almost at the seaward end of Queen Charlotte Sound, which Captain Cook visited repeatedly on his voyages. It was here that he claimed the country on behalf of Britain, as well as letting loose the first sheep in New Zealand. The cove is also the starting point of the 67km (42-mile) **Queen Charlotte Track**; you can hike the length of it (allow four days) staying in huts overnight, or get dropped off by water taxi and walk just a section.

TAKING A BREAK

For a good cup of coffee in Picton, try **Le Café** at 12–14 London Quay (tel: (03) 573 5588).

✚ 208 C2

Visitor Information Centre
✉ The Foreshore ☎ (03) 520 3113; www.destinationmarlborough.com
🕐 Nov–Mar Mon–Fri 8:30–6, Sat–Sun 8:30–5; Apr–Oct
Mon–Fri 9–4, Sat–Sun 10–3

Opposite:
The Seaward
Kaikoura
Range on
the south
coast of the
Marlborough
Sounds

Interislander
✉ Booking agents throughout the country ☎ (04) 498 3302;
www.interislander.co.nz 🕐 Sailings up to 10 times daily 🎫 Range of fares

Bluebridge
✚ 205 C4 ✉ 50 Waterloo Quay, Wellington ☎ (04) 471 6188;
www.bluebridge.co.nz 🕐 Sailings 4 times daily 🎫 Range of fares

MALBOROUGH SOUNDS: INSIDE INFO

Top tip You can fly from Wellington to Picton, Nelson or Blenheim and get a **bird's-eye view** of the landscapes of the Marlborough Sounds (▶ 35).

Hidden gem Some of the smaller islands of the sounds have been cleared of predators and turned into sanctuaries for endangered native species. Access is restricted to most islands but you can visit **Motura Island** on a guided tour.

In more depth On Picton's foreshore is the last remaining ship of the British East India Company, *Edwin Fox* (www.nzmaritime.co.nz/edwinfox.htm).

2 Abel Tasman National Park

New Zealand's smallest national park is also one of its most popular, drawing local and international visitors alike to its golden beaches, bush-covered hills, turquoise waters and granite outcrops.

The area was originally used seasonally by Maori, who came to gather food here and cultivate *kumara* (sweet potato). Inhabitants at a *pa* (fort) at **Taupo Point** were the first Maori to come into contact with Europeans when they were involved in a skirmish in 1642 with Dutch explorer Abel Tasman, after whom the park is named. The 22,530ha (55,647-acre) park was founded in 1942, largely through the efforts of a single local conservationist, Perrine Moncrieff, who had become concerned about logging in the area.

Best Foot Forward

Today, the park attracts large numbers of visitors in summer, not least because of its easy access and lovely beaches. Keen hikers can tackle the 51km (32-mile) **Abel Tasman Coastal Track** over three to five days, or those with less time can use the park's water-taxi service to get dropped off and walk short sections instead. The track is relatively easy, passing over forested headlands from bay to golden bay. The Department of Conservation manages the park huts and campsites that are found at regular intervals along the way (advance booking required). In addition, there is a 27km (18-mile) inland track that, like the coastal route, starts at Marahau and ends at Wainui, as well as shorter walks at Totaranui.

The park's coastal track covers 51km (32 miles)

Kayak Tours

An increasingly popular way of exploring the stunning bays and sculptured granite cliffs is from the sea by **kayak**. You can join a gentle half-day tour or, if you have more time, spend three days kayaking, swimming and camping on beaches as you go. Aside from the seals you'll spot basking on the rocks, you may also come across pods of dolphins or even an orca. Groups of two or more confident paddlers can also hire kayaks to explore independently. If you want to take things easier, there are **boat charter** options and **guided cruises**, or you can even fly direct to the luxurious Awaroa Lodge (► 132) for a relaxing break in this slice of paradise.

TAKING A BREAK

Awaroa Lodge (► 132) has an excellent restaurant, or if you join a kayak or boat tour food is usually provided as part of the package.

➕ 208 B2

Department of Conservation Visitor Centre
✉ Corner of King Edward and High streets, Motueka ☎ (03) 528 1810; www.doc.govt.nz ⏰ Mon–Fri 8–4:30 ❗ Hut passes can also be booked at the visitor information centre in Nelson (► 130)

Abel Tasman Aqua Taxi
✉ Marahau, RD2, Motueka ☎ (03) 527 8083, 0800 278 282 toll free; www.aquataxi.co.nz ⏰ Daily service (weather dependent) 💰 Expensive

Sea Kayak Company
✉ 506 High Street, Motueka ☎ (03) 528 7251, 0508 252 925 toll free; www.seakayaknz.co.nz ⏰ Daily (weather dependent) 💰 Expensive

Catamaran Sailing and Launch Charters
✉ 46 Martin Street, Monaco, Nelson ☎ (03) 547 6666; www.sailingcharters.co.nz ⏰ Daily (weather dependent)

Abel Tasman Seal Swim
✉ Kayak Abel Tasman Base, Main Road, Marahau, RD2, Motueka ☎ (03) 527 8022; www.sealswim.com ⏰ Nov–May daily 9:15, 11:15 💰 Expensive

---

ABEL TASMAN NATIONAL PARK: INSIDE INFO

Top tip The best time to visit the park is in February or March, after the school holidays have finished but while the weather is still warm and sunny.

Hidden gem Taupo Point, on Wainui Bay in the northwest of the park, has an information board describing the *pa* (fort) that existed here when Abel Tasman arrived in 1642. The beautiful beach adjoining the headland is popular with nudists and rarely busy.

In more depth If you have time, join a **seal swim** tour to Tonga Island. The seals may look ungainly on land, but their grace underwater is incredible to observe as you snorkel above them.

❸ Whale Watching in Kaikoura

The sperm whales that come to feed in the nutrient-rich waters off Kaikoura attracted whalers in the early 19th century, who hunted them down for their precious oil. Today, the whales are still the town's main drawcard, but visitors now come to shoot photos rather than harpoons.

Kaikoura is a small town on the northeast coast of the South Island, uninspiring in itself but backed by the stunning and precipitous Kaikoura Range, and with offshore waters that teem with a diverse range of marine wildlife. Early Maori named it after the abundant crayfish found here (*kai koura* means "eat crayfish"), but it was the seals and whales that reeled in the first Europeans.

From Hunting to Tourism

Fyffe House is the earliest building in Kaikoura and was built by George Fyffe, whose cousin Robert established the first whaling station here in 1842. Whale vertebrae were used as piles in the construction of the house, which is now open to visitors; in 2008, storms uncovered whale bones from the station's heyday on the beach in front.

The main industry of Kaikoura today is **whale watching** rather than whale hunting, which pulls in thousands of visitors year-round. Tour boats head 2km (1 mile) out to sea, where underwater canyons that plummet to depths of 1,500m (5,000 feet) and more come close to shore. Here, an upwelling of nutrients and minerals attracts all manner of sea creatures, including sperm whales, orca, pilot whales, humpbacks, dolphins, seals and sharks, as well as seabirds.

Wildlife Watching

The **sperm whales** are present year-round and are located with the aid of hydrophones and sharp eyes. Once a whale is spotted, the boat motors to within a respectful distance and the incredible leviathan can be observed resting at the surface for 10 minutes or so, before its vast tail rises up as it dives into the deep canyons to resume feeding. Several individuals may be spotted, as well as other species of whale, and you may also see **bottlenose dolphins** or even rare **Hector's dolphins** (see box). Back on land, you can visit the **seal colony** at the end of the peninsula beyond Fyffe House and walk

HECTOR'S DOLPHINS

Hector's dolphins are endemic to New Zealand and are the rarest marine dolphins in the world, numbering fewer than 8,000 individuals. They are also the smallest dolphin species at just 1.4m (4.6 feet) from nose to tail, and are instantly recognizable by their rounded dorsal fin.

A tour boat catches a glimpse of a sperm whale

along the cliffs there (see box), join a **Maori cultural tour** to learn more about the area's first inhabitants, or take to the sky for **aerial views** of the whales and the stunning coastline.

TAKING A BREAK

On your way to the seal colony, stop off at the open-air **Kaikoura Seafood BBQ** (tel: 027 376 3619).

+ 207 F5
Visitor Information Centre
⊠ West End ☎ (03) 319 5641; www.kaikoura.co.nz ⊙ Mon–Fri 9–5, Sat–Sun 9–4

Fyffe House
⊠ 62 Avoca Street ☎ (03) 319 5835; www.historic.org.nz ⊙ Oct–Apr daily 10–6; May–Sep Thu–Mon 10–4 ✋ Inexpensive

Maori Tours
⊠ 10 Churchill Street ☎ (03) 319 5567; www.maoritours.co.nz ⊙ Half-day tours daily 9, 1:30 ✋ Expensive

Whale Watch Kaikoura
⊠ Whaleway Station ☎ (03) 319 6767; www.whalewatch.co.nz ⊙ Daily 7:15, 10, 12:45 ✋ Expensive

Wings Over Whales
⊠ Kaikoura Airport, PO Box 55, Kaikoura ☎ (03) 319 6580; www.whales.co.nz ⊙ 30-min tours daily ✋ Expensive

Dolphin Encounter
⊠ 96 The Esplanade ☎ (03) 319 6777; www.dolphin.co.nz ⊙ Nov–Apr daily 5:30am, 8:30am, 12:30pm; May–Oct 8:30am, 12:30pm ✋ Expensive

WHALE WATCHING IN KAIKOURA: INSIDE INFO

Top tip The best time to go on a whale-watching tour is early in the morning, before the wind gets up and the sea is likely to be calmer.

Hidden gem A rewarding walk follows part of the **Kaikoura Peninsula Walkway** from the seal colony at Point Kean to Whalers Bay (25 minutes). The path leads up onto the cliffs, giving great views down to the seals basking below.

In more depth Large pods of dusky dolphins frequent Kaikoura's inland waters year-round. For the rare chance to see these acrobatic mammals up close join a **dolphin swim** tour.

At Your Leisure

4 Blenheim

Set on the wide plains of the Wairau River valley, Blenheim has risen to prominence in recent years as the centre of the Marlborough wine industry, known the world over for its Sauvignon Blanc. You can join a guided tour of the wineries in the area, stopping off for tastings and food among the vines, or pick up a map from the visitor information centre to create your own itinerary. Just outside town is the Omaka Aviation Heritage Centre, with a large collection of rare World War I planes that form the centrepiece of realistic dioramas created by special effects experts from film director Peter Jackson's Weta Workshop.

➕ 208 B1

Visitor Information Centre
✉ Railway Station, Blenheim ☎ (03) 577 8080; www.destinationmarlborough.com
🕓 Mon–Fri 8:30–5, Sat–Sun 9–3

Marlborough Travel
✉ PO Box 1000, Blenheim ☎ (03) 577 9997, 0800 990 800 toll free; www.marlboroughtravel.co.nz 🕓 Guided wine tours daily 💰 Expensive

Omaka Aviation Heritage Centre
✉ 79 Aerodrome Road, Blenheim ☎ (03) 579 1305; www.omaka.org.nz 🕓 Daily 10–4; closed 25 and 26 Dec, 1 Jan 💰 Moderate

5 Nelson

Nelson is one of the oldest settlements in New Zealand, established by the New Zealand Company back in 1841. This heritage can be seen in the row of cottages in South Street behind the cathedral (➤ 133) and in other mid-19th-century homes such as Broadgreen House in the nearby suburb of Stoke, and is covered more fully in the excellent Nelson Provincial Museum.

Today, Nelson has a lively arts and crafts scene – visit the Saturday morning market in Montgomery Square for fun, funky pieces to take home, or browse the exhibitions at the Suter Art Gallery.

The city also makes a great base from which to explore the diverse landscapes of the Abel Tasman National Park (➤ 126–127) and Nelson Lakes National Park (see opposite).

➕ 208 B2

Visitor Information Centre
✉ Millers Acre Centre, 75 Trafalgar Street, Nelson ☎ (03) 548 2304; www.nelsonnz.com
🕓 Nov–Mar daily 8:30–6; Apr–Oct Mon–Fri 8:30–5, Sat–Sun 9–4

Broadgreen House
✉ 276 Nayland Road, Stoke ☎ (03) 547 0403
🕓 Daily 10:30–4:30 💰 Inexpensive

Nelson has a number of arts and crafts outlets

The clear, fresh water of Waikoropupu Springs in Golden Bay

Nelson Provincial Museum
✉ Corner of Trafalgar and Hardy streets, Nelson ☎ (03) 548 9588; www.museumnp.org.nz ◷ Mon–Fri 10–5, Sat–Sun and public holidays 10–4:30 🎟 Donation

Suter Art Gallery
✉ 208 Bridge Street, Nelson ☎ (03) 548 4699; www.thesuter.org.nz ◷ Daily 10:30–4:30 🎟 Inexpensive; free Sat

6 Golden Bay
A winding drive 100km (60 miles) northwest of Nelson over the Takaka Hill takes you to sleepy Golden Bay. At Waikoropupu Springs just outside the main town of Takaka, the clearest fresh water in the world bubbles out of the ground at a rate of 14,000 litres (3,000 gallons) per second. The springs are sacred to Maori, so swimming in them is forbidden, but a viewing platform allows visitors to see underwater and a walking trail winds around the site.

The bay itself is dotted with shallow swimming beaches from the western end of Abel Tasman National Park (▶ 126–127) right round to the 30km-long (19-mile) Farewell Spit, the site of several whale strandings. On the outside of the spit is the wild and dramatic Wharariki Beach, reached via a 20-minute walk over ancient dunes.

Golden Bay is also the start (or end) of the 82km (51-mile) Heaphy Track, which traverses the remote Kahurangi National Park before emerging on the West Coast.
✚ 208 B2

Visitor Information Centre
✉ Willow Street, Takaka ☎ (03) 525 9136; www.nelsonnz.com ◷ Nov–Apr daily 9–5; rest of year Mon–Fri 9–5, Sat–Sun 9–4

7 Nelson Lakes National Park
Centred on the small settlement of St Arnaud, the Nelson Lakes National Park is a 102,000ha (252,000-acre) wilderness of mountain peaks, glacial lakes and alpine vegetation. It is popular in summer for hiking, boating and trout fishing, and in winter for skiing on the small Rainbow Ski Area.

The short walk through the Lake Rotoiti Nature Recovery Project is ideal if you're not stopping – look for bellbirds, fantails and kaka along the way.
✚ 208 B1

Department of Conservation Visitor Centre
✉ View Road, St Arnaud ☎ (03) 521 1806; www.starnaud.co.nz ◷ 26 Dec–6 Feb daily 8–6; 7 Feb–Easter 8–5; rest of year 8–4:30

Rainbow Ski Area
✉ PO Box 76, St Arnaud ☎ (03) 521 1861; www.skirainbow.co.nz ◷ Mid Jul–mid Oct daily 9–4

8 Hanmer Springs
At the thermal reserve in this alpine resort, natural hot springs feed a sequence of pools and you can choose how hot you want your soak. The pools have attracted visitors since 1859, and are particularly popular in winter, when you can have a hot bath in snowy surrounds. As well as the spa, aqua therapy centre and beauty treatments, there are numerous outdoor activities.
✚ 207 E5

Hanmer Springs Thermal Pool and Spa
✉ Amuri Avenue, Hanmer Springs ☎ (03) 315 0000; www.hanmersprings.co.nz ◷ Daily 10–9 🎟 Return pass: moderate

Where to... Stay

Prices
Expect to pay for two people sharing a double room per night:
$ under NZ$200 $$ NZ$200–$350 $$$ over NZ$350

MARLBOROUGH SOUNDS

Punga Cove Resort $-$$$
Punga Cove is a remote and beautiful spot. Tucked in a sandy cove in the Marlborough Sounds, on a hillside covered in *punga* (native tree ferns), the resort is accessible (just) by road, but most easily by boat.

Accommodation ranges from luxury suites with two bedrooms to cabins for backpackers on the Queen Charlotte Track (▶125). There's a restaurant with a million-dollar view of the cove and Queen Charlotte Sound, and also a shop, pool and sauna. Activities include walking, kayaking and fishing.

✚ 208 C2 ☒ Punga Cove, Endeavour Inlet ☎ (03) 579 8561; www.pungacove.co.nz

ABEL TASMAN NATIONAL PARK

Awaroa Lodge $$-$$$
Escape Nelson city to this relaxed luxury beachside lodge, 50km (30 miles) to the northwest in Abel Tasman National Park and accessible only by air, boat or on foot. Accommodation ranges from superior suites to family rooms, all well designed and tucked away in the bush. There is an excellent restaurant that uses local seafood as well as organic produce grown on site. Activities include beachcombing along Awaroa beach, hiking the Abel Tasman Track, sea kayaking and sailing.

✚ 208 B2 ☒ Awaroa Bay ☎ (03) 528 8758; www.awaroalodge.co.nz

KAIKOURA

Hapuku Lodge $$$
Some 12km (7 miles) north of Kaikoura is this unusual luxury lodge. Here, treehouses stand perched above a grove of kanuka trees, with views of mountains in one direction and out to sea in the other.

Three of the treehouses have a single bedroom with a king-size bed that can be converted into two singles, a seating area, a spa bath and a wood-burning stove. Two have an additional "lower branch" room that is connected to the upper level via an internal staircase, perfect for families. There are also six guest rooms in the main lodge and an open-plan apartment that sleeps up to six. Included in the price is a buffet Continental breakfast, and in the evening guests can enjoy delicious food made with fresh local ingredients.

✚ 207 F5 ☒ SH1 at Station Road, RD1 ☎ (03) 319 6559, 0800 524 568 toll free; www.hapukulodge.com

Nikau Lodge $$
Built from native timbers in 1925, Nikau Lodge today offers visitors to Kaikoura stylish bed-and-breakfast accommodation. There are seven guest rooms, five with a queen-size bed, one with a king that can be converted into two singles, and one with just a single. All have ensuite bathrooms, and the rooms upstairs have the bonus of spectacular mountain views. At the end of your day, soak in the garden hot tub before wandering down into town for dinner, a five-minute walk away.

✚ 207 F5 ☒ 53 Deal Street, Kaikoura ☎ (03) 319 6973; www.nikaulodge.com

BLENHEIM

Blue Ridge Estate $$

Situated very close to some of Marlborough's leading vineyards, this bed and breakfast has three guest rooms. All have ensuite bathrooms and direct access to the garden, with a private seating area, and the views look out over the estate's 8ha (20 acres) of grape vines to the mountains of the Richmond Range. The property is not suitable for children.

✚ 208 B1 ⊠ 50 O'Dwyers Road, Rapaura, RD3 ☎ (03) 570 2198; www.blueridge.co.nz

Hotel d'Urville $$–$$$

The heritage Public Trust Building in Blenheim offers a grand location for this boutique hotel. Much of the hotel is in the old bank vaults, and the 11 themed rooms have lofty ceilings, wooden floors and exotic furniture. The original central vault has been converted into a guest lounge with books and complimentary aperitifs. The restaurant and bar serve local food and wine.

✚ 208 B1 ⊠ 52 Queen Street ☎ (03) 577 9945; www.durville.com

NELSON

South Street Cottages $$–$$$

South Street, behind Nelson Cathedral, is distinguished by its diminutive 1860s cottages. Three of these cottages have been turned into self-contained holiday accommodation, providing a comfortable base in the heart of this historic city. Each has two bedrooms, one with a double bed and the other with a queen, as well as a fully equipped kitchen and garden courtyard. Also available is a nearby two-bedroom apartment, South Haven, and Haven Light, a one-bedroom waterfront villa on Wakefield Quay, designed around a pohutukawa tree and with fabulous views of the water.

✚ 208 B2 ⊠ South Street ☎ (03) 540 2769; www.cottageaccommodation.co.nz

Te Puna Wai Lodge $–$$

This early Victorian villa nestles in the hills above Nelson Port. The house has been lovingly refurbished, and rooms have adjoining bathrooms, oriental rugs and antique furnishings. The three rooms can be booked separately or together. Upstairs is a self-contained suite with fabulous sea views, while downstairs is a double room and a one-bedroom apartment with a kitchen.

✚ 208 B2 ⊠ 24 Richardson Street ☎ (03) 548 7621; www.tepunawai.co.nz

HANMER SPRINGS

Cheltenham House $$

Just around the corner from the hot pools is a 1930s heritage home with four spacious suites inside, two cottages in the garden, and a modern four-bedroom, three-bathroom villa that takes a maximum of eight guests. Each suite features antique furniture and king-size or twin beds. The cottages have queen-size beds and private bathrooms. This luxury bed and breakfast includes complimentary wines in the evening.

✚ 207 E5 ⊠ 13 Cheltenham Street ☎ (03) 315 7545; www.cheltenham.co.nz

The Heritage Hanmer Springs $–$$

Part of the Heritage hotel chain, the Heritage Hanmer Springs is a restored early 20th-century Spanish-style lodge that, like its sister establishments in Auckland and Queenstown, provides luxury accommodation. The standard rooms all have queen-size beds, while those opening onto the gardens also have an outside patio. The lodge has also six self-contained villas in its grounds. There is a bar and restaurant, outdoor pool and tennis courts, and it is just a short downhill walk to the town's thermal pools.

✚ 207 E5 ⊠ 1 Conical Hill Road ☎ (03) 315 0060, 0800 368 888 toll free; www.heritagehotels.co.nz

Where to...
Eat and Drink

Prices

Expect to pay per person for a three-course meal, excluding drinks:

$ under NZ$45 $$ NZ$45–$60 $$$ over NZ$60

MARLBOROUGH SOUNDS

The Mussel Pot $

Although the settlement of Havelock is tiny, the Mussel Pot is more than enough reason to stop. The set-up is casual, with wooden tables and benches inside and on the patio. On offer are "steamers" (whole steamed mussels) and "flats" (grilled half-mussels), both of which come with a choice of sauces and plenty of bread.

✚ 208 B2 ⊠ 73 Main Street, Havelock ☎ (03) 574 2824; www.themusselpot.co.nz ⏰ Nov–Mar daily 11:30–3:15, 5:30–10; Apr–Oct 11:30–2:30, 5–10

KAIKOURA

The Store at Kekerengu ($–$$)

Halfway between Blenheim and Kaikoura on State Highway 1 is this cafe-cum-crafts shop-cum-post office. The building fits well in the landscape, with bare wooden beams, and a double-sided fireplace and a bleached outside deck. It's a great place to stop for a light snack to break up your journey, or you can fill up on more substantial dishes such as crayfish and blue cod. In summer, sit outside and watch the surf crashing on the stony beach, or in winter warm yourself by the open fire. Local Marlborough wines feature big on the drinks list.

✚ 207 F5 ⊠ SH1, Kekerengu ☎ (03) 575 8600 ⏰ Nov–Apr daily 7:30–7:30; May–Oct 8–6

White Morph $$$

Adjacent to the motor inn of the same name on Kaikoura's Esplanade, and with views out to sea, is the town's only fine dining establishment. Like many other local restaurants it specializes in fresh seafood, including the crayfish after which the town is named. Seafood starters include bouillabaisse Pacifica and greenshell mussels in a coconut broth, and for mains there is a platter containing a selection of local *kai moana* (seafood). The restaurant has also won several awards for its beef and lamb dishes – great choices if you don't fancy fish.

✚ 207 F5 ⊠ 94 The Esplanade, Kaikoura ☎ (03) 319 5676; www.whitemorphrestaurant.co.nz ⏰ Nov–Apr daily 5:30–8:30, May–Oct 5:30–9:30

BLENHEIM

Herzog's $$$

This is no casual winery restaurant but a gourmet destination re-created by Hans and Therese Herzog in the style of their celebrated Swiss restaurant. The decor is opulent, with antiques, formal flower arrangements and the tables set with fine china and silverware. There's a fixed-price, five-course menu focused on seasonal produce, fish and game. With more than 550 labels, the wine cellar is one of the most extensive in New Zealand. The vineyard also has a bistro.

✚ 208 B1 ⊠ 81 Jeffries Road, Blenheim ☎ (03) 572 8770; www.herzog.co.nz ⏰ Mid Oct–mid May Tue–Sun 6:30pm–late; bistro: mid Oct–mid May Tue–Sun 12–5. Mid Dec–Mar Tue–Sun 12–5

Twelve Trees Restaurant $$

The restaurant at Allan Scott's striking rammed-earth winery is a popular place for lunch. Eat out on the sheltered garden terrace, or inside under the vaulted ceiling, where you can admire the artworks. The menu is simple and fresh, ranging from pear, blue cheese and kumara or bread and dips to local mussels, salmon and fresh salads. Allan Scott is a pioneer of viticulture in Marlborough and the producer of fine wines, so it's a good place to try them, too.

➕ 208 B1 ⊠ Allan Scott Wines and Estates, Jackson's Road, RD3, Blenheim ☎ (03) 572 7123; www.allanscott.com/restaurant ⏰ Daily 9–5 (lunch 11:30–3:30)

NELSON

The Boat Shed Café $$–$$$

A converted boat shed, with water lapping its foundations, this restaurant not surprisingly specializes in seafood. Choose from Nelson scallops and Tasman Bay crabs to salmon and crayfish come straight from the restaurant's holding tanks. Either dine inside or enjoy the views from the deck.

➕ 208 B2 ⊠ 350 Wakefield Quay, Nelson ☎ (03) 546 9783; www.boatshedcafe.co.nz ⏰ Mon–Fri 11–late, Sat, Sun 10–late

The Honest Lawyer $–$$

Styled on an English country pub, and built of locally quarried stone, the Honest Lawyer sits on a peninsula about 10 minutes' drive from Nelson. Quaint touches of lace curtains, open fireplace and bric-a-brac set the scene inside. Outside, a beer garden overlooks the estuary. The pub has 13 beers on tap, a good wine list and hearty pub food. You can also have breakfast, snacks and cream teas. There's accommodation on site with 10 rooms and three cottages.

➕ 208 B2 ⊠ 1 Point Road, Monaco, Nelson ☎ (03) 547 8850; www.honestlawyer.co.nz ⏰ Daily 7am–midnight (food until 9:30pm)

Morrison Street Café $$

A regular winner of Nelson's best cafe award, the Morrison Street Café is the perfect place to reboot your system with a coffee and cake. Alternatively enjoy a hearty weekend brunch, or relax over lunch in the courtyard, choosing from dishes such as Thai beef curry or mushroom risotto.

➕ 208 B2 ⊠ 244 Hardy Street, Nelson ☎ (03) 548 8110; www.morrisonstreetcafe. co.nz ⏰ Mon–Fri 7:30–4, Sat 8:30–4, Sun and public holidays 9–4

GOLDEN BAY

Mussel Inn $

This micro brewery has become something of a local institution. Quench your thirst on a Captain Cooker manuka beer, Apple Roughy cider or Lemming Aid (lemonade), all made on the premises, while you relax in front of the open fire, on the veranda or in the garden. Meals are simple but tasty and include pan-fried fish, homemade pies and the signature mussel chowder. The inn has won awards for its environmental stance, and has composting toilets and an anti-mobile phone policy. There is a good program of live music and other types of entertainment.

➕ 208 B2 ⊠ Onekaka, RD2, Takaka ☎ (03) 525 9241; www.musselinn.co.nz ⏰ Daily 11am–late; closed mid Jul–mid Sep

HANMER SPRINGS

Malabar $$

Chef Sudip Masra has brought a whole new range of flavours to Hanmer Springs from his native India, combining spices from the subcontinent with seasonings from Thailand and elsewhere in Asia to create exciting fusion dishes. You can start with a traditional Thai hot-and-sour tom yum soup or grilled scallop salad, before moving on to spice-encrusted rack of lamb or an Indian thali tray filled with a selection of curries and accompaniments.

➕ 207 E5 ⊠ Alpine Pacific Centre, 5 Conical Hill Road, Hanmer Springs ☎ (03) 315 7745 ⏰ Daily 12–3, 6–late; takeaway service also available

Where to...
Shop

The **Marlborough Art and Craft Trail** has more than 30 craftspeople (Railway Station, Sinclair Street, tel: (03) 577 8080). **Matua Valley** (New Renwick Road, tel: (03) 572 8642) sells wines, olive oil and souvenirs. **Sherrington Grange** (Mahau Sound, Picton, tel: (03) 574 2655) sells local cheese and honey. **Traditional Country Preserves** (Selmes Road, tel: (03) 570 5665) makes preserves and sells crafts. **Prenzel Distillery** (Riverlands Estate, tel: (03) 520 8215) makes liqueurs and fruit brandies.

Leighvander Cottage (The Village, RD1, Wairau Valley, tel: (03) 572 2851) has lavender-related products. On Sundays **Marlborough Farmer's Market**

has good local produce (A & P Park, Blenheim, tel: (03) 579 3599, Oct–Jun).

NELSON

At Nelson's **Saturday Market** (Montgomery Square, tel: (03) 546 6454) there's everything from dog outfits to organic produce. You can watch glassblowers at **Höglund Art Glass** (Lansdowne Road, Richmond, tel: (03) 544 6500).

The nearby **Grape Escape Complex** (McShanes Road, Appleby) includes the **Escape Gallery** (tel: (03) 544 4630), with local crafts, a cafe and chocolate shop. Get crafty yourself and choose world-class beads from the **Bead Gallery** (18 Parere Street, Nelson, tel: (03) 546 7807).

Where to...
Be Entertained

Visit some of the 45 wineries in the region using the **Marlborough Wine Trail map** from the Blenheim Visitor Centre (Railway Station, Sinclair Street, tel: (03) 577 8080).

Festivals

Marlborough Wine Festival is the culmination of a festival week in February. **Hunter's Garden Marlborough** is held in November.

NELSON

The Suter (208 Bridge Street, tel: (03) 548 4040) is the region's public art museum, with galleries, a craft shop, cafe and a theatre. Enjoy jazz at the **Victorian Rose** (281 Trafalgar Street, tel: (03) 548 7631),

or dance at the **Rock Bar** (165 Bridge Street, tel: (03) 546 8800). A number of wineries are open to visitors. Pick up a copy of the **Wineart guide map** from the visitor information centre (77 Trafalgar Street, tel: (03) 548 2304). This is a major hop-growing region: sample a brew at the organic **Founders** brewery (Founders Historic Park, 87 Atawhai Drive, tel: (03) 548 4638).

Festivals

Nelson's annual **Arts Festival** is held in October. Summer brings the annual **Jazz Festival** and, in odd-numbered years, the **Adam New Zealand Chamber Music Festival**. **The Sealord Nelson Summer Festival** is held from Christmas–Feb and includes a range of events.

Christchurch and the Southern Alps

Getting Your Bearings

If you thought the scenery of the North Island was magnificent and the people too nice to be true, prepare to be surprised. In the South Island, the mountains soar even higher, the forests are more vigorous, time seems to stand still and the landscapes will astonish you.

Christchurch is the South Island's largest city and a gateway to all other destinations in the south. The city was planned as an antipodean outpost of the Church of England, but has grown into a cosmopolitan community with a thriving cultural scene. Around the city, the Canterbury Plains are New Zealand's largest stretch of flat land and one of its most important agricultural areas. Some of the country's biggest farms use the land here for anything from traditional sheep and dairy farming to boutique vineyards and olive groves.

The plains were built up over millions of years from silt carried by rivers from the Southern Alps, the South Island's mountainous backbone, which separates the drier eastern regions from the humid and lush West Coast.

Most of New Zealand's national parks are in the South Island, so whichever way you go from Christchurch you will find spectacular land- or seascapes and see amazing wildlife. If you head north to Kaikoura, you will share the ocean with hundreds of dolphins and whales; heading south to Aoraki/Mount Cook, you'll walk through a wonderland of snow-capped peaks; and going west through Arthur's Pass to the rugged West Coast, you could be taking a stroll on a glacier within minutes of leaving the beach.

CHRISTCHURCH EARTHQUAKE

The earthquake that struck in early 2011 caused considerable damage to the central business district of Christchurch and nearby Lyttelton. Several major attractions and buildings were affected and at the time of writing the future of some were uncertain. Descriptions and information relating to Christchurch and Lyttelton have not been rewritten since the earthquake and it is recommended that you check online sources for the current status of these areas before travelling. Attractions known to be heavily damaged and likely to remain closed for some time include: Christchurch Cathedral, Christchurch Art Gallery, Christchurch Arts Centre, Canterbury Museum and Lyttelton Timeball Station.

Page 137: Akaroa harbour and town on Banks Peninsula

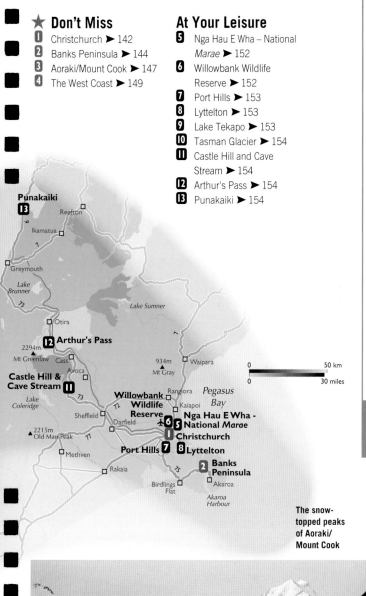

★ Don't Miss

At Your Leisure

Punakaiki
13
Reefton
Ikamatua
Greymouth
Lake Brunner
73
Otira
12 **Arthur's Pass**
2294m Mt Greenlaw
Cass
Avoca
934m Mt Gray
Waipara
Lake Sumner
7
Castle Hill & Cave Stream **11**
Lake Coleridge
73
Sheffield
72
Darfield
Rangiora
Kaiapoi
Pegasus Bay
Willowbank Wildlife Reserve
6 **5** **Nga Hau E Wha – National *Marae***
1 **Christchurch**
2215m Old Man Peak
71
Methven
Port Hills **7** **8** **Lyttelton**
Rakaia
75
2 **Banks Peninsula**
Birdlings Flat
Akaroa
Akaroa Harbour

0 — 50 km
0 — 30 miles

The snow-topped peaks of Aoraki/Mount Cook

In Five Days

If you're not quite sure where to begin your travels, this itinerary recommends five practical and enjoyable days exploring Christchurch and the Southern Alps, taking in some of the best places to see using the Getting Your Bearings map on the previous page. For more information see the main entries.

Day 1

Morning

Start your exploration of **①** Christchurch (see panel ➤ 138) by visiting **Cathedral Square** and joining a tour of **Christchurch Cathedral** (➤ 142). Take the tram to the Arts Centre, with its Gothic Revival buildings, and browse the galleries and craft shops (and the market, if it's the weekend). Have lunch at one of the cafes at the Arts Centre.

Afternoon

Visit the **Canterbury Museum** (➤ 143) and check out the **Christchurch Art Gallery** (➤ 142–143) for interesting exhibitions. Wander through the **Botanic Gardens** and the magnificent **Hagley Park** (above, ➤ 143). Join a wildlife or cultural evening tour at **⑥ Willowbank Wildlife Reserve** (➤ 152), take a walk or drive along the summit road on the **⑦** Port Hills (➤ 153) to watch the sun set behind the Southern Alps.

Day 2

Explore **②** Banks Peninsula (➤ 144–146) and its French settlement, Akaroa. On your way, stop at the Hilltop Tavern, about 60km (35 miles) from Christchurch, for the first view of the peninsula. Take SH75, the coastal route to Akaroa and join a harbour cruise to see some **Hector's dolphins**. Have lunch and browse the craft shops in Akaroa. Return to the hilltop via the summit road and explore the eastern bays of the peninsula on the way.

Day 3

Morning
Leave Christchurch early to drive to **3 Aoraki/Mount Cook** (above, ➤ 147–148), via **9 Lake Tekapo** (➤ 153) – the main roads are SH1 and SH8 – or take an early flight to Mount Cook airport. Explore the area and the glaciers that flow into the valley and join a walk or boat trip on the glacier lake.

Afternoon
Take a scenic flight over New Zealand's tallest mountain range and, weather permitting, land on **10 Tasman Glacier** (➤ 154) for a short walk. In the late afternoon, walk into the **Hooker Valley** along the glacial moraine, and across two swing bridges, for some of the best sunset views of Aoraki/Mount Cook.

Day 4

Morning
Fly back to Christchurch and travel to **4 the West Coast** (➤ 149–151) through **12 Arthur's Pass** (➤ 154). Either take the **TranzAlpine Express** (➤ 28–30), or drive along SH73, if you want to stop for short walks in the **Southern Alps**. Explore the limestone formations at **11 Castle Hill and Cave Stream** (➤ 154) on the way.

Afternoon
Have lunch in **Greymouth**, then head south along SH6 and visit greenstone-carving and glass-blowing workshops in **Hokitika** (➤ 149–150).

Day 5

Continue exploring the rainforests, lakes and beaches of the West Coast south of Hokitika. Walk to the face of either **Franz Josef or Fox glaciers** (➤ 150–151), and if you feel energetic, join a walking tour or a helicopter excursion to the top of Fox Glacier. You can take a scenic flight to get a bird's-eye view of Aoraki/Mount Cook and Mount Tasman. Alternatively, walk to **Lake Matheson** (➤ 187–189) for some of the best views of the Aoraki/Mount Cook range.

◻ Christchurch

Christchurch is like a lost corner of old England. Willows line the Avon River as it meanders through the city's heart, a lofty neo-Gothic cathedral rises from the central square, and many streets carry the names of English cathedral cities.

If you are arriving by air, you will see this city of gardens snuggling up against the Port Hills (➤ 153) and spilling out onto the largest area of flat land in New Zealand, the Canterbury Plains. Farming has always been Canterbury's economic backbone and Christchurch is hemmed in by a patchwork of fields that stretch between the wind-lashed eastern coastline and the foothills of the Southern Alps.

Punting in Hagley Park

Exploring Christchurch
(See panel ➤ 138).
Start your visit at lively **Cathedral Square**, where there's usually some street entertainment going on. The square is surrounded by numerous stately buildings including the Gothic Revival cathedral.

From Cathedral Square, walk along **Worcester Boulevard** or catch a ride on the restored tram to the Christchurch Art Gallery. Its collection totals more than 5,500 items, housed on two floors of exhibition space. There is also a sculpture garden, two retail outlets and a cafe and wine bar.

Further along is the **Arts Centre**, whose huddled cluster of Gothic Revival stone buildings exudes an almost medieval atmosphere. It once housed the University of Canterbury but today accommodates a thriving arts scene, with several galleries, craft shops, performance venues and eateries (➤ 157). There are free guided tours of the Arts Centre, which take place daily (10–3:30), or you can browse at your leisure. A weekend market is also held here.

Just across Rolleston Avenue is the **Canterbury Museum**, with displays on natural history and the Antarctic, and the entrance to what is, arguably, the early settlers' most precious gift to the modern city – **Christchurch Botanic Gardens** and **Hagley Park**. The 165ha (407-acre) park, the city's largest, has a golf course among its facilities. The native plants in the vast botanic gardens were gleaned from all over the country, and range from regenerating bush to a rose garden. The gardens are particularly lovely in the evening light, when the low rays shine through the trees' branches and cast reflections on the lake.

TAKING A BREAK

You can get a fine cup of coffee on ambient New Regent Street, a pedestrian zone with art deco-influenced facades.

✚ 207 E4 (see panel ➤ 138)

Visitor Information Centre
✉ Old Chief Post Office, Cathedral Square West ☎ (03) 379 9629; www.christchurchnz.com ⏺ Dec–Apr daily 8:30–6, May–Nov 8:30–5

Christchurch Cathedral
✉ Cathedral Square ☎ (03) 366 0046; www.christchurchcathedral.co.nz ⏺ Daily 9–5 🍴 Cafe ($) ⓦ Free; balconies and spire: inexpensive

Christchurch Art Gallery
✉ Worcester Boulevard ☎ (03) 941 7300; www.christchurchartgallery.org.nz ⏺ Thu–Tue 10–5, Wed 10–9 🍴 Cafe and wine bar ($$) Wed–Thu 9:30am–10pm, Fri–Sat 9:30am–11pm, Sun–Tue 9:30–5 ⓦ Free

Christchurch Arts Centre
✉ 2 Worcester Boulevard ☎ (03) 363 2836; www.artscentre.org.nz ⏺ Information office: daily 9:30–5

Canterbury Museum
✉ Rolleston Avenue, at Botanic Garden entrance ☎ (03) 366 5000; www.cantmus.govt.nz ⏺ Oct–Mar daily 9–5:30; Apr–Sep 9–5 ⓦ Donation; discovery centre and exhibitions: inexpensive

Christchurch Botanic Gardens
✉ Rolleston Avenue ☎ (03) 941 8999; www.ccc.govt.nz ⏺ Botanic Gardens: daily 7am–one hour before sunset; conservatories: daily 10:15–4; information centre: Mon–Fri 9–4, Sat–Sun 10:15–4 ⓦ Free

---

CHRISTCHURCH: INSIDE INFO

Top tips Trams travel regularly along a 2.5km (1.5-mile) loop that takes in all inner-city attractions. Passes (moderate; valid for two consecutive days) are available from the conductor and you can hop on and off as you please.
■ The region's **dry northwesterly winds** are similar to Europe's föhn and can cause headaches for some people.

Hidden gems Christchurch is known as **the garden city**. Visit Mona Vale gardens, or walk through Riccarton Bush, one of the last remnants of native lowland forest in Canterbury and the site of the first European settlement.

2 Banks Peninsula

Banks Peninsula was once an island and, although it has been connected to the mainland for thousands of years, it has retained an independent spirit and a distinctive landscape, with many secluded bays and golden beaches.

The biggest settlement, **Akaroa**, has a distinct Gallic flavour, with street names such as Rue Jolie and Rue Lavaud, the L'Aube hill as a backdrop and a romantic atmosphere reminiscent of a fishing village on the Côte d'Azur. French whaling captain Jean Langlois fell in love with the peninsula when he landed here in 1838 and promptly negotiated a land sale with the resident Maori chiefs. When he returned with French settlers two years later, British officials had claimed sovereignty under the Treaty of Waitangi (➤ 10). The French stayed, nevertheless, and left an indelible mark on the town.

It's fun just to walk Akaroa's narrow picturesque streets, to sample local food and wine or to enjoy some of the water activities available. In summer, a catamaran cruise of the Akaroa harbour is particularly special because large pods of New Zealand's smallest dolphin, the Hector's dolphin, come into the sheltered waters to calve and will often swim alongside the boat.

Take a Road Trip

Although there is public transport to Akaroa, it is worth driving the 85km (53 miles) from Christchurch so that you can stop for sweeping views over the peninsula and to explore some of the hidden bays. Take State Highway 75 through

A Maori statue guards the shores of Akaroa

Taitapu to **Little River**, about halfway between Christchurch and Akaroa. This sleepy township near the head of **Lake Forsyth** is worth a brief stop for a coffee, before the road narrows and starts winding up to the hilltop. The views from the summit are stunning, sweeping across the entire Akaroa harbour and the small Onawe peninsula. Remnants of the once lush native forests still nestle in the humid gullies.

Volcanic Beginnings

From this viewpoint it becomes obvious that Banks Peninsula was born from a violent volcanic eruption. The land flows down in all directions to the sea, which has sculpted the coastline into rocky cliffs and sandy beaches and filled the crater to create long, narrow Akaroa harbour. The cogwheel-shaped volcanic cone was originally an island, until the land bridge was formed by shingle and debris, washed down from the Southern Alps and onto the Canterbury Plains, about 20,000 years ago. In 1769, Captain James Cook mistakenly named it Banks Island because the isthmus connecting the peninsula to the mainland was so low; the truth was discovered by Europeans only in 1809, when another explorer, Captain Chase, tried to sail through the gap.

The volcanic beginnings of Banks Peninsula can be seen in the landscape

The Summit and Coastal Routes

At the hilltop, the road forks: SH75 on the right is the coastal route – the faster way of getting to Akaroa – and the other route is the Summit Road, which skirts the peninsula's spine with turn-offs to several smaller bays. As you drop down to the coast on SH75, the first bay you'll find is **Barrys Bay**, where, on alternate days from October to May, you can watch cheese being produced by the cheesemaker there, and sample and buy the finished product (tel: (03) 304 5809).

On the way back to Christchurch, take the **Summit Road** and explore **Le Bons Bay**, a safe and sheltered beach with a scattering of holiday homes, or secluded **Okains Bay**, with its small museum that houses an impressive collection of ancient Maori treasures. Take the turn-off to **Birdlings Flat**, about

8km (5 miles) from Little River. You may find semi-precious stones among the pebbles on the long and untamed beach, and it's a beautiful place to watch the sun set over the ocean.

TAKING A BREAK

Turn left into the Grehan Valley as you enter Akaroa to get to **Tree Crop Farm** (Grehan Valley Road, tel: (03) 304 7158), a quirky place with extensive wild gardens crossed with footpaths. The entry charge includes a coffee or berry juice. The farm also offers romantic accommodation in a historic 1850s cottage or in huts in the grounds.

➕ 207 F4

Visitor Information Centre
✉ Post Shop Building, 80 rue Lavaud, Akaroa ☎ (03) 304 8600; www.akaroa.com ⏰ Oct–Mar daily 9–5, Apr–Sep Mon–Fri 9–5, Sat–Sun 9–4

Akaroa Harbour Cruises
✉ Main Wharf, Akaroa ☎ (03) 304 7641; www.canterburycat.co.nz ⏰ Mid Oct–mid Apr daily 11, 1:30, mid Dec–mid Mar 11, 1:30, 3:40 💲 Expensive

Hinewai Reserve
✉ Long Bay Road, RD3, Akaroa ☎ (03) 304 8501
⏰ Casual walks: 24 hours 💲 Free; donations to Maurice White Native Forest Trust ❓ Bring sturdy footwear for track walking. Lodge available overnight by arrangement

Akaroa Museum
✉ 71 rue Lavaud, Akaroa ☎ (03) 304 1013 ⏰ Mid Oct–Easter daily 10:30–4:30, rest of year 10:30–4
💲 Inexpensive

Grassy hilltops provide excellent grazing

BANKS PENINSULA: INSIDE INFO

Top tips Banks Peninsula has a comprehensive network of roads for a rural area, but the Summit Road is narrow and windy, so **drive with care**. Some roads may be difficult to negotiate after rain.
■ Pick up a copy of **Akaroa: An Historic Walk** (inexpensive) from Akaroa Information Centre on Rue Lavaud. It gives details of more than 40 historic buildings in the area.

Hidden gem Hinewai Reserve is a 1,050ha (2,594-acre) conservation project southeast of Akaroa with good walking tracks through remnants of native forest. A series of 31 other small reserves is scattered over the peninsula; some are easy to explore on foot. Ask for a map at the visitor information centre.

In more depth Visit the Akaroa Museum to find out more about the area's history and culture. Three historic buildings, including Langlois-Eteveneaux House, which was partly made in France, make up some of the complex.

3 Aoraki/Mount Cook

New Zealand's highest mountain rises from the icy landscape of Aoraki/Mount Cook National Park. The pyramid of Aoraki – "cloud-piercer" – dominates all the land around it.

The Mount Cook lily

More than one-third of the park's 700sq km (270sq miles) is covered in permanent snow or ice. Of New Zealand's 27 peaks over 3,000m (10,000 feet), 19 are huddled together in this area and Aoraki/Mount Cook, which towers above other peaks at 3,754m (12,313 feet), is the centrepiece of this sparkling landscape.

Mount Cook might not be as high as many peaks in the European Alps, but it's a difficult mountain to climb, being exposed to ferociously rapid weather changes along the Main Divide, the mountainous chain that separates the eastern and western coasts of the South Island. It is even a difficult mountain to see: as its Maori name suggests, it often has its head in the clouds. Most visitors get only a drive-by glimpse of the giant as they travel from Christchurch to Queenstown, but if you enjoy walks and outdoor activities, it's worth exploring the area around Mount Cook village.

FEELING PEAKY
The first people to ascend the formidable peak were locals Jack Clarke, Tom Fyfe and George Graham, who reached the summit on 25 Dec, 1894, but several famous climbers, including Sir Edmund Hillary (➤ 24), have since sharpened their skills on Aoraki/Mount Cook.

Take to the Skies
For a good view of the mountains, take a **ski plane** from Mount Cook Airport, near Mount Cook village, or a **helicopter** from Glentanner Park, about 15 minutes from the village. You can choose different routes through the national park but all will give you stunning views of the massive plateau from which Aoraki rises, with the Tasman Glacier (➤ 154), the largest ice flow in the southern hemisphere outside Antarctica, along its side. Whichever way you go up, you can **land on a glacier** and go for a short walk in the snow. Once the engines are turned off, the silence can be quite eerie.

Explorations by Water

If you want to go **boating on a glacial lake**, join a guided sea-kayaking tour or take a trip in a small, motorized inflatable to explore the lake at the mouth of the **Mueller Glacier**. The glacier flows into the **Hooker Valley** at Mount Cook village and forms a small lake, eventually narrowing into a river. The water is a milky azure from the "glacial flour" or dust ground off the mountains as the frozen river flows over them. As the glacier slowly melts, large chunks of ice also break off (you can explore some of these) and you may also see some avalanches crashing down from the surrounding peaks.

A glacial lake in Mount Cook National Park

TAKING A BREAK

The **Sir Edmund Hillary Alpine Centre** at The Hermitage Hotel has a self-service cafe/bar serving light meals and drinks.

✚ 206 C4

Park Visitor Centre
✉ 1 Larch Grove, Mount Cook village ☎ (03) 435 1186; www.doc.govt.nz 🕐 Oct–Mar daily 8:30–6; Apr–Sep 8:30–5

Mount Cook Ski Planes
✉ Mount Cook Airport, Mount Cook village ☎ (03) 430 8034, www.mtcookskiplanes.com

Glacier Sea Kayaking
✉ Trips depart from the Old Mountaineers' Café and Bar, next

door to the visitor centre ❓ Book at the Park Visitor Centre, YHA or Hermitage Hotel ☎ (03) 435 1890; www.mtcook.com

Helicopter Line
✉ Glentanner Park, Mount Cook village ☎ (03) 435 1801; www.helicopter.co.nz

Alan's 4WD Tours
❓ 2.5-hour trip to the flats above Tasman Glacier; information or bookings at the Park Visitor Centre, Hermitage Hotel or YHA ☎ (03) 435 1601; www.mountcooktours.co.nz

AORAKI/MOUNT COOK: INSIDE INFO

Top tips Mount Cook village is an excellent base for short walks: pick up a brochure at the Park Visitor Centre. Be sure to check the weather before you set out, as it can change quickly.

■ There are no banking facilities and few shops in the national park, so **bring food and cash**.

In more depth The Hermitage Hotel (► 155) is home to the Sir Edmund Hillary Alpine Centre, with a 3D movie on Aoraki/Mount Cook, a planetarium, a museum dedicated to the region and to Sir Ed (► 24), and a cafe and bar.

4 The West Coast

On a calm and sunny day, the West Coast is a wonderland of snowy peaks, glistening lakes and lush rainforests. But "The Coast" – as New Zealanders refer to the narrow strip of land between the Tasman Sea and the South Island's mountainous spine – also experiences some ferocious weather, bringing more than 5,000mm (200 inches) of rain a year and sometimes whipping the surf into a mighty ocean.

Westland could be called Wetland. The area's rainfall is surpassed only by Fiordland (► 166–168), New Zealand's largest national park, with which south Westland shares the honour of World Heritage status. You can often see clouds looming over the western side of the mountains as soon as you reach Arthur's Pass (► 154). They rarely reach the golden hills on the eastern side of the Main Divide, dissolving instead into rain as they reach the wall of mountains. The rain however is what gives the coast its exuberant freshness and vigour in the form of the region's forests, pastures, lakes and imposing glaciers.

Greymouth's Fortunes
Travelling from Christchurch, you meet the coast at **Greymouth**, a port on the River Grey and the region's largest town, with about 10,000 inhabitants. Founded on gold and continued on coal, it now survives on timber, fishing and tourism. Although not exciting, it is a handy base for exploring the area. Follow SH6 south towards Hokitika, and about 10km (6 miles) south of Greymouth you will see the turn-off to **Shantytown**, a re-creation of an 1880 gold-rush town, where you can still pan for gold – great for children.

Hokitika and the Landscape Beyond
In **Hokitika**, about 40km (25 miles) south of Greymouth, the memorial clock tower marks the town centre and there's

On a calm day perfect reflections are cast on the waters of Lake Matheson

a scattering of arts and crafts studios along Tancred and Revell streets. Several stone- and bone-carvers and glass-blowers have opened their workshops to the public and you can watch your souvenirs evolve in their hands. This is also where the annual Wildfoods Festival (➤ 12) takes place.

South of Hokitika the scenery becomes grander and the population sparser. The mountain ranges rise gradually as you approach the **Aoraki/Mount Cook massif**, with New Zealand's highest peaks, Aoraki/Mount Cook (➤ 147–148) and Mount Tasman. The road moves away from the ocean to wind through pastureland, past glacier-carved lakes and along wind-battered rainforests. Trees along this coastal seam have a distinct eastward lean, their branches reaching for the mountains.

The Southern Alps' Glaciers

After about 150km (90 miles) you'll reach the Southern Alps' glacier region, an impressive vista of ragged mountains with large snowfields and ice walls. There are more than 60 glaciers in the Westland National Park alone, and about 3,000 throughout the Southern Alps, but most are inaccessible to anybody but mountaineers. **Franz Josef and Fox glaciers**, however, stretch their icy tongues so far down the ranges they could almost lick the sea.

> **TRAMPING**
> Fox Glacier is a short drive from the mirroring waters of **Lake Matheson** and the untamed beauty of **Gillespies Beach** (➤ 187–189).

If you have never seen a glacier up close it is worth walking for a few minutes to get a good view of the frozen pinnacles, crevasses and ice falls. Pick up information about guided walks and scenic flights at the information centres at Franz Josef or at Fox village, 25km (16 miles) further south. These are both tiny resort towns with just a main street lined with eateries and tour-operators' shops. The car park for the Franz Josef Glacier is 5km (3 miles) inland from the main road, and the first lookout is a 20-minute return walk. At the larger Fox Glacier, you'll find a car park 4km (2.5 miles) from the main road and similar options, from short walks to a one-hour excursion to the glacier's terminal face.

The ever-moving Franz Josef Glacier

TAKING A BREAK

The **Lake Mahinapua Hotel** (tel: (03) 755 8500) is just south of Hokitika, on SH6 opposite the turn-off to Lake Mahinapua. It's a typical colonial building, plain inside, but the pub is a great place to drink with the locals and enjoy some salty West Coast repartee.

🚹 207 D5

Greymouth Visitor Information Centre

🚹 207 D5 ✉ Corner of Herbert and Mackay streets ☎ (03) 768 5101; www.greydistrict.co.nz
🕐 Nov–Mar Mon–Fri 8:30–6, Sat 9–5, Sun and public holidays 10–5; Apr–Oct Mon–Fri 8:30–5:30, Sat 9–5, Sun and public holidays 10–4

Shantytown

🚹 207 D5 ✉ Rutherglen Road, Greymouth ☎ (03) 762 6634, 0800 742 689 toll free; www.shantytown.co.nz 🍴 Everybody's Tearooms ($) 🕐 Daily 8:30–5 💵 Moderate

Franz Josef Visitor Centre

🚹 207 D4 ✉ Main Road, Franz Josef ☎ (03) 752 0796; www.doc.govt.nz 🕐 Nov–Mar daily 8:30–6; Apr–Oct 8:30–5

Franz Josef Glacier Guides

🚹 207 D4 ✉ Main Road, Franz Josef ☎ (03) 752 0763, 0800 484 337 toll free; www.franzjosefglacier.com 🕐 Daily, weather-dependent

Guiding Fox Glacier

🚹 206 C4 ✉ Main Road, Fox Glacier ☎ (03) 751 0825, 0800 111 600 toll free; www.foxguides.co.nz 🕐 Daily, weather-dependent

White Heron Sanctuary Tours

🚹 207 D4 ✉ SH6 (PO Box 19), Whataroa ☎ (03) 753 4120, 0800 523 456 toll free; www.whiteherontours.co.nz 🕐 Heron tours daily during breeding season late Oct–early Mar; nature tours and jet boating year-round 💵 Expensive

---

WEST COAST: INSIDE INFO

Top tips Consider joining **a guided walk or helicopter flight to the glacier surface**. No mountain experience is required and you will be equipped with a pair of boots, instep crampons and an alpenstock.
- If you are planning a glacier excursion, or even just approaching one, bring warm clothing and stay behind the safety barriers.

Hidden gems The road between Hokitika and the glaciers passes several **glacial lakes**. Lake Mahinapua, the first glacial lake on the route south from Hokitika (from SH6, turn right to Ruatapu), is fringed by tall stands of kahikatea. About 40km (25 miles) further south, SH6 runs along the shores of Lake Ianthe, which offers picnic spots and a small campsite. Further south, about 10km (6 miles) before Franz Josef Glacier, is Lake Mapourika.

In more depth Visit the **breeding area of the kotuku**, the majestic white herons, which nest in New Zealand only at Okarito Lagoon. The breeding area is accessible only for guided tours as the birds are protected. The best time to visit is between November and February, when the birds are on their nests. You can organize a guide at White Heron Sanctuary Tours at the address above.

At Your Leisure

A sculpture in the grounds of Nga Hau E Wha

5 Nga Hau E Wha – National *Marae*

(See panel ➤ 138). The *marae* is the South Island's largest Maori cultural centre and offers introductions to Maori protocol, customs and history. Nga Hau E Wha stands for the four directions of the wind, signifing that the *marae* welcomes visitors from all corners of the world.

Tours of two carved buildings – the *whare nui* (meeting house) and *whare wananga* (house of learning) – are available, as are cultural evenings and *hangi*.

➕ 207 E4 ✉ 250 Pages Road, Christchurch
☎ (03) 388 7685 🕐 Mon–Fri 8–4; cultural evenings: 6:45 🚌 5, from Cathedral Square
💰 Moderate. Booking essential; tours require numbers of 20 or more to run

6 Willowbank Wildlife Reserve

On the edge of Christchurch city near the airport is the Willowbank Wildlife Reserve, which through its exhibits explains the natural history of New Zealand and the impact introduced species have had on the indigenous wildlife. Highlights include the Alpine Walk-Through Aviary with its resident kea (alpine parrots), and the Nocturnal House, home to New Zealand's iconic bird, the kiwi. The park also takes part in the Department of Conservation's Kiwi Recovery Programme, hatching and rearing kiwi eggs to boost populations in the wild. Evenings are one of the best times to visit, when you can join a guided tour to see Willowbank's nocturnal inhabitants waking up for the night or join in the Ko Tane Maori cultural performance, before dining in the on-site restaurant.

➕ 207 E4 ✉ 60 Hussey Road, Christchurch
☎ (03) 359 6226; www.willowbank.co.nz
🕐 Daily 9:30am–10pm; guided evening nature tours: hourly 5:30–10; Ko Tane shows: 5:30, 6:30 🚌 11 💲 Expensive

7 Port Hills

The Port Hills separate Christchurch and its seaside suburb Sumner from Lyttelton port. They are the crater rim of a dead twin volcano, whose eruption created Lyttelton harbour and Banks Peninsula (➤ 144–146). They're the only significant elevation in Christchurch, offering views of beaches and the Canterbury Plains from the Summit Road.

Drive up Dyers Pass Road to find the Sign of the Takahe, a magnificent neo-Gothic restaurant. Completed in 1949, it was the first of a string of roadhouses planned from

Christchurch to Akaroa, although only four were built. At the top of the pass is the second, the Sign of the Kiwi, now a tearoom.

Further along Summit Road, there are views of the Avon-Heathcote Estuary, and of New Brighton Beach. Christchurch visitor information centre (➤ 143) has free maps of the Port Hills roads.
➕ 207 E4

8 Lyttelton

(See panel ➤ 138). The picturesque port of Lyttelton is connected to Christchurch by road and rail tunnels. It's best known for its castle-like Timeball Station, built in 1876 by local prisoners. The timeball was lowered each day to signal 1pm local time, enabling sailors to check the accuracy of their chronometers, used to calculate longitude. It was replaced by radio time signals in 1934. During the 1970s, the station was restored and is now one of only five worldwide in working order. Once again, the ball drops at 1pm each day.
➕ 207 E4

Visitor Information Centre
✉ 20 Oxford Street, Lyttelton ☎ (03) 328 9093; www.lytteltonharbour.info 🕐 Daily 9–5
🚌 28 from Christchurch Convention Centre

Lyttelton Timeball Station
✉ 2 Reserve Terrace, Lyttelton ☎ (03) 328 7311; www.timeball.co.nz 🚌 28 from Cathedral Square 🕐 Daily 10–5:30
💲 Inexpensive ⚠ Steep steps

9 Lake Tekapo

Lake Tekapo, between Christchurch and Aoraki/Mount Cook, is a lovely place for a break. The town has sweeping views over the glacier-fed lake; its radiant turquoise colour is thanks to minerals and dust deposited by the icy rivers from the Southern Alps.

The pretty little Church of the Good Shepherd beside the lake was built in the 1930s and is a memorial to the pioneer farmers of the Mackenzie Country.

Snow-capped Mount Rollerton, the highest peak in Arthur's Pass National Park

⑩ Tasman Glacier

The Tasman Glacier is the largest ice flow in the southern hemisphere outside Antarctica: it stretches for 27km (17 miles), and is 3km (2 miles) wide and 600m (1,968 feet) deep. Unusually, its last few kilometres are almost flat, and are covered with debris from its higher sections. The unsealed Tasman Valley Road ends at a car park about 8km (5 miles) from Mount Cook village, from where it is a 20-minute walk to a lookout point over the glacier's terminus. Guided tours are available – enquire at the visitor information centre at Mount Cook village (➤ 148).
🞤 206 C4

⑪ Castle Hill and Cave Stream

If you are driving to Arthur's Pass on SH73, take a break after about 110km (70 miles) to explore Castle Hill and Cave Stream. Limestone formations run through the length of the east coast of the South Island and in several places form bizarre-looking outcrops. Castle Hill features vast gardens of sculpted limestone, weathered into amazing shapes, including gargoyles and scallops. At Cave Stream, a small river has diverted underground and carved out a 362m (1,188-foot) tunnel. The cave is easily accessible, but you must go in a group with an experienced guide (tours are often organized by nearby accommodation). Don't walk into the cave during or after heavy rain.
🞤 207 E4 ✉ Signposted on SH73
☎ www.doc.govt.nz

⑫ Arthur's Pass

Just 90 minutes' drive from Christchurch, Arthur's Pass National Park is a 1,145sq km (442sq-mile) wilderness straddling the Southern Alps, which form a rugged spine along the length of South Island and separate the dry eastern coast from the temperate forests of the West Coast. It is a popular weekend destination for Christchurch residents, with skiing, hiking or mountaineering being popular pursuits. The main centre, Arthur's Pass village, is the starting point for many walks and is also a good place to have a break if you are on your way to the West Coast (➤ 149–151), either along SH73 or aboard the TranzAlpine train (➤ 28–30).
🞤 207 D4

Department of Conservation Visitor Centre
✉ SH73, Arthur's Pass ☎ (03) 318 9211; www.doc.govt.nz 🕐 Nov–Mar daily 8–5; rest of year 8:30–4:30 ❓ Information on park walks, maps and route guides; information panels on the history of the area and the natural history of the park; up-to-date online weather information

⑬ Punakaiki

Pancake rocks are the main feature of this small settlement, about 40km (25 miles) north of Greymouth. Stratified limestone stacks jut from the beach, and blowholes throw up columns of spray in rough weather. A 10-minute wheelchair-accessible track leads to geological forms weathered into curious shapes. Down the road, the 30-minute Truman Track leads through a coastal forest to reach the coastline. At low tide, walk down the beach past a succession of reefs, caves and waterfalls.
🞤 207 D5 ☎ www.punakaiki.co.nz

Where to…
Stay

Prices

Expect to pay for two people sharing a double room per night:

$ under NZ$200   **$$** NZ$200–$350   **$$$** over NZ$350

CHRISTCHURCH

See panel ▶ 138.

Beaufort House $$–$$$

Originally built in 1916 as a stately home for a prominent surgeon and city councillor, Beaufort House is a listed historic building with distinctive Gothic touches and furnished with antiques of the era. There are five stunning, spacious suites with large beds, flat-screen televisions and luxury fittings. There are several public rooms and a residents' bar. It is just a five-minute walk to Cathedral Square.

➕ 207 E4 ✉ 2 Latimer Square, Christchurch ☎ (03) 365 8847; www.beauforthouse.co.nz

The Château on the Park $–$$

This hotel is unashamedly romantic, with architecture reminiscent of a French chateau. The swimming pool is surrounded by lavender bushes, you cross a moat to get to the bar. Set in a residential suburb beside Hagley Park (▶ 142–143), it's a short drive from the city centre.

➕ 207 E4 ✉ 189 Deans Avenue, Riccarton ☎ (03) 348 8999; www.chateau-park.co.nz

The George Hotel $$$

A small luxury hotel on the banks of the Avon, The George has 53 deluxe rooms and suites with views over Hagley Park. Some bedrooms have balconies and spa baths and the Residence wing is set in a traditional English-style garden. The emphasis is on understated elegance and good service. The fine-dining Pescatore (▶ 156), which specializes in seafood, has been named one of New Zealand's top 10 restaurants, and the hotel's brasserie is renowned for its breakfasts.

➕ 207 E4 ✉ 50 Park Terrace ☎ (03) 379 4560; www.thegeorge.com

BANKS PENINSULA

Maison de la Mer $$–$$$

This elegant house in the centre of Akaroa has been beautifully restored in French country style and offers three luxurious suites, all with harbour and beach views. Upstairs are the Fleur de Lys suite, with a private sunroom, and the Provence suite, with a spa bath. The self-contained Boathouse has its own kitchen and deck. Breakfasts are included.

➕ 207 F4 ✉ 1 rue Benoit, Akaroa ☎ (03) 304 8907; www.maisondelamer.co.nz

AORAKI/MOUNT COOK

The Hermitage Hotel $–$$$

The spectacularly situated Hermitage is one of New Zealand's most famous hotels. The original hotel was destroyed in a flood in 1913; the second burned down in 1957. The present hotel consists of a stone alpine lodge, a new luxury wing, and a modern lodge, motel and chalets. For a spectacular view of Aoraki/Mount Cook, book one of the luxurious rooms in the Aoraki Wing or, in summer, a table at the Panorama Restaurant. There's a choice of restaurants and bars, a gift shop, sauna and tennis courts.

➕ 206 C4 ✉ Terrace Road, Mount Cook village ☎ (03) 435 1809, 0800 686 800 toll free; www.hermitage.co.nz

Where to...
Eat and Drink

Prices
Expect to pay per person for a three-course meal, excluding drinks:
$ under NZ$45 $$ NZ$45–$60 $$$ over NZ$60

CHRISTCHURCH

See panel ▶ 138.

Mona Vale $$

This is an elegant homestead restaurant/café set within the gardens beside the Avon River. Built as a private home at the turn of the 19th century, it is a popular restaurant, with indoor and alfresco seating. Try the famous Devonshire teas, or high tea on Tuesday afternoons. Evening group dining is available by prior arrangement.

✚ 207 E4 ⊠ 63 Fendalton Road, Christchurch ☎ (03) 348 9660; www.monavale.co.nz ⊘ Oct–Apr daily 9.30–5, May–Sep 9.30–4

Pescatore $$$

This iconic Christchurch restaurant within The George Hotel has panoramic views over Hagley Park. It is formal dining in a minimalist interior and is considered one of New Zealand's best contemporary dining experiences. Executive Chef Andrew Brown has created unique seasonal menus, which are matched with top vintages from Pescatore's wine list, honoured by *Wine Spectator* magazine as being one of the world's best restaurant lists.

✚ 207 E4 ⊠ 50 On Park ☎ (03) 371 0257; www.thegeorge.com/pescatore ⊘ Tue–Sat 6pm–late

Yamagen $$$

Yamagen offers the best of Japanese dining using the finest New Zealand produce and presented traditionally or with the flair of teppan-yaki cooking. The teppan chefs can cook up to 10 dishes at a time on the teppan grills in theatrical style. The atmosphere is exciting and fun for those sitting around the grill, or more intimate at your own table. Try the chilli chicken, which has been on the menu for 20 years.

✚ 207 E4 ⊠ Crowne Plaza, corner of Kilmore and Durham streets, Christchurch ☎ (03) 365 7799 ⊘ Sat–Thu 6–late, Fri 12–2.30, 6–late

BANKS PENINSULA

French Farm Winery and Restaurant $

Make a detour just to visit this striking French provincial-style building in its beautiful rural setting. Wines from the little vineyards in the valley are made on site and feature on the wine list. The a la carte menu includes salads with Akaroa salmon, local cheeses and platters to share. In summer, an alfresco restaurant serves wood-fired pizzas.

✚ 207 F4 ⊠ French Farm Valley Road, Duvauchelle ☎ (03) 304 5784; www.frenchfarm.co.nz ⊘ Sep–May daily 10–4

WEST COAST

Café de Paris $–$$

French chef Pierre Esquilat and his Kiwi wife Joy run this little bit of *Rive Gauche* on the West Coast. An airy cafe during the day, serving coffee and pastries and light lunches, it offers an a la carte menu in the evening. Look for classics like French onion soup, along with West Coast venison and wild pig.

✚ 207 D5 ⊠ 19 Tancred Street, Hokitika ☎ (03) 755 8933; www.cafedeparis.net.nz ⊘ Daily 7:30am–late

Where to...
Shop

CHRISTCHURCH

See panel ▶ 138.

City Centre

Christchurch's main shopping area is a pleasant network of pedestrian malls intersecting Colombo Street and fringing Cathedral Square. Between the Bus Exchange and the Avon River, **City Mall** is a landscaped pedestrian precinct that takes in parts of High and Cashel streets and arcades like **Shades Atrium** and the **Guthrey Centre**. Here you will find speciality shops, international chains, food courts, cafes, bookshops and department stores.

Ballantynes (corner of City Mall and Colombo Street, tel: (03) 379 7400) is a Christchurch institution,

an old-fashioned, family-run department store.

The High Street is a great place to browse for bargains in books and music, antiques, art and funky fashion. The precinct is also home to top designers **Victoria Black** (201–203 High Street, tel: (03) 379 1197) and **Workshop** (230 Tuam Street, tel: (03) 379 7305). Pick up picnic goods at **Copenhagen Bakery** (119 Armagh Street, tel: (03) 379 3935), which specializes in pastries and breads.

Sheepskins and knitwear, leather goods, All Blacks paraphernalia, and paua and greenstone (pounamu) jewellery can be found in the shops clustered around Cathedral Square. There's also a craft market here on Thursdays and Fridays. Nearby New Regent Street

boasts boutiques and cafes, built in Spanish Mission style.

The centre of New Zealand's high-tech sports and leisurewear industry, Christchurch is the home of labels such as Fairydown, Macpac, and Canterbury of New Zealand. Major outlets are **R & R Sport** (54 Lichfield Street, tel: (03) 365 2178), **Bivouac Outdoor** (661 Colombo Street, tel: (03) 366 3197), **Kathmandu** (40 Lichfield Street, tel: (03) 366 7148) and **Rugby Post** (97 Worcester Street, tel: (03) 365 4604). The **Swanndri Store & Outlet** (75 Clarence Street, Riccarton, tel: (03) 341 3945) has traditional bush shirts.

The **Arts Centre** (Worcester Boulevard, tel: (03) 366 0989), in the Gothic Revival buildings of the old Canterbury University, has galleries, shops, theatres, cinemas and cafes. Browse around the 30 art and craft outlets, where you can also meet the artists. The weekend **Arts Centre Market** has 80 stalls, with entertainment, crafts and food.

Suburbs

Merivale, north of the city, is a chic shopping centre, with 40 boutiques in **Merivale Mall** (189 Papanui Road, tel: (03) 355 9692), top designer fashion store **Quinns** (195 Papanui Road, tel: (03) 355 7349), and antiques shops, cafes and bars. **Traiteur** (corner of Aikmans and Papanui roads, tel: (03) 355 7750), is a European-style butchers.

The **Riccarton Rotary Market**, held on Sunday from 9am to 2pm at Riccarton Park Racecourse (Racecourse Road, tel: (03) 339 0011), has more than 300 stalls selling crafts, food, clothing, jewellery and bric-a-brac. **Dress Smart Hornby** (409 Main South Road, Hornby, tel: (03) 349 5750) has more than 50 stores, each with 30–70 per cent off normal prices.

Near the airport, **Untouched World** (155 Roydvale Avenue, tel: (03) 358 3809) is a striking complex of retail store, restaurant, garden and wine bar. It carries ethical clothing, products and food.

Where to...
Be Entertained

CHRISTCHURCH

See panel ▶ 138.

Look for listings in the Mega Guide section of *The Press* on Fridays and its Weekend Guide on Saturdays. For a lively night out, head for the area known as The Strip.

Arts

The Court Theatre (Arts Centre, Worcester Boulevard, tel: (03) 963 0870) usually has at least one production in season. The heritage **Isaac Theatre Royal** (145 Gloucester Street, tel: (03) 366 6326) is used by visiting theatre and dance companies. The **Town Hall** (86 Kilmore Street, tel: (03) 366 8899) is the venue for performances by **Southern Opera**

(tel: (03) 363 3131), **Christchurch Symphony** (tel: (03) 379 3886), the **Christchurch City Choir** (tel: (03) 366 6927) and visiting performers. Lunchtime concerts are held at the **Arts Centre Great Hall** (tel: (03) 363 2836) and the **Music Centre of Christchurch** (140 Barbadoes Street, tel: (03) 377 5000). For jazz, try **Fat Eddies** (179 Tuam Street, tel: (03) 943 2833), the **Twisted Hop** (6 Poplar Street, tel: (03) 962 3688), and the **Dux de Lux** (corner of Hereford and Montreal streets, tel: (03) 366 6919), which also hosts soul/reggae bands.

The **Christchurch Art Gallery** (▶ 142) and **CoCA** (66 Gloucester Street, tel: (03) 366 7261) specialize in New Zealand works. At the **Arts Centre** (2 Worcester Boulevard, tel: (03) 366 0989) you can watch

artisans creating works in a variety of media and then buy them direct.

Sports

Major rugby fixtures and test cricket are played at **AMI Stadium** (30 Stevens Street, tel: (03) 379 1765), and the **Canterbury Crusaders** (Super 14 rugby union) have a passionate local following. Book tickets through **Ticket Direct** (tel: 0800 224 224 toll free). For horse racing, go to **Riccarton Park Racecourse** (Racecourse Road, tel: (03) 366 0000), or catch the harness racing at **Addington Raceway** (Jack Hinton Drive, tel: (03) 338 9094). The Estuary at Ferrymead is good for windsurfing and parasailing, while Sumner has surf and swimming beaches. Canterbury rivers offer salmon fishing, jet boating and rafting. In the city, there's boating on the Avon. Head to the Port Hills for walks, mountain biking and paragliding.

Christchurch is 90-minutes' drive from the ski fields. **Mount Hutt**

(tel: (03) 302 8811) is the largest commercial field, or for a real Kiwi experience, try the club fields in the **Craigieburn ranges** (information/booking tel: (03) 318 8711), where the facilities are basic but you can stay overnight.

Golfers should try the city course in **Hagley Park** (tel: (03) 379 8279) or the 36-hole twin course at **Harewood** (371 McLeans Island Road tel: (03) 359 8843).

Wine and Beer Trails

Canterbury and Waipara (an hour's drive north of Christchurch) are distinctive wine-growing regions. Most wineries welcome visitors. Contact the visitor centre for a wine trail map, or join a half- or full-day guided tour with **Canterbury Wine Tours** (tel: (03) 315 7522).

Festivals

The arts, literature, jazz, comedy, buskers, flowers, wine and food, summertime – Christchurch has festivals for all of them, and more.

The Wild South

Getting Your Bearings

The southern regions of the South Island are often bypassed by visitors – yet they feature some of the wildest and most scenic places on Earth. Many of the more remote areas may have remained unexplored to this day, had it not been for a stampede of fortune seekers, attracted by the lure of gold.

Like moths heading for the flame, miners swarmed to the southern parts of New Zealand in the mid-19th century, abandoning the exhausted gold fields of California and New South Wales. Their picks and shovels shaped the landscape from Queenstown to Dunedin and their adventurous spirit is still alive in Queenstown, where you can challenge your body and mind amid stunning scenery – and then relax and enjoy the deserved rewards of fine food and wine.

Queenstown is also a gateway to Fiordland, New Zealand's largest national park and a World Heritage area of majestic mountains and seascapes. Towering peaks, icy lakes and sheer-sided fjords, carved by glaciers and separated by narrow, densely forested valleys, combine to create a landscape of unmatched grandeur.

The central part of the southern South Island is where the gold-miners' heritage is best preserved by a dry and sunny climate. Here, modern pioneers have successfully established the world's southernmost vineyards and orchards. On the southeastern coast, Dunedin combines Scottish charm with scenic appeal and easy access to rare wildlife.

Milford Sound · 2723m Mt Tutoko
Sutherland Sound · 1692m Mitre Peak · Milford Sound
George Sound · 1966m Barrier Peak
Charles Sound · 2036m Mt McDougall
Secretary Island · 1484m Double Peak · Lake Te Anau · Te Anau
Doubtful Sound · Te Anau Downs
2 Fiordland · Te Anau
Manapouri · Lake Manapouri · 94
Resolution Island
Lake Monowai
West Cape · Cameron Mountains · Lake Hauroko
Puysegur Point · Lake Poteriteri

★ Don't Miss

At Your Leisure

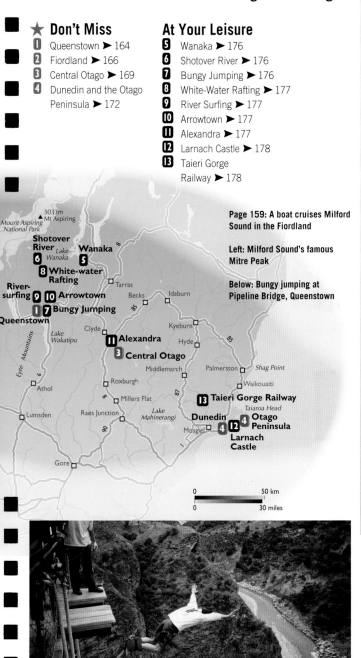

Page 159: A boat cruises Milford Sound in the Fiordland

Left: Milford Sound's famous Mitre Peak

Below: Bungy jumping at Pipeline Bridge, Queenstown

In Five Days

If you're not quite sure where to begin your travels, this itinerary recommends five practical and enjoyable days exploring the Wild South, taking in some of the best places to see using the Getting Your Bearings map on the previous page. For more information see the main entries.

Day 1

Start the morning by exploring the buzzing downtown of **1** **Queenstown** (➤ 164–165). Then walk along the shores of beautiful **Lake Wakatipu** (➤ 164) and join a cruise on the vintage steamship **TSS Earnslaw** (➤ 165). Have lunch at a cafe in town.

After lunch, drive to **6** **Shotover River** (➤ 176) to see the magnificent canyon or to test your nerves with a bungy jump. Then join a tour and explore the region's gold-digging history. Try **8** white-water rafting, jet boating (above), or **9** **river surfing** (➤ 177). Alternatively, visit the old gold-mining town of **10** **Arrowtown** (➤ 177) or the family attractions in **5** **Wanaka** (➤ 176).

In the evening catch the **Skyline gondola** (➤ 165) for night-time views of the lake and city. Have dinner at one of the restaurants downtown or visit the nearby Gibbston Valley Winery (➤ 180).

Day 2

If you want to experience the scenic road to **Milford** (➤ 194–196), fly to Te Anau and drive from there. Otherwise, fly directly to Milford and spend the day exploring **2** **Fiordland** and the majestic **Milford Sound** (➤ 166–168). Join a cruise to see the Fiordland crested penguins and resident

dolphins, and to get close to Mitre Peak and the 146m (479-foot) **Stirling Falls** (➤ 167). Other activities at Milford Sound include kayaking excursions and a trip to an underwater observatory to view Fiordland's awe-inspiring marine life. Return to Te Anau in the evening.

Day 3

Drive through ruggedly scenic **3 Central Otago** (➤ 169–171) and visit orchards or vineyards to taste the produce of New Zealand's fruit bowl. Stop in small rural places such as **Cromwell**, **Clyde** and **11 Alexandra** (➤ 177–178) for meal breaks and to explore the area's gold-rush history. Continue driving to the wildlife capital, **4 Dunedin** (➤ 172–175).

Day 4

Explore the southern city's Victorian architecture and Scottish heritage. Spend the morning investigating the Octagon, St Paul's Cathedral, the Dunedin Public Art Gallery and the University of Otago campus. Take the train journey along the **13 Taieri Gorge** (➤ 178) in the afternoon.

Day 5

Explore the untamed beauty of the **4 Otago Peninsula** (➤ 174–175), with its seaside towns and wildlife. Visit **12 Larnach Castle** (left, ➤ 178) and the royal albatross colony at **Taiaroa Head** (➤ 174). On the way back, join a tour to see yellow-eyed penguins, or walk to Sandfly Bay to watch the birds return from the ocean and waddle up to their nests. Take a break at the pretty town of **Portobello** (➤ 174).

① Queenstown

For a few crazy years after the discovery of gold here in 1862, Queenstown's fortunes were extracted from the Shotover River. But, with its rugged beauty and wild waters, the river has become Queenstown's modern gold mine, and the gold rush has given way to the adrenalin rush.

Queenstown is a magnet for thrill seekers. Every year it welcomes a million international visitors, most coming to part with their money so that they can swoop down a river in a raft, whizz off in a jetboat, or take a gut-wrenching freefall or hair-raising helicopter ride. With ubiquitous tour operators promising adventure activities ranging from bungy jumping to snowboarding, the alpine resort buzzes all year round (see At Your Leisure, ➤ 176–178 for individual recommendations). Queenstown is only the size of a sprawling village, but it has a cosmopolitan atmosphere and rivals the capital Wellington with its variety of downtown cafes and restaurants.

Skippers Canyon

There's a proud gold-mining heritage too. Of all the Wakatipu diggings, the most reliable was **Skippers Canyon**, a beautiful gorge cut by the Shotover into soft schist about 27km (17 miles) from Queenstown. The area around Skippers was still being dredged for gold in 1992, but now only the school building and cemetery remain. The last gold digger, Joe Scheib, established **Skippers Park** (➤ 176), and his family continues to gather gold-rush relics and explain the history of gold mining in the area at Winky's Museum.

Bungy jumping is just one of the high-adrenaline sports you can try in Queenstown

Picture Perfect Boat Trips

Queenstown's enviable position on the shores of **Lake Wakatipu**, framed by the majestic Southern Alps, means that

some of New Zealand's most picturesque scenery is within reach. So, if you are looking for something less energetic, take a cruise on the vintage steamship **TSS Earnslaw**. The ship has been ploughing Lake Wakatipu since 1912, transporting goods for run holders (farmers) and conveying passengers. You can explore the engine room and fireboxes, browse old photographs or just enjoy the stunning scenery. The *Earnslaw* makes daily excursions to a high country farm at Walter Peak, where you can join a farm tour, have a barbecue lunch or go for a horse trek. A gondola ride up **Bob's Peak** is a perfect finale to an action- and scenery-filled day. Evening light colours the view across the city, Lake Wakatipu and Coronet Peak, and the Remarkables to the Cecil and Walter peaks.

A tour boat powers through Shotover Gorge passing beneath Edith Cavell Bridge

TAKING A BREAK

Try some wholesome foods, check your email and hang out with the cool crowd at funky **Vudu Café** (23 Beach Street, tel: (03) 442 5357; www.vudu.co.nz).

✚ 206 B3

Queenstown Visitor Information Centre
✉ Clocktower Building, cnr Shotover and Camp streets ☎ (03) 442 4100; www.queenstown-vacation.com ⏰ Dec–Mar daily 7:30–6:30; Apr–Nov 7:30–6

TSS *Earnslaw*
✉ Steamer Wharf, end of Shotover Street ☎ (03) 249 7416, 0800 656 501 toll free; www.realjourneys.co.nz ⏰ Oct–mid Apr daily 10, 12, 2, 4, 6, 8, May–Sep 12, 2, 4 💲 Expensive

Skyline Gondola
✉ Brecon Street ☎ (03) 441 0101; www.skyline.co.nz ⏰ Daily 9–late 💲 Expensive

---

WILD SOUTH: INSIDE INFO

Top tip If you want to try **white-water rafting** but aren't so sure about the risks, opt for the **Kawarau River** rather than the Shotover. The Kawarau is a high-volume river with no exposed rocks in the rapids and is therefore gentler.

Hidden gem Queenstown's gardens rarely feature in tourist brochures but they are worth a visit. Extensive lawns and rose gardens mix with sports grounds on a small peninsula on the eastern side of Queenstown Bay, off Park Street.

In more depth Taste some of the award-winning wines from this southern-most wine-growing region. Pick up a wine trail map from the visitor centre.

2 Fiordland

Fiordland is pure wilderness. The best way to discover the raw beauty of New Zealand's largest national park is to explore Milford Sound. Brooding and serene, it's the most northern of Fiordland's 14 glacier-carved fjords and the only one accessible by road. Although Milford Sound and its landmark Mitre Peak are often photographed, the mountains, rainforests and waterfalls still leave visitors in awe.

The South Island's southwestern tip is New Zealand's least explored part, and is one of the greatest wildernesses of the southern hemisphere. Together with the Westland/ Tai Poutini (► 149), Mount Aspiring and Aoraki/Mount Cook (► 147–148) national parks, Fiordland makes up the World Heritage Area called **Te Wahipounamu** – "the place of greenstone". The scenery is the result of over 500 million years of sculpting, with the landscape relentlessly ground, split, pressurized and washed down by the elements.

A Natural Wonderland – Milford Sound

Te Wahipounamu covers 10 per cent of New Zealand's total area and most of its wilderness is difficult, sometimes almost impossible, to reach. **Milford Sound's** dramatic splendour provides a window to this natural wonderland. You can reach

Virgin forest clings to the sheer mountain slopes in Milford Sound

Milford by air, road or on foot. The sound is the end point of the Milford Track, a four-day walk established by 19th-century pioneers who discovered New Zealand's highest waterfall, the **Sutherland Falls**, and who were the first to cross overland to Milford. The track is extremely popular, so numbers are strictly limited and accommodation is only in huts along the route (no camping is permitted). You will have to organize the walk well ahead, particularly during the summer months.

The road to Milford (➤ 194–196) is a spectacular alpine drive, with many

Visitors can begin to grasp the vastness of the Fiordland from boat trips

points of interest and short nature walks along the 120km (74 miles) from Te Anau. The road is open to campervans and trailers, but presents challenging driving: it is sometimes closed because of avalanche danger or high winds, so check with the **Fiordland Visitor Information Centre** in Te Anau.

All Aboard

After the remoteness of the journey, the bustle of Milford's main bus terminal and car park may come as a bit of a shock. Milford's small wharf is the departure point for all cruises, which vary from **one-hour boat trips** to **overnight voyages** (➤ 168). The exact route depends on weather conditions, but generally each trip will take you to Milford Sound's mouth and a short distance out onto the Tasman Sea. On the way, the boats pass below towering **Mitre Peak** (1,692m/5,550 feet) and cruise close to lush rainforests that cling to the sound's sheer rock walls. Chances are that bottlenose dolphins will join the boat within a short distance of the wharf; sightings of seals and Fiordland crested penguins are also common. Weather permitting, the ship will be steered under the magnificent **Stirling Falls**, which drop sheer into the sea.

A Rich Ecosystem

Thanks to a top layer of fresh water, courtesy of the phenomenal 6,000mm (235 inches) of annual rainfall, Milford Sound is a special ecosystem below the surface, as well as above. The relatively warm, tea-coloured top layer allows rare marine organisms, such as black coral, to grow at shallower depths than elsewhere, and you can get a glimpse of them at the **Milford Deep** in Harrison's Cove, accessible by cruise. Here, you descend 10m (30 feet) to the viewing room, whose large windows give outstanding **close-ups of the marine life** at a depth that would otherwise be inaccessible. If that isn't enough splendid scenery, you can fly back to Queenstown and see the entire national park below.

TAKING A BREAK

Walk to Bowen Falls, about 10 minutes from the wharf, to have a **picnic at Cemetery Point**. The area was named after its mounds of debris brought from the falls, which resemble graves. However, there are actually three real graves there, containing fatalities from the old whaling and sealing days.

➕ 206 A2

Fiordland Visitor Information Centre

➕ 206 B2 ✉ Lakefront Drive, Te Anau ☎ (03) 249 7924; www.doc.govt.nz 🕐 Nov–Apr daily 8:30–6, May–Oct 8:30–4:30 🚌 SH94 to Te Anau branches off the main Invercargill to Queenstown Road (SH6). Intercity offers regular bus services to Te Anau

Milford Sound's Mitre Peak

Real Journeys

➕ 206 B2 ✉ Lakefront Drive, Te Anau ☎ (03) 249 7416, 0800 656 501 toll-free; www.realjourneys.co.nz 🕐 Daily 💷 Expensive ❓ Bus tours, flights and cruises of Milford and Doubtful sounds and Lake Manapouri depart from Milford Sound, Te Anau and Queenstown; booking essential

Milford Sound Red Boat Cruises

➕ 206 B3 ✉ Milford Wharf, Milford Sound ☎ (03) 441 1137, 0800 264 536 toll-free; www.redboats.co.nz 🕐 Daily 💷 Expensive

Mitre Peak Cruises

➕ 206 B3 ✉ Visitor Terminal, Milford Sound ☎ (03) 249 8110; 0800 744 633 toll free; www.mitrepeak.com 🕐 Daily 💷 Expensive

---

FIORDLAND: INSIDE INFO

Top tips Milford Sound changes its mood as quickly as the weather, so **bring rain gear and sun protection**. Don't forget an **insect repellent**, as sandflies can be a nuisance throughout Fiordland.

■ Consider a **coach-cruise-fly combination** to get the best out of a short visit. There are a number of operators who offer trips from Te Anau or Queenstown.

Hidden gem Doubtful Sound, further south, will appeal to those looking for an experience with fewer companions. Doubtful is not as easily accessible and can only be reached by crossing Lake Manapouri by boat and taking a bus over Wilmot Pass, but its unspoiled and remote wilderness makes up for the effort.

In more depth Overnight cruises will give you an idea of Milford Sound after daytime visitors have gone – and you might hear an unforgettable dawn chorus.

3 Central Otago

Central Otago stretches out across a rugged plateau sheltered by the Southern Alps. The wide, open landscape is fringed only by rolling foothills and luminous skies. There is something romantic about "Central", with its Tuscan-style golden hills and tiny villages, old stone buildings and gold-rush relics.

GOLDEN OPPORTUNITY
Central Otago's gold rush isn't over yet, and the Macraes mining company still extracts about 5 tonnes of gold each year.

Summer temperatures can climb well over 30°C (86°F) and parch the landscape, while in winter they regularly drop below freezing and the foothills get a dusting of snow. The arid climate has helped preserve many gold-mining remnants, and provides ideal conditions for fruit growing and viticulture.

Hit the Road

Plan at least a day to cover the 280km (174 miles) between Queenstown (➤ 164–165) and Dunedin (➤ 172–175), allowing time for stops. Several old gold-mining sites along the way are worth exploring, as are some of the wineries and orchards. The banks of the **Clutha River** provide ideal picnic spots and short walks.

On your way out of Queenstown, stop at the visitor information centre for a guide to **Central Otago's wineries** and a map of the **Otago Goldfields Heritage Trail**, which links more than 20 sites with gold-mining history.

Arrowtown and the rolling foothills of the Central Otago plateau

From Queenstown, follow State Highway 6 along the Kawarau River. If you want to explore one of the best-preserved Chinese gold-mining settlements, make a short detour to charming **Arrowtown** (► 177); otherwise, drive along the **Kawarau Gorge** to see the river's **Roaring Meg rapids** and stunning canyon. About 18km (11 miles) from Queenstown you will pass another gold-rush legacy – a stone-piered suspension bridge, which was built in 1880 and today doubles as a platform for bungy jumpers (► 176–177).

Chinese prospectors once lived in these small huts

Visiting Cromwell and Clyde

The steep slopes of the gorge are in stark contrast to the flat valley area of **Gibbston**, planted with row after row of grapevines, and the expansive **Cromwell Flats**. **Cromwell**, about 50 minutes from Queenstown, sits at the confluence of the Clutha and Kawarau rivers. When gold was discovered here in 1862, several thousand miners arrived within days and transformed the settlement. More recently, parts of Cromwell disappeared under Lake Dunstan, when the **Clyde Dam** was built as part of the Clutha River hydropower scheme. Many historic huts had to be painstakingly removed and re-erected in what is now called **Old Cromwell**, a popular attraction. Along SH6 is **The Big Picture**, which features an interactive film about local winemakers, tastings and lessons on how to distinguish between wine aromas.

From Cromwell, State Highway 8 will take you to **Clyde**, a small town whose streets are lined with 19th-century stone buildings, and **Alexandra**, a pleasant town on the banks of the Clutha and the district's commercial hub (► 177–178).

Along the Clutha River

From here you can either follow SH8 or take SH85, nicknamed **the Pigroot**, to Dunedin (► 172–175). The Pigroot winds through rolling hills and sleepy townships to reach the dramatic **Maniototo Plains**. The faster way to Dunedin is along SH8 and the mighty **Clutha**, New Zealand's largest river. The Clutha is 87km (54 miles) shorter than the Waikato River in the North Island but it carries almost twice as much water. Between Alexandra and Roxburgh, the Clutha flows through a narrow gorge that can only be seen from a boat or a foot track, but even a short walk provides some stunning views.

TAKING A BREAK

Speargrass Inn (tel: (03) 449 2192), between Alexandra and Roxburgh, offers rooms, food and crafts.

✛ 206 C2

Visitor Information Centre
✛ 206 C2 ✉ 21 Centennial Avenue, Alexandra ☎ (03) 448 9515; www.centralotagonz.com 🕐 Nov–Mar daily 9–6; Apr–Oct 9–5

The Big Picture
✛ 206 C3 ✉ Corner of Sandflat Road and SH6, Cromwell ☎ (03) 445 4052; www.bigpicturewine.com 🕐 Daily 9–6 💷 Moderate

Old Cromwell Town
✛ 206 C3 ✉ Melmore Terrace, Cromwell ☎ (03) 445 0212; www.cromwell.org.nz 🕐 Site: 24 hours; shops and cafe: daily 10–3 💷 Free

A 19th-century stone cottage near the town of Alexandra

4 Dunedin and the Otago Peninsula

Dunedin's early wealth and Scottish heritage have left a tangible mark. The first impression is of a cityscape dominated by spires, gables and roofs bristling with turrets. This is also the gateway to the Otago Peninsula, a place of untamed natural beauty and a sanctuary for rare wildlife.

Set between rolling hills and the rugged coastline, Dunedin is the capital of the southern province of Otago, which is best known for its pioneering gold-mining history, rugged scenery, and fertile orchards and vineyards.

The city clings to the walls of a natural amphitheatre, enclosing a harbour whose narrow channel extends to the tip of the Otago Peninsula and beyond Port Chalmers. Dunedin's prosperity in the second half of the 19th century resulted in a Victorian city in the middle of the southern Pacific and, despite modern intrusions, much of the original architecture remains intact. Historic buildings have been given a new lease of life, serving as public venues and municipal buildings. Many grand old homesteads have been restored and wooden villas are scattered through the hilly suburbs.

Scottish Influence

Dunedin's Scottish heritage is also evident throughout the city. This is one of only a handful of places in New Zealand with a kilt shop, stocking more than 500 tartans. Dunedin also boasts its own pipe band, and still has haggis ceremonies and a population that speaks with

THE OTHER SIDE OF THE WORLD

Dunedin is the old Gaelic name for Edinburgh, but, apart from street names and the original architecture, it has little in common with the Scottish capital. Locals claim that Dunedin is hillier, smaller and closer to the sea – and that it has a better climate than Edinburgh.

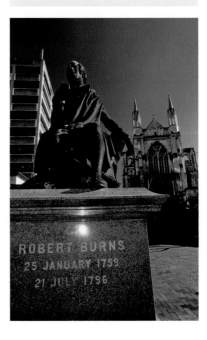

ROBERT BURNS
25 JANUARY 1759
21 JULY 1796

Opposite: A statue of poet Robert Burns is just one example of the pervading Scottish influence seen around the city

Above: The bluestone buildings of Dunedin University

a distinctly rolling accent. Much of Dunedin's architecture is modelled on Scottish and other British examples: New Zealand's first university, the University of Otago, resembles the University of Glasgow buildings; the college buildings of Otago Boys' High School have the air of a British public school; and even the former prison was modelled on architect Norman Shaw's design for Scotland Yard in London.

The City's Sights

Start your exploration in the heart of the city, the eight-sided **Octagon**, through the middle of which runs Dunedin's main street, changing from Princes Street on the south to George Street on the north. Rather fittingly, a **sculpture of poet Robert Burns** overlooks the Octagon's small central park – "with his back to the kirk and his face to the pub". The Oban Hotel, which Burns once faced, is no more, but behind him towers **St Paul's Anglican Cathedral**. Walk up the marble steps to see its soaring limestone-vaulted nave. Apart from Italian marble floor tiles, most of the stone and timber used to build the cathedral came from New Zealand, most notably the near-white Oamaru limestone, which you will find in public buildings and sculptures throughout the country. Next to the cathedral, the ground floor of the **Civic Centre** houses Dunedin's **visitor information centre**. On the other side of the cathedral is the **Dunedin Public Art Gallery**, which has a large collection of paintings by Frances Hodgkins.

It is a short walk along George Street to the **University of Otago** campus. Dunedin is very much a university town – during term time its population of just under 120,000 swells by about 17,000, and students are one of the driving forces behind the city's vibrant cafe and cultural scene. The campus itself is constantly bursting at the seams, with new buildings going up on the fringes, but a walk through the inner group of historic slate-roofed bluestone buildings, huddled beside the Leith stream, will give a sense of its Victorian origins.

If you're going to take the vintage train journey to the Taieri Gorge (➤ 178), allow time to inspect Dunedin's **railway station**, a monument to Edwardian architecture and testimony to the settlers' faith in railways. Inside, the Royal Doulton mosaic-tile floors and stained-glass windows depict railway motifs and the monogram of New Zealand Railways.

The Otago Peninsula

A tour of the Otago Peninsula is a must, even if you only have time to drive to **Taiaroa Head**. You should get a chance to observe albatrosses, penguins, seals and Stewart Island shags in the wild, just a few minutes from the city. Taiaroa Head is the only mainland breeding colony of **royal albatrosses** in the world. Albatross chicks are raised here every year but can only be seen as part of a guided tour to the observatory.

It takes about 45 minutes to drive to Taiaroa Head along the coastal route, which winds past many bays on the harbour side of the peninsula, each with spectacular views of the city. If you take the inland route, the views are even better, as you're overlooking the entire peninsula, with its rocky shores within the harbour and its steep cliffs and secluded sandy beaches on the seaward side. You can also inspect Larnach Castle (➤ 178) before you reach the peninsula's main settlement, **Portobello**, where the road continues to Taiaroa Head. A few minutes before you reach the albatross colony, a sign points to **Penguin Place**, an ecotourism venture where visitors can observe yellow-eyed penguins from hides and trenches dug into the dunelands.

TAKING A BREAK

Visit **Glenfalloch Woodland Garden**, about 9km (6 miles) from Dunedin along the coastal route to Portobello. The

Visitors approach Taiaroa Head by water

narrow walking tracks wind through shrubs, trees and herbaceous borders. The gardens have a cafe and wine bar, open Nov–Apr daily 11–3:30 (tel: (03) 476 1006; www.glenfalloch.co.nz).

🔀 207 D2

Dunedin Visitor Information Centre
✉ 20 Princes Street, Dunedin
☎ (03) 474 3300;
www.dunedinnz.com
🕐 Mon–Fri 8:30–5, Sat–Sun 8:45–4, public holidays 9–5

Taiaroa Head has a rare colony of breeding royal albatrosses

Dunedin Public Art Gallery
✉ 30 The Octagon, Dunedin ☎ (03) 477 4000; www.dunedin.art.museum
🕐 Daily 10–5 📙 Free

St Paul's Cathedral
✉ The Octagon, Dunedin ☎ (03) 477 2336; www.stpauls.net.nz
🕐 Services: Sun 8am, 10am, 7pm; Tue 8am; Wed 10am; Thu 8am, 6pm; Fri 8am

Royal Albatross Colony
✉ Taiaroa Head, Otago Peninsula ☎ (03) 478 0499; www.albatross.org.nz
🕐 Visitor centre: Wed–Mon 9:30–5, Tue 10:30–5. Tours of the albatross colony: 24 Nov–Mar Wed–Mon 9am–sunset, Tue 10:30am–sunset; Apr–16 Sep Wed–Mon 10am–sunset, Tue 10:30am–sunset; booking essential
🚌 Peninsula bus, tour buses 📙 Expensive

Penguin Place Yellow-Eyed Penguin Reserve
✉ Penguin Place, Harington Point Road, Otago Peninsula ☎ (03) 478 0286; www.penguinplace.co.nz 🕐 Oct–Mar tours every 30 mins 10:15am–90 mins before sunset; Apr–Sep tours every 30 mins 3:15–4:45pm
📙 Expensive

DUNEDIN AND THE OTAGO PENINSULA: INSIDE INFO

In more depth Visit the **Otago Settlers Museum** (31 Queens Gardens, Dunedin; tel: (03) 477 5052; www.otago.settlers.museum; daily 10–5; free) to find out more about the Scottish families who influenced Dunedin's development or to join a guided city tour.

■ If you're interested in natural history or the area's Maori cultural heritage, the **Otago Museum** (419 Great King Street, Dunedin, tel: (03) 474 7474; www.otagomuseum.govt.nz; daily 10–5; donation; Discovery World: inexpensive) has some good displays.

Hidden gem **Sandfly Bay** is an enchanting beach on the seaward coast of the Otago Peninsula, where you can watch yellow-eyed penguins return to their nests in the evening.

At Your Leisure

There are numerous places to take the plunge around Queenstown

5 Wanaka

Some 55km (35 miles) northeast of Queenstown, lakeside Wanaka offers a couple of great family attractions. Puzzling World has mazes, optical illusions and plenty of hands-on puzzles to keep idle minds busy. Out at the airport, meanwhile, is the New Zealand Fighter Pilots Museum, dedicated to the country's World War II air aces and with vintage aircraft on display. Some of the planes fly in the biennial Warbirds Over Wanaka air show (➤ 182).
🕂 206 C3

Puzzling World
✉ 188 Main Highway, Wanaka
☎ (03) 443 7489; www.puzzlingworld.co.nz
🕐 Nov–Apr daily 8:30–5:30, May–Oct 8:30–5
🎫 Inexpensive

New Zealand Fighter Pilots Museum
✉ Wanaka Airport, SH6, Luggate ☎ (03) 443 7010; www.nzfpm.co.nz 🕐 Daily 9–4 (extended hours in Jan) 🎫 Inexpensive

6 Shotover River

The Shotover River gorges are the mini Grand Canyons of the south but some of their landscaping was done by hand, pick and shovel during the gold-mining days. The most stunning gold-rush relics are at Skippers Park, about 27km (17 miles) from Queenstown. At Winky's Museum in the park you'll find rusty horseshoes, century-old bath taps, pots and bottles and – bizarrely – a miner's boot with the poor fellow's foot bones still in it. Try your luck with a gold pan and you will almost certainly take home a flake or two. The road to Skippers Park can be dangerous and hire cars are not insured for the route.
🕂 206 B3

Skippers Canyon
✉ Skippers Canyon, Shotover River
☎ (03) 442 9434, 0800 226 966 toll free;
www.skipperscanyonjet.co.nz 🕐 Tours mid Jun–mid Sep daily 9, 1; Sep–Jun 8:30, 12, 3:30
🎫 Expensive

7 Bungy Jumping

Thrill seekers inspired by the exploits of AJ Hackett (➤ 25) will be satisfied near Queenstown. The original bungy site is a bridge across the Kawarau River, 43m (141 feet) high and the only place where jumpers can splash into the water. The next highest jump is the Ledge, adjacent to Queenstown's gondola station (➤ 165), at 47m (154 feet), and with spectacular views across

White-water rafting on the Shotover River

to the Remarkables mountains and down to Queenstown 400m (1,300 feet) below. The highest jump in Queenstown is the Nevis Highwire, where you leap from a gondola suspended 134m (440 feet) above the Nevis River.

AJ Hackett Bungy
🚹 206 B3 ✉ Bungy Centre, corner of Camp and Shotover streets, Queenstown ☎ (03) 442 4008; www.ajhackett.com 🕐 Daily; courtesy transport to bungy jump location 💲 Expensive; T-shirt included

8 White-Water Rafting

Rafting companies operate year-round on the Kawarau and Shotover rivers, except when the water levels are too high. Up to eight people – confident swimmers only – fit into each boat. There's a brief introduction on how to paddle, how to float safely downriver and how to help scoop others out. Generally, the Kawarau River is the safer option, with no exposed rocks. Book at the Queenstown information centre.

Challenge Rafting
🚹 206 B3 ✉ Queenstown Visitor Information Centre, corner of Shotover and Camp streets, Queenstown ☎ (03) 442 7318, 0800 423 836 toll free; www.raft.co.nz 🕐 Daily 💲 Expensive

9 River Surfing

River surfing, or sledging, gives you a some control over how you navigate the rapids, equipped with a wetsuit, helmet, fins and a body board. Each trip starts in calm water with an introduction to the equipment and techniques. From there you can either stay in the quieter sections, slowly floating down the Kawarau River, or tackle four rapids of varying difficulty. Basic swimming skills are needed.

Serious Fun River Surfing
🚹 206 B3 ✉ 39 Camp Street, Queenstown ☎ (03) 442 5262, 0800 737 468 toll free; www.riversurfing.co.nz 🕐 Daily 9am, 2pm; booking required, courtesy transport to river 💲 Expensive

10 Arrowtown

Arrowtown is a faithfully restored early gold-mining settlement, set against the backdrop of a majestic mountain range and the golden, tussock-covered high country. The town's main street, lined with historic houses, shops and saloons, could be mistaken for a Western film set. A few minutes from the centre, on the banks of Bush Creek, are the remains of a Chinese gold-mining camp, indicating the harsh life of Chinese diggers, who often came to work the tailings for any gold undetected by earlier miners.

🚹 206 B3 ☎ www.arrowtown.com

11 Alexandra

Like most Central Otago towns, Alexandra sprang up virtually overnight after the discovery of gold

Larnach is New Zealand's only castle

nearby. While many of the historic buildings remain, Alexandra has developed into a tranquil but modern town and the commercial hub of Central Otago. It's now an oasis of orchards among rocky hills, owing its current prosperity to fruit production and the growing reputation of local wines.

🕂 206 C2 ☎ www.alexandra.co.nz

🄬 Larnach Castle

Built by the 19th-century banker and merchant baron William Larnach, this is New Zealand's only castle, and was one of the most expensive buildings in the country when construction was completed. From 1871 Larnach employed more than 200 workmen and spent a reputed NZ$426,000. The castle's best-known features are its elaborate ceilings, carved by English and Italian craftsmen. After Larnach's suicide in 1898, the castle was used as a cabaret venue, a tourist resort and a psychiatric hospital. The Barker family bought it in 1967, restoring the buildings and gardens.

🕂 207 D2 ✉ 145 Camp Road, Otago Peninsula ☎ (03) 476 1616; www.larnachcastle.co.nz ⏱ Castle: daily 9–5; gardens: Oct–Easter daily 9–7; Easter–Sep daily 9–5

🖑 Castle: moderate; gardens: inexpensive. Accommodation offered (➤ 179)

🄬 Taieri Gorge Railway

A vintage train takes passengers through the spectacular Taieri Gorge, inland from Dunedin. As the railway winds for 58km (36 miles) to Pukerangi, the landscapes change from rolling pastures to steep cliffs of layered schist rock. In the narrowest part of the gorge, the train passes between sheer cliffs on one side and a sudden drop on the other. From Pukerangi, the land flattens into the Taieri river plains that continue to Middlemarch, a small rural settlement. The train has an open viewing carriage and makes stops at sightseeing spots. Most people take the four-hour return trip to Pukerangi or six-hour return to Middlemarch, but you can continue to Queenstown by bus.

🕂 207 D2 ✉ Dunedin Railway Station, Anzac Avenue, Dunedin ☎ (03) 477 4449; www.taieri.co.nz ⏱ To Pukerangi: Oct–Apr Mon–Thu, Sat 9:30, 2:30, Fri, Sun 2:30; May–Sep daily 12:30. To Middlemarch: Oct–Apr Fri, Sun 9:30. To Palmerston: Oct–Apr Wed, Sat 9:30; May–Sep occasional days 🖑 Expensive

Taieri Gorge Railway

Where to...
Stay

Prices
Expect to pay for two people sharing a double room per night:
$ under NZ$200 $$ NZ$200–$350 $$$ over NZ$350

QUEENSTOWN

Driftwood $$
Textile artist Vicky Wills has created a slice of paradise in a secluded lakeside setting beneath the Remarkables mountain range, yet still only a brief 15 minutes' drive south of Queenstown. There are two loft studios each with king-size beds, kitchen facilities, bathtubs and log fires and an elegant three-bedroom house. Guests can choose to relax in the native bush garden or explore Lake Wakatipu by kayak.
➕ 206 B3 ✉ 40 Cedar Drive, Wakatipu ☎ (03) 442 7088; www.driftwood.net.nz

The Heritage Queenstown $–$$$
This alpine-lodge style complex is a short walk from town and has lovely views over Lake Wakatipu and the Remarkables. Suites have kitchen facilities, and there are also 40 villas. In winter, there's a roaring fire in the restaurant; in summer you can dine on the balcony.
➕ 206 B3 ✉ 91 Fernhill Road ☎ (03) 442 4988; www.heritagehotels.co.nz

CENTRAL OTAGO

Mt Rosa Lodge $$$
This luxurious bed and breakfast is set in the Gibbston Valley, famous for its wines, and looks out over Mt Rosa Station, one of the largest vineyards in Central Otago. There are three tastefully decorated guest rooms, each with its own private access and outdoor terrace, ensuite bathroom, king-size bed and sitting area. A gourmet breakfast is served, and your hosts can also provide picnic hampers and dinner by arrangement. Aside from visiting wineries, other outdoor activities include golf, fly fishing and skiing in winter.
➕ 206 C3 ✉ Gibbston Back Road, RD1 ☎ (03) 441 1484; www.mtrosalodge.co.nz

DUNEDIN

Larnach Lodge $–$$$
This re-created colonial wooden farm building in the grounds of Larnach Castle (▶ 178) has a stunning view of the harbour and the Otago Peninsula. Twelve rooms are ensuite and decorated in period style. Six more rooms, located in the converted coach house, have shared bathroom facilities. Guests can have dinner in the castle (arrange it by 5pm), and a free tour during opening hours. Breakfast is also included.
➕ 207 D2 ✉ Larnach Castle, 145 Camp Road, Dunedin ☎ (03) 476 1616; www.larnachcastle.co.nz

Lisburn House $–$$
This cosy bed and breakfast, three minutes' drive south of the city centre in the suburb of Caversham, was built in 1865 as a townhouse and is one of Dunedin's finest remaining examples of Victorian Gothic architecture. Its exterior has been beautifully preserved, while the interior features a wood-panelled dining room, open fireplaces and a sweeping staircase. There are three large bedrooms, each with queen-size four-poster bed and private bathroom. The Claddagh restaurant is open for both lunch and dinner.
➕ 207 D2 ✉ 15 Lisburn Avenue, Dunedin ☎ (03) 455 8888; www.lisburnhouse.co.nz

Where to...
Eat and Drink

Prices

Expect to pay per person for a three-course meal, excluding drinks:

$ under NZ$45 $$ NZ$45–$60 $$$ over NZ$60

The Bathhouse $$$

Built to commemorate the coronation of King George V in 1911, The Bathhouse is now a nostalgic cafe on the beach. Tables and chairs are set on the boardwalk, and the glass frontage gives views over the lake and mountains.

This casual, relaxed cafe is licensed and has beer on tap. It is open for breakfast, lunch, dinner and serves tapas-style dishes of New Zealand-inspired cuisine using lamb and salmon.

➕ 206 B3 ✉ 15 Marine Parade, Queenstown Bay ☎ (03) 442 5625; www.bathhouse.co.nz ⏰ Daily 9am–late

Gibbston Valley Winery $

One of Central Otago's pioneering vineyards, Gibbston Valley makes the most of its site in the scenic Kawarau Gorge. There's a stylish restaurant, a tasting facility and a shop. Local and seasonal ingredients are used in such dishes as the Mediterranean platter and pan-fried South Island salmon. Each dish has a suggested wine match.

➕ 206 B3 ✉ Gibbston, R01, SH6 ☎ (03) 442 6910; www.gvwines.co.nz ⏰ Daily 12–3; wine tours: 10–4

Saffron $$$

This friendly restaurant receives rave reviews. Try the scampi from Stewart Island to start, followed by a trio of Thai curries, and a goats'-cheese sorbet served with dates poached in Amaretto to finish. The extensive wine list favours local wines, but there's a good selection of French vintages available too. Saffron's sister restaurant next door, serves pizzas and pasta to families.

➕ 206 B3 ✉ 18 Buckingham Street ☎ (03) 442 0131; www.saffronrestaurant.co.nz ⏰ Daily 11am–late

Pier 24 $$–$$$

Located on the ocean front in St Clair Beach Resort, chefs Michael Coughlin and Greg Piner bring a touch of culinary genius to each dish. In the summer when the doors are open wide, this becomes coastal alfresco dining or in winter, hide behind the glass and watch the storms. The main menu changes regularly, but look out for Southland lamb with parmesan and rocket gnocchi and the always-popular creme brûlée.

➕ 207 D2 ✉ 24 Esplanade, St Clair Beach, Dunedin ☎ (03) 456 0555; www.stclairbeachresort.com ⏰ Oct–Mar daily 7am–late, Apr–Sep 8am–10:30pm

Plato $$

Housed in a former seafarer's hostel on the waterfront in Dunedin, Plato is a relaxed restaurant serving imaginative dishes using seasonal, usually local ingredients, especially seafood. Dinner choices include pan-fried lamb's kidney to start, followed by sole with spinach and greenshell mussels, and cappuccino brûlée. To wash it down, opt for any of the outstanding New Zealand wines on offer.

➕ 207 D2 ✉ 2 Birch Street ☎ (03) 477 4235; www.platocafe.co.nz ⏰ Dinner: daily 6pm–late; brunch: Sun 11am–2pm

Where to...
Shop

QUEENSTOWN

Queenstown is geared for tourists, with most shops in the **Queenstown Mall** area open till late and many offer packing and posting services. Prices may be on the high side.Sports and outdoor equipment are readily available but try **Outside Sports** (36 Shotover Street, tel: (03) 441 0074) or **Queenstown Sportsworld** (17 Rees Street, tel: (03) 442 8452).

Stroll down the pedestrian Queenstown Mall for rugby paraphernalia at **Champions of the World** (11 The Mall, tel: (03) 441 1122), a branch of **Louis Vuitton** (12 The Mall, tel: (03) 441 8002), and souvenirs, books and cafes. **O'Connell's Shopping Centre** (corner of Camp and Beach streets,

tel: (03) 442 7760) has 25 stores under one roof, offering everything from food to fashion.

At the **Jade Factory** (22 Beach Street, tel: (03) 442 8688) you can watch carvers produce jewellery and sculptures in traditional and contemporary designs. The gift centre also sells woodcarvings.

For picnic items head for the **Mediterranean Market** (corner of Gorge and Robins roads, tel: (03) 442 4161).

ARROWTOWN

Buckingham Street is lined with boutiques, galleries and souvenir shops housed in pretty cottages. Gold-mining themed souvenirs can be found at **The Gold Shop** (No. 29, tel: (03) 442 1319) or buy

an original piece of New Zealand art from **Arrowtown Gallery** (No. 40–44, tel: (03) 442 1755). For knitwear, there's **The Wool Press** (No. 40, tel: (03) 442 1355), while **Ikon** (No. 50, tel: (03) 409 8364) sells New Zealand designer clothing. Follow the Wakatipu Arts Trail to buy direct from artists – ask for a leaflet at the **Lakes District Museum** (No. 49, tel: (03) 442 1824).

DUNEDIN

George Street is the main shopping area, with a mix of chain stores and highly individual local stores. Dunedin celebrates its Scottish roots at **The Scottish Shop** (17 George Street, tel: (03) 477 9965). **Meridian Shopping Mall** (267–287 George Street, tel: (03) 474 7500) houses Arthur Barnett's department store, K-Mart, fashion chains and food outlets.

For designer clothing, head for **Plume** (310 George Street,

tel: (03) 477 9358). Browse for designer objects at **Things** (326 George Street, tel: (03) 477 4427) and **Acquisitions** (286 George Street, tel: (03) 477 0623). For collectables, try **Queens Gardens Antique Centre** (16 Queens Gardens, tel: (03) 742 5010).

Near the Octagon, is the **Lure Jewellery Workshop** (1st Floor, 1 Stuart Street, tel: (03) 477 5559), where you can watch five jewellers creating pieces of contemporary New Zealand jewellery. For work by New Zealand artists, try **Milford Galleries** (18 Dowling Street, tel: (03) 477 7727), **Moray Gallery** (55 Princes Street, tel: (03) 477 8060) or **Brett McDowell Gallery** (5 Dowling Street, tel: (03) 477 5260).

Up near the university, **Everyday Gourmet** (446 George Street, tel: (03) 477 2045) is a good place to buy deli food. The **University Book Shop** (378 Great King Street, tel: (03) 477 6976) has two floors of books for all ages and interests and a continuous clearance sale.

Where to...
Be Entertained

QUEENSTOWN

For listings of what's on, see the free *Mountain Scene*, published every Thursday, or call in at the Queenstown visitor centre (corner of Shotover and Camp streets, tel: (03) 442 4100).

Skiing

Queenstown is a major ski resort, with two fields on its doorstep: **Coronet Peak** (tel: (03) 442 4620) and **The Remarkables** (tel: (03) 442 4615). Others are about an hour away near Wanaka. You can hire gear in the city or on the field.

Wine Trails

Central Otago, the world's southernmost wine-making region, has more than 30 vineyards. Pick up a wine trail map from the visitor centre or ask about guided tours.

Golf

There are five golf courses around Queenstown: **Millbrook Resort** (tel: (03) 441 7000), **Queenstown Golf Club** (tel: (03) 442 9169), **Frankton Golf Club** (tel: (03) 442 3584), **Arrowtown Golf Club** (tel: (03) 442 1719) and **The Hills** (tel: (03) 409 8290).

Nightspots

Lasseters Wharf Casino (Steamer Wharf, tel: (03) 441 1495) is open till 3am and **SkyCity Casino** (Beach Street, tel: (03) 441 0400) till 4am. You may be asked for ID.

The city's coolest bar – literally – is **Minus 5** (Steamer Wharf, tel: (03) 442 6050) and it is made entirely of ice. For live music, try **Subculture** (13–14 Church Street, tel: (03) 442 7685), which hosts international bands.

Festivals

The **Clyde Wine and Food Harvest Festival** is held at Easter, while June/July brings the hugely popular annual **Queenstown Winter Festival**. The biennial **Warbirds Over Wanaka**, held at Easter, is the largest air show in the southern hemisphere (www.warbirdsoverwanaka.com).

DUNEDIN

Check Thursday's edition of the *Otago Daily Times* for listings or ask at the visitor centre (20 Princes Street, tel: (03) 474 3300).

Arts and Entertainment

Dunedin's professional theatre company, **Fortune** (231 Stuart Street, tel: (03) 477 8323), has regular seasons of plays.

Concerts of classical music are given regularly by the **Southern Sinfonia** (110 Moray Place, tel: (03) 477 5623).

Dunedin Casino operates in the restored 1880s Southern Cross Hotel (118 High Street, tel: (03) 477 4545). There's a dress code.

Sports

Otago waterways are perfect for fishing trout. Professional guides supply transport, gear, tackle and the necessary fishing licence. Golf is available at several courses: contact the visitor centre. **Carisbrook Stadium** is the city's major sporting venue. A new stadium is being built for the 2011 Rugby World Cup.

Festivals

The city's **Summer Festival** is held Jan–Feb, followed in March by the **Fringe Festival**. The **Cadbury Chocolate Carnival** takes place in July, while October sees the annual **Rhododendron Festival** and the biennial **Otago Festival of the Arts**.

Walks and Tours

1 Wellington City to Sea Walkway

Walk

This walk, with its stunning views of the city and harbour, covers the first third of a 12km (7-mile) route that leads from the heart of central Wellington to the capital's southern coastline and the picturesque suburb of Island Bay. You can pick up a detailed description and map of the entire walkway at the Wellington Visitor Information Centre (▶ 106).

DISTANCE 4km (2.5 miles) **TIME** 1.5–2 hours **START POINT** Bolton Street Memorial Park ✚ 205 B4
END POINT Aro Street ✚ 205 A1 **GETTING BACK** From Aro Street, catch the No. 9 bus

**Page 183: A waterfall as seen from a boat cruise at Milford Sound
Left: Wellington skyline as seen from the botanic gardens**

1–2

Turn from The Terrace, one of Wellington's central arteries near Parliament (▶ 104–106), into Bolton Street. The Bolton Street Memorial Park is just a few metres uphill on your right. From 1840 to 1892 this was the only cemetery for non-Catholics in Wellington, unusually allowing all faiths in one burial ground.

Walk up the steps to the small **chapel**, a replica of the original 1866 Anglican mortuary. Inside are displays about the main killers of the

TAKING A BREAK
You're never short of a cafe to rest in when exploring Wellington. Round off your walk with a snack at the **Aro Café** (90 Aro Street, tel: (04) 384 4970).

of the chapel, the Anglican part of the old cemetery is still mostly intact and you'll find some beautiful tombstones. On the right, there is a memorial plaque for the people in the mass grave below.

Follow the walkway on the right of the chapel to the **Denis McGrath Bridge**, which crosses the motorway. Turn right after the bridge to follow Robertson Way through a heritage rose garden and uphill past the Jewish cemetery to a lookout point over Thorndon (▶ 107). A few metres further uphill, at an iron gate, is the **Seddon Memorial**, a tall obelisk in honour of Richard John Seddon, who arrived in New Zealand as a gold-miner and eventually became the country's Premier in 1893.

19th century – disease, fire, poverty, earthquakes, tides and battle – and burial records of prominent citizens, including some of the founders of Wellington, who are interred in the cemetery (chapel open daily 10–4).

When a motorway was built through the cemetery in the 1960s, the original chapel was removed and the remains of almost 4,000 early settlers were shifted to a mass grave below the current chapel. On the left side

Wellington Harbour

2–3

From the Seddon Memorial towards the gate of Anderson Park. As you pass the sports grounds on your right you can already see the Lady Norwood Rose Garden and the Botanic Garden's **Begonia House** (open daily 9–5 in summer; 9–4 in winter). Here, the traffic noise finally subsides, particularly around the small Japanese-style Peace Flame water garden to the left of the rose garden.

Leave the Begonia House and cafe on your right, and follow the Serpentine Way uphill (a sign points to the Cable Car) as it winds through remnants of native forest. After about five minutes, it meets a narrow track; turn left into the Junction Path towards the **Sculpture Park**. Path names are not always on raised signposts so look for flat plaques on the lawn. Pass several sculptures, then continue along Manuka Way for a few metres before turning right into Scrub Path. The path skirts around the hilltop, where you'll see the large **meteorological station**. Follow the markers along Scrub Path, then turn right onto Hill Path and climb up the steps (made of railway sleepers) and, at the top, turn right into Australian Path. This takes you to the top of the hill and the **Sundial of Human Involvement,** the **Carter Observatory** (▶ 110), several

smaller historic observation domes and the top terminal of the **Cable Car** with its museum (▶ 110).

3–4

The magnificent views from the Cable Car take in Wellington's central city, the waterfront, Matiu/Somes Island (▶ 111) and the distant Rimutaka Ranges.

Walk out onto the road and past a planted traffic island to turn left onto a footpath signposted to Rawhiti Terrace. Cross Rawhiti Terrace and continue down another footpath to Kelburn Parade and the **Victoria University** buildings. Veer left to Salamanca Road and

Spectacular views can be seen from the Cable Car

cross it to enter **Kelburn Park**. Walk around the left side of the sports field and turn left and downhill at the large fountain. Follow the track through bush, past squash courts, through another part of Wellington's green belt and up a few steps to Salamanca Road. Then turn left and cross the road, and walk back up on the other side to Mount Street.

At the top of Mount Street, at the Student Union Building, turn left and stroll through the **Roman Catholic Cemetery**, where early settlers were buried. When you reach Waiteata Road, at the bottom of the cemetery hill, turn right and follow the markers past university buildings, around the back of a student apartment block, its car park and a gym to the Boyd Wilson sports field. Walk along the field and turn left down a path past Te Aro School to the southern and more residential end of The Terrace. From there, turn right to follow The Terrace for a few metres until it intersects with Abel Smith Street. Cross the street and walk past several small houses to Aro Street Park and the Aro Valley.

Aro Street, with its colonial villas, shops and cafes, is one of Wellington's favourite historic streets. This walk ends here, so stop for a coffee unless you want to take the long official route all the way to the sea.

2 LAKE MATHESON
Walk

DISTANCE 2.5km (1.5 miles) for lake circuit **TIME** 1.5 hours for lake circuit
START/END POINTS Car park at Lake Matheson ➕ 206 C4 **GETTING THERE** At Fox Glacier turn into Cook Flat
Road and after about 5km (3 miles) turn right to Lake Matheson car park

Lake Matheson is renowned for providing the best opportunity to see New Zealand's highest mountains without having to brave the harsh alpine environment. On a calm day, the reflections on the lake are magical, but even if the surface is ruffled, the views to the Southern Alps are magnificent. A short drive away is Gillespies Beach, which represents the wild essence of the West Coast, with pounding surf and enchanted landscapes of bleached driftwood.

1–2

The best time to see the reflections of Aoraki/Mount Cook and Mount Tasman on Lake Matheson is early in the morning or late in the evening. The lake circuit starts from a car park about 6km (4 miles) from Fox Glacier village. The path skirts the entire lake, undulating between the swampy shoreline and forest, to three main viewing platforms.

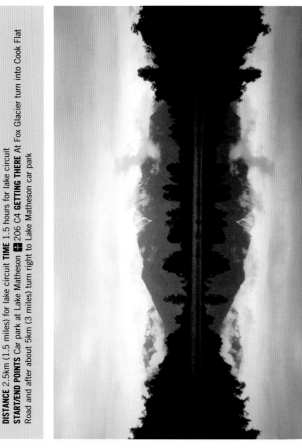

Mount Cook and Tasman perfectly reflected in Lake Matheson

of towering flax bushes, until it reaches the lake and the jetty after about 20 minutes. At the **jetty** lookout, the entire lake comes into view for the first time. Lake Matheson was carved out by the retreating Fox Glacier, which left a hole at the head of a small side valley about 14,000 years ago. It used to be an important food-gathering place for Maori people, who put out eel traps in the lake and hunted the forest for wood pigeons and the weka (wood hen). When the Europeans arrived, they cleared the grassy river flats for farmland, but the lake's forest fringe remains and is now part of Westland/Tai Poutini National Park.

As you continue from the jetty, the lake disappears from view briefly. After about 10 minutes, a raised boardwalk brings you to the water's edge, as it skirts around the lakefront and crosses the swampy outlet at the back of the lake. From there a few steps lead up to the **View of Views** platform, which overlooks the entire lake, across to the Fox valley and mountain ranges. You'll get good views of the mountains from any of the viewpoints, but this is the best spot to get the postcard image of the peaks reflected in the water.

Sheltered by dense forests, the lake's surface is calm on most days. Reflections are particularly clear on this lake due to the tannin leached from fallen vegetation and the humus-rich soil which has stained the water a dark brown colour.

The wetlands around the lake are home to introduced waterfowl, as well as native songbirds such as the melodious bellbird, who you are likely to hear during the walk.

Gillespies Beach with its ocean-worn tree stumps

At the start, the track crosses a **swing bridge** over Clearwater River and cuts through dense, low forest along the outlet stream, sometimes giving way to patches

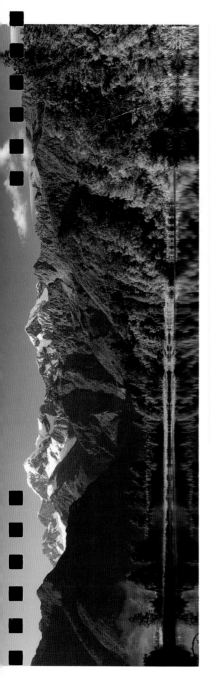

2-3

From the View of Views it is five minutes to the next lookout, **Reflection Island** – although not really an island but a small platform jutting out onto the water. The rest of the loop track keeps to the forest and eventually brings you back out to the farmland, punctuated by the tall kahikatea swamp tree. On frosty, misty mornings, these isolated, gnarled trees are another scenic setting for photographs of the mountain ranges.

Stunning landscapes surround Lake Matheson

WALKING AT GILLESPIES BEACH

From Lake Matheson, drive along Cook Flat Road for 9km (6 miles), turn right and follow Gillespies Beach Road (unsealed) for 11km (7 miles), then turn right to the car park. Walk through the dunes to the beach and head north. The beach has a wild beauty, with roaring surf and skeletal trees scattered along the high-tide mark. It's named after James Edwin Gillespie, who detected gold here in 1865. Rusting gold dredgers are still visible, but they are gradually sinking into the mire. After about an hour you'll reach the estuary fed by the Waikowhai Stream. Cross the trestle bridge and either explore the lagoon's dark tidal swamps or follow the path further north to the tunnel and lookout point. From there you can drop back down to the beach and walk for 30 minutes to the fur seal colony at Galway Beach. This is mainly a winter haul out for immature males, so while there may be hundreds there in winter, it can be difficult to find any in summer.

3 Around East Cape
Tour

The East Cape, first to greet the rising sun, remains isolated and sparsely populated. A tour along the Pacific Coast Highway (SH35) takes you along a string of azure bays and deserted beaches, interspersed with small Maori townships. The area is steeped in Maori history and you will find numerous meeting houses and churches. The jagged Raukumara Range provides a formidable backdrop to the coastal scenery.

DISTANCE 334km (207 miles) **TIME** 1–2 days for a leisurely tour
START POINT Opotiki, eastern Bay of Plenty ✚ 209 E4 **END POINT** Gisborne, Poverty Bay ✚ 209 F4

1–2
Start your journey at **Opotiki**, a small farming township at the confluence of the Waioeka and Otara rivers. The extensive coastline at this eastern end of the Bay of Plenty is lined with safe, sandy beaches and is punctuated by rocky volcanic outcrops. Opotiki marks the intersection between SH2,

For the next 20km (12 miles) the road follows the coast, opening up to views across the Bay of Plenty at Maraenui Hill, until you reach the mouth of the **Motu River**, renowned for white-water rafting and jet boating.

3–4

Te Kaha, 70km (43 miles) from Opotiki, is a small town set in a delightful cove that was once the scene of inter-tribal battles. As recently as 1930, open-boat whaling still operated here and whales were landed

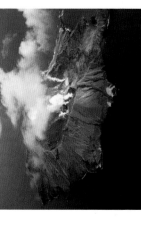

A bird's-eye view of White Island

which continues to Gisborne through the Waioeka Gorge, and the more scenic SH35, which winds its way around the spectacular East Cape to the same destination.

As you leave Opotiki, you'll get good views out to **White Island** (▶ 91), 48km (30 miles) offshore. About 6km (4 miles) from Opotiki, at the sandy beaches of **Tirohanga**, there are remnants of terraces of an ancient and extensive *pa*, a Maori fortified village, clearly visible on Tirohanga Bluff. The partly unsealed Motu Road, now a popular mountain-bike track along the Waiaua River, turns off SH35 about 11km (7 miles) from Opotiki, climbing through rugged, bush-covered country to Matawai, on SH2, which is about two hours' drive away.

2–3

After passing several stretches of sandy beaches and rocky inlets, you reach **Torere**, about 23km (14 miles) from Opotiki. Holy Trinity Church, beside the meeting house, is worth a short stop in order to compare its relative simplicity with the ornate wooden St Mary's Church at Tikitiki, further along the route.

Map labels:
Mawhai Point
Arero
Tolaga Bay
Cooks Cove Walkway
Waihau Bay
Whangara
Waimata
Te Karaka
Ormond
998m ▲ Tutamoa
Whatatutu
Waipaoa
Motu
Matawai
Otoko
Gisborne
Poverty Bay
35
7
2
Waioeka

0   20 km
0   10 miles

excursions. The grey shell of the derelict freezing works (an abattoir) near the old wooden wharf recalls the days of intensive coastal shipping at the cape before the road was developed.

Rocky inlets and sandy coves are dotted along the East Cape

Built in about 1894, it shows a strong European influence in its architectural design.

4–5
For the next 15km (9 miles) the road snuggles into the curves of the coastline, looking out to the rocky inlets and glistening beaches of **Waihau Bay** and **Oruaiti Beach**, until it turns away from the coast at Whangaparaoa, near **Cape Runaway**, the eastern extremity of the Bay of Plenty. It was named by Captain Cook in October 1769 when five Maori warrior canoes paddled out towards his ship. Cook ordered grapeshot to be fired over the warriors' heads, scaring them into a quick retreat.

Whangaparaoa is a place of mythical significance to Maori as the landing place of two of the seven ancient canoes that brought the first people to populate Aotearoa (New Zealand). From Whangaparaoa, SH35 briefly leaves the coast as it skirts across to **Hicks Bay**, 148km (92 miles) from Opotiki, offering viewpoints, bush walks and deep-sea fishing

The Anglican Church at Raukokore

on the beach. It's now a holiday resort and home of hero Willie Apiata (➤ 11). Te Kaha's richly carved Tukaki meeting house features an intricate lintel. Pretty **Whanarua Bay**, about 18km (11 miles) further along the Pacific Coast Highway, has a number of secluded beaches.

About 10km (6 miles) from Whanarua Bay, at **Raukokore**, the Anglican Church stands imposingly on a lone promontory near the sea.

5–6

From Hicks Bay continue for another 12km (7 miles) to **Te Araroa**, which has a visitor information centre, postal facilities, shops, a petrol station and, in its school grounds,

The East Cape lighthouse

reputedly the biggest pohutukawa tree in the country, thought to be 600 years old. It has a girth of over 19m (62 feet) and is named Te Waha o Rerekohu after an old tribal chief.

At Te Araroa, you'll find the turn-off to the **East Cape lighthouse**, at mainland New Zealand's most eastern point. The detour, a 44km (27-mile) return trip on an unsealed road, takes about 50 minutes, and you'll have to go up 700 steps from the car park to the lighthouse, but the effort is well rewarded with the views towards **East Island**. Originally, the lighthouse was on East Island but the rocky outcrop has no beaches, and when four men drowned trying to land supplies, the lighthouse was shifted to its present site.

Tikitiki, 25km (15.5 miles) from Te Araroa, is a small settlement on the banks of the Waiapu River, best known for St Mary's Church, one of the most ornate Maori churches in New Zealand. It was built in 1924 as a memorial to World War I soldiers from the local Ngati Porou tribe, still the main tribe on the East Coast.

6–7

The centre for the Ngati Porou is the small town of **Ruatoria**, 20km (12 miles) further on at the foot of the tribe's sacred mountain

Mount Hikurangi: At 1,752m (5,747 feet), Mount Hikurangi is the North Island's highest non-volcanic peak. You can get good views from the Ihungia rest area, about 20km (12 miles) further along the highway; because of the peak's sacred status you need permission to climb it.

Further along, **Waipiro Bay village**, reached via an unsealed loop road off the highway, was once the busiest town on the coast; today, it's a slow-paced settlement where most activity revolves around the *marae*. **Te Puia Springs**, 231km (143 miles) from Opotiki, has a lake and hot pools near by, and **Tokomaru Bay**, 242km (150 miles) from Opotiki, is a crumbling but picturesque town with a beach and cliffs at the end of the bay. For the next 40km (25 miles) you'll pass several beaches before reaching **Tolaga Bay** and the **Cooks Cove Walkway**, south of the township. The easy 6km (4-mile) return trip crosses private land to where Cook dropped anchor to repair the *Endeavour* and take on water supplies (allow 2.5 hours; the walk is closed during lambing season, August to Labour Weekend). For the rest of the 54km (33-mile) journey to Gisborne, the road passes several tranquil beaches and settlements, including Whangara, where *Whale Rider* was filmed (▲ 19).

4 Scenic Drive on Milford Road

Tour

Driving on State Highway 94, the road to Milford Sound, is a journey of superlatives. It leads through the **Te Wahipounamu World Heritage** area, one of the greatest wilderness areas left in the southern hemisphere, with the highest mountains, largest glaciers, tallest forests, wildest rivers, most rugged landscape and deepest lakes.

DISTANCE 120km (74 miles) **TIME** 2.5 hours' driving time; allow about 6 hours to take in sights and short walks along the way **START POINT/END POINT** Te Anau ✛ 206 B2

1–2

For the first 30km (19 miles) to Te Anau Downs, the road follows the edge of **Lake Te Anau**, a long, narrow lake with three side arms stretching out towards the peaks of the Southern Alps. From the small wharf, the road leaves the lake to wind gently through pastures with fenced paddocks, grazing livestock

and pockets of native forest dominated by the small-leaved southern beech.

After about 50km (31 miles), you reach the first lookout point out to the **Eglinton**

The Earl Mountains are reflected perfectly in the aptly named Mirror Lakes

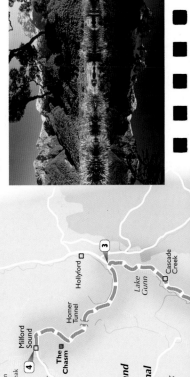

From the Mirror Lakes, it's only 5km (3 miles) to Knobs Flat, which has campsites, toilets and the last card phone before Milford.

2–3

Take a break at **Knobs Flat** to see the displays on local nature and on the history of the road to Milford, particularly the construction of Homer Tunnel, which you'll enter later (see box below).

As you leave Knobs Flat, the landscape starts changing from hilly pastures to an increasingly dense native rainforest and soaring, partly snow-covered peaks.

About 78km (48 miles) from Te Anau, just before the road meets Lake Gunn, a 45-minute nature walk provides an opportunity to see typical vegetation before the road climbs beyond the tree line. A few minutes into the nature walk, a 500-year-old beech log has a mark on one of its year rings to indicate its size when Captain Cook made his first visit to New Zealand.

Several longer walks fork off Milford Road, including the popular Routeburn and Greenstone tracks, before you reach the junction with the unsealed no-exit Lower Hollyford Road.

A DIFFICULT JOB

Homer Tunnel was started during the Depression in the 1930s, and the men endured great hardship, working in an area prone to landslides, earthquakes and avalanches. It took almost 20 years to hew the tunnel through the sheer rock, and several men died when the air blast from an avalanche destroyed most of their camp.

Valley, a frequently mist-shrouded river valley. The ranges and forests close in as you reach **Mirror Lakes,** about 58km (36 miles) from Te Anau. Stretch your legs on a five-minute boardwalk beside several small glacial lakes. The lakes provide reflective views of the Earl Mountains. Look out for the Mirror Lakes sign, which is upside down so that you can read the reflection. This is a favourite habitat for waterfowl and wetland plants. Beech trees are the main feature of Fiordland forests.

This leads to the **Humboldt Falls** and the head of the Hollyford Track.

3–4
The last few kilometres before Milford are the most scenic (though the risk of avalanche means you can't stop until you get to the Chasm). You should turn your lights on as you approach **Homer Tunnel**, about 19km (12 miles) from Milford. Here, the mountains form a solid rock wall in front of you, free of vegetation but awash with hundreds of waterfalls fed by snowfields and glaciers. The water runs through the rock and drips down inside the tunnel, as the hand-hewn passage was left unlined. Sections of the 1,207m (3,959-foot) tunnel now have large sheets of metal to divert the water down the sides, where it forms two small creeks running alongside the traffic. As you come out of the tunnel the view opens out to a narrow U-shaped valley and the road continues on a steep downhill run to Milford, through a precipitous zigzag past imposing mountains streaming with water. The road frequently narrows to one-way bridges to cross creeks that can swell to roaring rivers. One of the best short walks along Milford Road is **the Chasm**, about 9km (6 miles) from Milford,

a 20-minute walk along the Cleddau River to two footbridges with views of a series of waterfalls.

From the Chasm, the road passes a stretch of steaming beech forest and a river viewpoint at the Tutoko Bridge, before finally reaching **Milford Sound** (➤ 166–168), with Mitre Peak dominating the view.

BEFORE YOU SET OUT...
■ Milford Road can be busy in high season, so a start before 8am from Te Anau is a good idea.
■ The road may be closed due to winds or avalanches (mostly June to November); check roadside information signs in Te Anau.
■ Fill your tank and buy food and drink before you leave Te Anau. There are no petrol stations or shops on the road to Milford Sound.
■ Buy the annotated Milford Road World Heritage Highway Guide map (NZ$1; available from Fiordland National Park Visitor Centre, Te Anau).
■ For up-to-date road advice and weather reports: Transit Highway Information Line: 0800 444 449 toll free; www.milfordroad.co.nz; www.fiordland.org.nz

The beautiful Milford Sound lies at the end of this scenic drive. Page 197: An Auckland policeman provides directions

Practicalities

BEFORE YOU GO

WHAT YOU NEED

	Required: Some countries require a passport to remain valid for a minimum period (usually at least 6 months) beyond the date of entry – check before booking	UK	Germany	USA	Canada	Australia	Ireland	Netherlands	Spain
● Required									
○ Suggested									
▲ Not required									
△ Not applicable									
Passport/National Identity Card		●	●	●	●	●	●	●	●
Visa (Visa regulations can change – check before booking)		▲	▲	▲	▲	▲	▲	▲	▲
Onward or Return Ticket		●	●	●	●	●	●	●	●
Health Inoculations		▲	▲	▲	▲	▲	▲	▲	▲
Health Documentation		▲	▲	▲	▲	▲	▲	▲	▲
Travel Insurance		●	●	●	●	●	●	●	●
Driving Licence (national, plus translation for Spanish nationals)		●	●	●	●	●	●	●	●
Car Insurance Certificate (included if car is hired)		▲	▲	▲	▲	▲	▲	▲	▲
Car Registration Document		▲	▲	▲	▲	▲	▲	▲	▲

WHEN TO GO

Auckland

High season   Low season

JAN	FEB	MAR	APR	MAY	JUN	JUL	AUG	SEP	OCT	NOV	DEC
23°C	23°C	22°C	20°C	18°C	15°C	13°C	14°C	16°C	18°C	19°C	22°C
73°F	73°F	72°F	68°F	64°F	59°F	55°F	57°F	61°F	64°F	66°F	72°F

☀ Sun   ⛅ Sunshine and showers   🌧 Wet   ☁ Cloudy

The temperatures given above are the **average daily maximum** for each month.

New Zealand's main travel season is during the warmer months, generally from November to March, but ski resorts like Queenstown are busy throughout the year. The warmest months are December, January and February, and the coldest are June, July and August. The north of New Zealand is often described as "Mediterranean", with short winters and long summers. The south has long winters with plenty of snow. The best time to travel is after January, as the weather in late summer and autumn tends to be more stable than during spring. Winter and spring have more rain, which can cause floods in some areas.

GETTING ADVANCE INFORMATION
Websites

■ Pure New Zealand (Tourism New Zealand) www.newzealand.com

■ Tourism Auckland www.aucklandnz.com

■ Tourism Rotorua www.rotoruanz.com

■ Christchurch and Canterbury Tourism www.christchurchnz.com

■ Positively Wellington Tourism www.wellingtonnz.com

■ Queenstown Tourism www.queenstown-nz.co.nz

GETTING THERE

By Air Auckland, Wellington and Christchurch are the main international airports.
From the UK Air New Zealand has direct flights to Auckland, and Qantas, Cathay Pacific, Emirates and Singapore Airlines have good connections.
From the rest of Europe Flights from many European cities to Los Angeles, Singapore and Hong Kong give good connections to New Zealand.
From the US and Canada United Airlines, Air New Zealand offer direct flights to Auckland, with other airlines providing code-share services.
From Australia Air New Zealand, Virgin's Pacific Blue, Emirates and Qantas fly to all main centres and Jetstar flies to Christchurch.

Travel times New Zealand is a 3.5-hour flight from eastern Australia. From the west coast of the United States, a direct flight to New Zealand takes around 12 hours. Flights from Europe to New Zealand head either via the US or destinations in Asia, from where they take around 10 hours.

Ticket prices Prices are highest in December and January, but you can get cheaper tickets between Christmas and New Year. Prices drop during the cooler months from May to August.

TIME

New Zealand Standard Time is 12 hours ahead of Greenwich Mean Time (GMT), and 2 hours ahead of Australian Eastern Standard Time.
Daylight Saving Time Clocks are put forward by one hour on the last Sunday of September and wound back on the first Sunday of the following April.

CURRENCY AND FOREIGN EXCHANGE

Currency The unit of New Zealand currency is the dollar; $1=100 cents. Notes are printed in English and issued in 5, 10, 20, 50 and 100 dollar denominations. Coins are issued in denominations of 10, 20 and 50 cents (all silver), 1 and 2 dollars (gold). Although the New Zealand dollar (also referred to as the kiwi dollar) has gained against major overseas currencies in recent years, the country remains a fairly low-cost holiday destination. There is no restriction on the amount of foreign currency that can be brought in or taken out of New Zealand, but every person who carries more than $10,000 in cash in or out is required to complete a Border Cash Report. **Foreign currency** can be exchanged at banks, some hotels and Bureau de Change kiosks, which are found at international airports and most city centres. The best **exchange rates** are given by the trading banks: BNZ, National Bank, ANZ, Westpac. You can withdraw money from **ATM machines** with international credit cards and ATM cards as long as they have a four-digit PIN encoded. All major **credit cards** can be used. **Travellers' cheques** are accepted at hotels, banks and some stores. All goods and services are subject to 15 per cent **Goods and Services Tax** (GST), included in the displayed price. You can't claim this tax back, but when a supplier ships a major purchase to your home address the GST will not be charged.

For information on New Zealand, a copy of the New Zealand vacation brochure, or the contact details of the nearest travel agent with New Zealand expertise:	**In the UK** ☎ 020 7930 1662 **In the USA** ☎ 1800 252 981 toll free	**In Canada** ☎ 613/238 5991 toll free **In Australia** ☎ 310/395-7480

WHEN YOU ARE THERE

NATIONAL HOLIDAYS

1 Jan	New Year's Day
2 Jan	New Year's Holiday
6 Feb	Waitangi Day
Mar/Apr	Good Friday*
Mar/Apr	Easter Sunday
25 Apr	Anzac Day*
1st Mon Jun	Queen's Birthday
Last Mon Oct	Labour Day
25 Dec	Christmas Day*
26 Dec	Boxing Day

* Many restaurants and attractions close on these days

ELECTRICITY

New Zealand operates on a 230V AC, 50 hertz mains supply, three-pin plug system. Most hotels provide 110V AC sockets for shavers only, and hardware or electronics shops stock adaptors.

OPENING HOURS

○ Shops
● Offices
● Banks
● Post Offices
● Museums/Monuments
● Pharmacies

8am 9am 10am noon 1pm 2pm 4pm 5pm 7pm

□ Day   □ Midday   □ Evening

In addition to the opening hours shown left, pharmacies and stores are open on Saturday 9–12 or 9–4 and some shops are open on Sunday. Bigger towns may have late-night shopping on Thursday or Friday until 8:30 or 9pm. Some smaller shops close at lunchtime on Saturdays. Local convenience stores (dairies) are usually open 7am–8pm seven days.

TIPS/GRATUITIES

Tipping is not generally expected, but may be given to reward excellent service:

Restaurants	Not expected
Cafes/bars	Not expected
Tour guides	Not expected
Taxis	Not expected
Hairdressers	Not expected
Chambermaids	Not expected
Porters	Not expected
Toilets	Not expected

MAORI WORDS TO TRY

Maori is the second official language in New Zealand behind English. Few people speak it fluently, but everyone knows some key words and phrases. Try these words and the locals will love you:

Kia Ora	Hi, g'day
Haere Mai	Welcome
Ka Pai	Good, fine
Haere Ra	Goodbye

TIME DIFFERENCES

GMT	New Zealand	USA (East)	USA (West)	Germany	Australia (Sydney)
12 noon	12 midnight	7 am	4 am	1 pm	10 pm

STAYING IN TOUCH

Post Auckland's main post office is at 24 Wellesley Street, tel: (09) 379 6710. In Wellington, the main office is at 7–27 Waterloo Quay, tel: (04) 496 4999, in Christchurch, it is at 53–59 Hereford Street, tel: (03) 365 0336, and in Dunedin it is at 233 Moray Place, tel: (03) 474 0932.

Public telephones Telecom operates the public telephone service and most call boxes use Telecom phone cards, available from shops. For directory enquiries dial 018, and for international directory enquiries dial 0172. The International country dialling code is 64.

International Dialling Codes
Dial 00 followed by

UK:	44
USA/Canada:	1
Ireland:	353
Australia:	61
Germany:	49

Mobile providers and services Major cell phone providers are Vodafone, Telecom and 2 Degrees. SIM cards for each network are available for purchase at electronic stores and mobile phone retail stores. Pre-paid SIM cards start at around NZ$20. Using a local phone number, incoming calls are free.

WiFi and internet Internet speeds are not as fast in New Zealand as other countries, but if you're not downloading large files you'll find it works just fine. Maximum download speeds can be up to 24Mbps. WiFi is now fairly standard all over the country. In many cases access is free – or for the price of a coffee at a local cafe. When you log on you will be shown the networks in your immediate area and can pre-pay for an hour, day or month.

PERSONAL SAFETY

New Zealand is generally safe, but don't take safety for granted. Thieves are attracted to areas where tourists congregate, so take care with valuables.

■ Don't leave valuables in your car within plain sight. Opportunistic thieves only need a few seconds to take a handbag, laptop or even luggage.

■ In the outdoors, the weather can change quickly from one extreme to the other.

■ Prepare carefully for outdoor excursions: take appropriate clothing for any kind of weather, protect yourself from the sun and bring a first-aid kit. For automatic weather forecasts call 0900 99909.

■ Leave an itinerary with friends and family.

■ Hitchhiking is not illegal but strongly discouraged. If you do plan on hitchhiking, go in pairs or a group and leave your contact details and travel plans with friends/family or trusted locals you have met.

Police assistance:
☎ 111 from any phone

EMERGENCY TELEPHONE NUMBERS

POLICE 111

FIRE 111

AMBULANCE 111

HEALTH

 Insurance A doctor's visit costs about $55. Make sure your travel insurance covers hospital care. Accidents (but not illnesses) are covered by the Accident Compensation Corporation (ACC), which ensures that residents and tourists alike are not charged for any medical treatment required as a consequence of an accident suffered in New Zealand. This covers both physical and psychological damage. In cases of minor injuries, for example a sprained ankle, you may have to contribute to the cost of the initial doctor's visit and physiotherapy. The ACC scheme means you can't sue anybody for damages.

 Dental services Dentists are expensive, so make sure your travel insurance covers dental treatments.

 Weather The sun can be harsh in New Zealand, even through cloud. Make sure you apply sunscreen and wear a hat.

 Drugs Painkillers can be bought over the counter at pharmacies, but antibiotics have to be prescribed.

 Safe water While tap water is safe to drink, some streams are infected with giardia and E-coli, which can cause serious intestinal illness. If you're unsure, treat the water before drinking.

RESTRICTED GOODS

Many types of goods such as food, wooden items and outdoor gear need to be declared on entering New Zealand. Check the list on your Passenger Arrival Card.

CONCESSIONS

Students/Children Most museums offer discounted prices for children between five and 14 as well as university students (with valid ID). There are also family concessions, which cover two adults and up to four children, and under-fives can usually get in free.
Senior citizens Discounted prices are available for some attractions, public transport and accommodation.

TRAVELLING WITH A DISABILITY

Wheelchair access and toilet facilities for people with disabilities are a legal requirement for new accommodation establishments. Many government facilities and attractions are similarly equipped. Quarantine laws prevent overseas visitors from bringing guide dogs. Cities have a Total Mobility (wheelchair transporter) taxi service operated by the main taxi companies. Some tour companies can adapt adventure activities for people with disabilities. For further information visit Weka, the New Zealand Federation of Disability Centres' website: www.weka.net.nz

CHILDREN

Most attractions, particularly museums, have hands-on activities designed for kids. Hotels and restaurants are generally child friendly, but some bed and breakfasts are designed for couples rather than families.

TOILETS

All attractions have public toilets, which can also be found in many public areas, such as city squares, parks and playgrounds. Most public toilets have access for wheelchairs and many have baby-changing facilities.

EMBASSIES AND HIGH COMMISSIONS

UK
☎ (04)
924 2888
(Wellington)

USA
☎ (04)
462 6000
(Wellington)

Ireland
☎ (09)
977 2252
(Auckland)

Australia
☎ (04)
473 6411
(Wellington)

Canada
☎ (04)
473 9577
(Wellington)

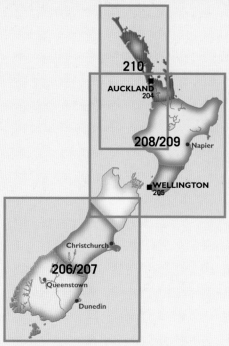

210

AUCKLAND
204

208/209

• Napier

■ WELLINGTON
205

Christchurch •

206/207

Queenstown

Dunedin •

To identify the regions, see the map on the inside of the front cover

Streetplans

————— Motorway

————— Main/other road

————— Railway

— ⌂ — Ferry route

●——● Cable car

    Park/garden/cemetery

✝ Church

[i] Tourist information

✉ Post Office

▣ Featured place
of interest

204	0 500 metres
	0 500 yards

205	0 300 metres
	0 300 yards

Regional Maps

═════ Major route

▒▒▒▒▒ Motorway

————— National road

————— Main/secondary road

– – – – Marine reserve

    National Park

    Forest

    Built-up area

    Glacier

▲ Height in metres

□ City/town/village

✈ Airport

▣ Featured place
of interest

206-210	0 50 km
	0 30 miles

Atlas

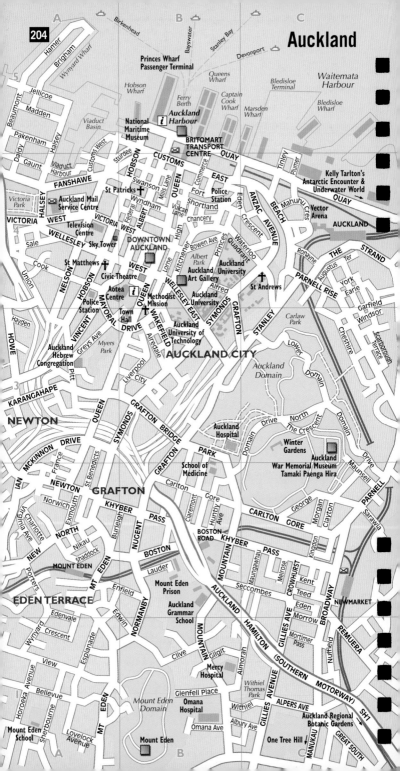

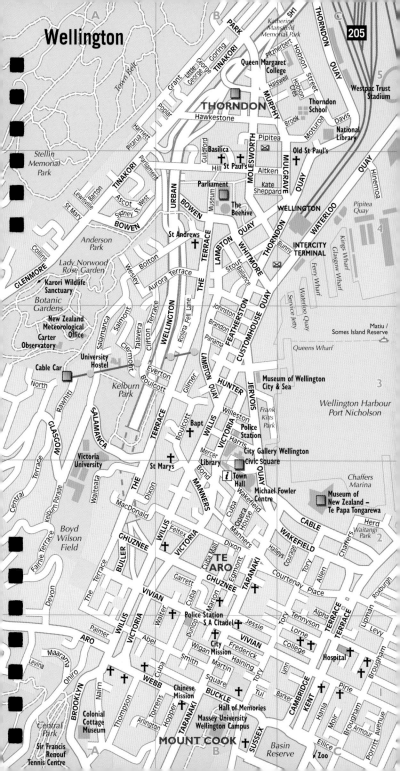

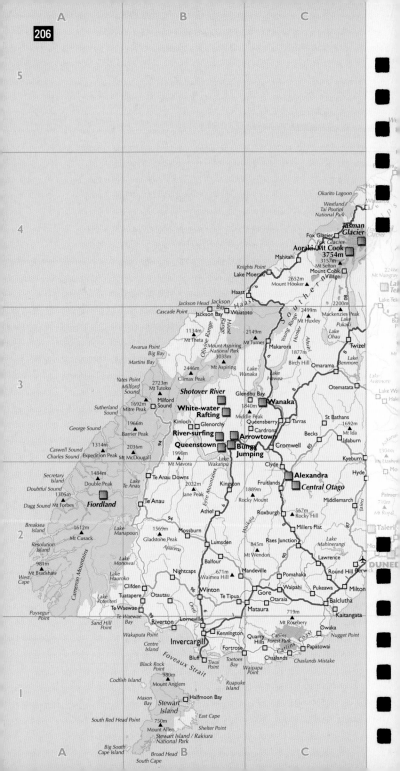

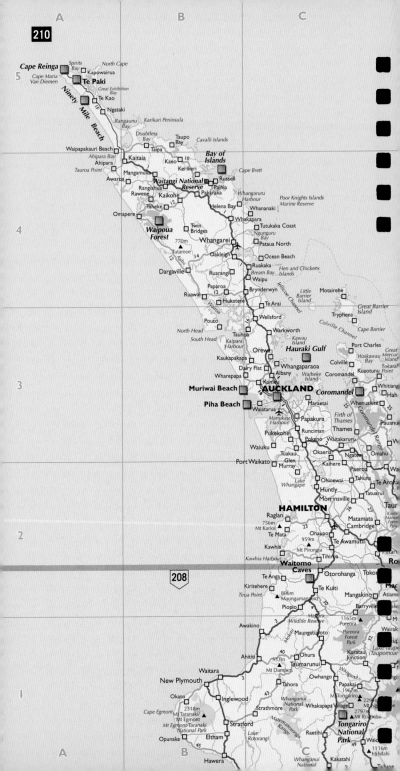

208

5

A   B   C

Cape Reinga
Spirits Bay
Cape Maria Van Diemen
North Cape
Te Paki
Kapowairua
Te Kao
Great Exhibition Bay
Ngataki
Rangaunu Bay
Karikari Peninsula

Waipapakauri Beach
Doubtless Bay
Taupo Bay
Cavalli Islands
Kaitaia
Taipa
Ahipara Bay
Ahipara
Tauroa Point
Kaeo
Bay of Islands
Kerikeri
Cape Brett
Awanui
Mangamuka
Russell
Rangiahua
Waitangi National Reserve
Paihia
Rawene
Kaikohe
Pakaraka
Whangaruru Harbour
Taheke
Helena Bay
Poor Knights Islands Marine Reserve
Omapere
Wananaki
Whakapara
Whangaruru
Waipoua Forest
Twin Bridges
Tutukaka Coast
770m
Tutamoe
Whangarei
Ngunguru Bay
Pataua North
Dargaville
Oakleigh
Ocean Beach
Ruarangi
Ruakaka
Hen and Chickens Islands
Paparoa
Waipu
Little Barrier Island
Ruawai
Brynderwyn
Motairehe
Hukatere
Te Arai
Great Barrier Island
Pouto
Wellsford
Tryphena
North Head
Tauhoa
Warkworth
Cape Barrier
South Head
Kaipara Harbour
Kawau Island
Colville Channel
Orewa
Port Charles
Hauraki Gulf
Kaukapakapa
Colville
Waikawau Bay
Kuaotunu
Dairy Flat
Whangaparaoa
Coromandel
Whitianga
Wharepapa
Albany
Waiheke Island
Kumeu
Muriwai Beach
AUCKLAND
Coromandel
Whenuakite
Piha Beach
Maraetai
Pauanui
Waiatarua
Firth of Thames
Manukau Harbour
Papakura
Thames
Pukekohe
Runciman
Waitakaruru
Waiuku
Pokeno
Okaeria
Omahu
Tuakau
Kaihere
Port Waikato
Glen Murray
Ngatea
Paeroa
Lake Whangape
Ohinewai
Tahuna
Te Aroha
Huntly
Tatuarui
Morrinsville
Raglan
HAMILTON
Matamata
756m
Mt Karioi
Ohaupo
Cambridge
Te Mata
959m
Kawhia
Mt Pirongia
Te Awamutu
Kawhia Harbour
Tihiroa
Waitomo Caves
Rotorua
Te Anga
Otorohanga
Kiritehere
Te Kuiti
Tirua Point
Mangakino
Piopio
806m
Maungamangero
Barryville
Awakino
Mokau Wildlife Reserve
1165m
Pureora
Maungatapoto
Pureora Forest Park
Ahititi
40
Ohura
533m
Kuratau Junction
Lake Taupo Taupomoana
Waitara
Taumarunui
Whangani
New Plymouth
Mt Damper
Papakai
Okato
Tahora
Owhango
1967m
2518m
Inglewood
Whakapapa Village
Mt Tongariro
2290m
Cape Egmont
Mt Taranaki
Strathmore
Mt Ngauruhoe
Mt Egmont
Whanganui National Park
2797m
Mt Egmont/Taranaki National Park
Lake Rotorangi
Matemateaonga Range
Mt Ruapehu
Opunake
Eltham
Tongariro National Park
1116m
Hihitahi
Hawera
Kakatahi
Whanganui National

Acknowledgements

The Automobile Association would like to thank the following photographers, companies and picture libraries for their assistance in the preparation of this book.

Abbreviations for the pictures credits are as follows – (t) top; (b) bottom; (c) centre; (l) left; (r) right; (AA) AA World Travel Library.

2(i) AA/M Langford; 2(ii) AA/A Belcher; 2(iii) Auckland War Memorial Museum; 2(iv) AA/A Belcher; 2(v) AA/P Kenward; 3(i) AA/P Kenward; 3(ii) AA/A Belcher; 3(iii) Auckland War Memorial Museum; 4/5 AA/M Langford; 5c AA/M Langford; 5r AA/P Kenward; 6/7 AA/P Kenward; 7 AA/P Kenward; 8t AA/A Belcher; 8b AA/P Kenward; 9 AA/A Belcher; 10 AA/A Belcher; 11 AA/M Langford; 13 Photolibrary Group; 14t AA/A Belcher; 14c AA/A Belcher; 14b New Zealand Tourist Board; 15t AA/M Langford; 15b AA/A Belcher; 16t AA/M Langford; 16c AA/M Langford; 16b AA/M Langford; 17 © New Line/Everett/Rex Features; 18 © BuenaVista/Everett/Rex Features; 19 © Action Press/Rex Features; 20 Patrick Riviere/AFP/Getty Images; 21 © Everett Collection/Rex Features; 23 Ross Land/Getty Images; 24 Fabrice Coffrini/AFP/Getty Images; 25 AA/A Reisinger & V Meduna; 26 AA/A Belcher; 27 altrendo travel/Getty Images; 28/29 Photolibrary Group; 30 AA/A Belcher; 31l AA/A Belcher; 31c AA/P Kenward; 31r AA/P Kenward; 45l Auckland War Memorial Museum; 45c AA/A Belcher; 45r AA/M Langford; 47 AA/M Langford; 48t AA/A Belcher; 48b AA/A Belcher; 49 AA/M Langford; 50 AA/A Belcher; 52 AA/P Kenward; 53 AA/A Belcher; 54 AA/A Belcher; 55 Auckland War Memorial Museum; 56 Auckland War Memorial Museum; 57 Auckland War Memorial Museum; 58t AA/M Langford; 58b AA/A Belcher; 60 AA/A Belcher; 61 AA/A Belcher; 62 AA/A Belcher; 63 AA/M Langford; 64 AA/M Langford; 65 AA/M Langford; 66t AA/M Langford; 67b AA/P Kenward; 68 AA/M Langford; 75l AA/A Belcher; 75c AA/P Kenward; 75r AA/A Belcher; 76 AA/M Langford; 77 AA/A Belcher; 78t AA/A Belcher; 78b AA/A Belcher; 79 AA/M Langford; 80 AA/A Belcher; 82 AA/M Langford; 83 AA/M Langford; 84 AA/M Langford; 85 AA/M Langford; 86 AA/A Belcher; 87 AA/P Kenward; 88 AA/M Langford; 89 AA/A Belcher; 90 AA/P Kenward; 92 AA/M Langford; 93 Photolibrary Group; 99l AA/A Belcher; 99c AA/A Belcher; 99r AA/A Belcher; 101 AA/A Belcher; 102t AA/A Belcher; 102b AA/P Kenward; 103 AA/A Belcher; 104 AA/A Belcher; 105 AA/A Belcher; 106 AA/A Belcher; 107 AA/P Kenward; 108t AA/A Belcher; 108b AA/A Belcher; 109 AA/A Belcher; 110 AA/M Langford; 111 AA/A Belcher; 112 Photolibrary Group; 119l AA/P Kenward; 119c AA/M Langford; 119r AA/P Kenward; 120 AA/M Langford; 121 AA/M Langford; 122 AA/A Belcher; 123 AA/P Kenward; 124 AA/P Kenward; 126 AA/P Kenward; 129 AA/P Kenward; 130 AA/M Langford; 131 AA/M Langford; 137l AA/A Belcher; 137c AA/M Langford; 137r AA/P Kenward; 139 AA/M Langford; 140 AA/M Langford; 141 AA/A Belcher; 142 AA/M Langford; 144 AA/A Belcher; 145 AA/A Belcher; 146 AA/A Belcher; 147 AA/M Langford; 148 AA/M Langford; 149 AA/A Belcher; 150 AA/A Belcher; 152/153 AA/N Hanna; 154 AA/A Belcher; 159l AA/P Kenward; 159c AA/M Langford; 159r AA/M Langford; 160 AA/A Belcher; 161 AA/A Belcher; 162 AA/A Reisinger & V Meduna; 163t D Wall/Alamy; 163b AA/A Belcher; 164 AA/A Belcher; 165 AA/A Reisinger & V Meduna; 166 New Zealand Tourist Board; 167 AA/P Kenward; 168 AA/A Belcher; 169 AA/A Belcher; 170 AA/P Kenward; 171 AA/A Belcher; 172 AA/A Belcher; 173 AA/A Belcher; 174 AA/P Kenward; 175 AA/P Kenward; 176 AA/A Reisinger & V Meduna; 177 AA/A Reisinger & V Meduna; 178t AA/A Belcher; 178b AA/A Belcher; 183l AA/A Belcher; 183c AA/P Kenward; 183r AA/P Kenward; 184 AA/A Belcher; 185 AA/A Belcher; 186 AA/A Belcher; 187 AA/M Langford; 188 Photolibary Group; 189 Jochen Schlenker/Robert Harding; 191 AA/P Kenward; 192l © Will Newitt/Alamy; 192r D H Webster/Robert Harding; 193 © Arco Images GmbH/Alamy; 194 AA/A Belcher; 196 AA/P Kenward; 197l AA/A Belcher; 197c AA/M Langford; 197r AA/A Belcher; 201t AA/A Belcher; 201c AA/M Langford; 201b AA/A Belcher.

Every effort has been made to trace the copyright holders, and we apologize in advance for any accidental errors. We would be happy to apply any corrections in the following edition of this publication.

SPIRALGUIDES

Questionnaire

Dear Traveler

Your comments, opinions and recommendations are very important to us. So please help us to improve our travel guides by taking a few minutes to complete this simple questionnaire.

Send to: **Spiral Guides, MailStop 64, 1000 AAA Drive, Heathrow, FL 32746–5063**

Your recommendations...

We always encourage readers' recommendations for restaurants, nightlife or shopping – if your recommendation is added to the next edition of the guide, we will send you a FREE AAA Spiral Guide of your choice. Please state below the establishment name, location and your reasons for recommending it.

_____

_____

_____

_____

_____

Please send me AAA Spiral _____

(see list of titles inside the back cover)

About this guide...

Which title did you buy?

_____ **AAA Spiral**

Where did you buy it? _____

When? m m / y y

Why did you choose a AAA Spiral Guide? _____

_____

_____

_____

_____

Did this guide meet your expectations?

Exceeded ☐   Met all ☐   Met most ☐   Fell below ☐

Please give your reasons _____

_____

_____

_____

_____

continued on next page...

Were there any aspects of this guide that you particularly liked?

Is there anything we could have done better?

About you...

Name (Mr/Mrs/Ms)

Address

Zip

Daytime tel nos.

Which age group are you in?

Under 25 ☐ 25–34 ☐ 35–44 ☐ 45–54 ☐ 55–64 ☐ 65+ ☐

How many trips do you make a year?

Less than one ☐ One ☐ Two ☐ Three or more ☐

Are you a AAA member? Yes ☐ No ☐

Name of AAA club

About your trip...

When did you book? m m / y y When did you travel? m m / y y

How long did you stay?

Was it for business or leisure?

Did you buy any other travel guides for your trip? Yes ☐ No ☐

If yes, which ones?

Thank you for taking the time to complete this questionnaire.

All information is for AAA internal use only and will NOT be distributed outside the organization to any third parties.